TRANSFORMATIONAL TRUTH:

A BIBLICAL APOLOGETIC
VOLUME II

TRANSFORMATIONAL TRUTH:

A BIBLICAL APOLOGETIC
VOLUME II

I Peter 3:15 "Be ready always to give an answer."

Dr. Andrew T. Knight

ALSO BY DR. ANDREW T. KNIGHT

Transformational Truth:A Biblical Apologetic, Volume I

Children's Ministry Leadership

Leadership the Lord's Way

Available at: www.AndrewKnight.org

Copyright © 2020 by Dr. Andrew Thomas Knight
All rights reserved

ISBN 978 – 1 – 7325777 – 4 – 9

Centurion Education Foundation
P.O. Box 87
New Smyrna Beach, FL 32170

Made in America

DEDICATION

This book is a continuation of the research that was done in the area of biblical apologetics in Transformation Truth Vol. I. The first subject that is discussed in this second volume is biblical philosophy. We all have a philosophy of life, and that philosophy came from somewhere and usually someone that has influenced them. When I was a boy, my grandpa Shawhan would tell me life stories of when he was in WWI and later in business. While in port in New York City, my grandpa went to hear Billy Sunday preach, and he trusted Christ as his personal Savior. In Grampa's personal life, he never used alcohol and warned me of the harm that it does. He would tell me how he would never sell any farm equipment at his dealership on Sundays because it was the Lord's Day. It made no difference to him if he lost business. He was always going to do the right thing! What my grandpa was teaching me was to have a public and a private life that was godly. I have never stopped thinking about those life stories that my grandpa taught me. Thank you, Grandpa Shawhan, for sharing your profound stories, which have helped shape my philosophy of life.

CONTENTS

ALSO BY DR. ANDREW T. KNIGHT v

DEDICATION vii

CONTENTS viii

CHAPTER ONE A BIBLICAL PHILOSOPHY 16

   INTRODUCTION 16

      Biblical Basis of Philosophy 17

      Biblical Philosophy 19

      Knowledge 26

         Old Testament 27

         New Testament 28

      Truth 29

      Philosophy of Education 33

      Western Thought 38

   CONCLUSION 45

A BIBLICAL PHILOSOPHY: QUESTIONS ONE 47

      A Biblical Philosophy—Questions One 48

      A Biblical Philosophy—Answers One 51

CHAPTER TWO A BIBLICAL WORLDVIEW OF EVIL, SUFFERING, AND MIRACLES ... 54

   INTRODUCTION 54

      The Problem of Evil 55

      The Problem of Suffering 66

      The Morality of God 73

      Basis of the morality of God 73

      The Problem of Miracles 87

         The Ten Plagues 94

         The Wilderness 94

   CONCLUSION 100

A BIBLICAL WORLDVIEW OF EVIL, SUFFERING, AND MIRACLES: QUESTIONS TWO ... 102

      A Biblical Worldview of Evil, Suffering, and Miracles—Questions Two 103

A Biblical Worldview of Evil, Suffering, and Miracles—Answers Two 106

CHAPTER THREE CALVINISM, ARMINIANISM, AND PRESUPPOSITIONAL APOLOGETICS **109**

INTRODUCTION *109*
Calvinist Beliefs 110
Predestination 110
Election 115
Infralapsarian Election 118
Limited Atonement 122
Unlimited Atonement 124
Arminian Beliefs 127
Historical Background 127
Beliefs Defined 128
Conflicted Beliefs 131
Beliefs Debated 132
Biblicist Beliefs 133
Predestination 133
Perseverance 134
Election 136
Limited Atonement 136

CONCLUSION *137*

CALVINISM, ARMINIANISM, AND PRESUPPOSITIONAL APOLOGETICS: QUESTIONS THREE **139**

Calvinism, Arminianism, and Presuppositional Apologetics—Questions Three 140
Calvinism, Arminianism, and Presuppositional Apologetics—Answers Three 142

CHAPTER FOUR A BIBLICAL WORLDVIEW OF MANHOOD AND WOMANHOOD . **144**

INTRODUCTION *144*
Perception of the Problem 144
Description of the Problem 145
The Problem in Biblical Perspective 146
Old Testament 147
New Testament 148
Biblical Manhood 149
Masculine Identity 149

- Masculine Leadership 153
- Biblical Womanhood 154
  - Feminist Mind 154
  - Adam's Helper..155
  - Godly Examples..157
- CONCLUSION 160

A BIBLICAL WORLDVIEW OF MANHOOD AND WOMANHOOD: QUESTIONS FOUR..162

- A Biblical Worldview of Manhood and Womanhood—Questions Four........163
- A Biblical Worldview of Manhood and Womanhood—Answers Four 165

CHAPTER FIVE A BIBLICAL WORLDVIEW OF SEX AND MARRIAGE 168

- INTRODUCTION..168
  - Perception of the Problem 168
  - Description of the Problem 169
  - The Problem in Biblical Perspective 170
    - Old Testament..171
    - New Testament..173
  - A Biblical Husband 175
  - A Biblical Wife 176
  - Biblical Intimacy 178
- CONCLUSION...180

A BIBLICAL WORLDVIEW OF SEX AND MARRIAGE: QUESTIONS FIVE 181

- A Biblical Worldview of Sex and Marriage—Questions Five 182
- A Biblical Worldview of Sex and Marriage—Answers Five..........................184

CHAPTER SIX A BIBLICAL WORLDVIEW OF COUNSELING IN THE LOCAL CHURCH 186

- INTRODUCTION..186
  - Where Should Biblical Counseling Happen?..................................186
  - What is Biblical Counseling?...188
  - Who Should do Biblical Counseling? 192
  - Preventative Biblical Counseling 195
  - Premarital Biblical Counseling..199
  - Biblical Counseling for Addictions 203
  - Biblical Counsel for Divorcees 206
  - Biblical Counseling for Strong Marriages 208

CONCLUSION..209

A BIBLICAL WORLDVIEW OF COUNSELING IN THE LOCAL CHURCH: QUESTIONS SIX **211**

    A Biblical Worldview of Counseling in the Local Church—Questions Six 212
    A Biblical Worldview of Counseling in the Local Church—Answers Six.........215

CHAPTER SEVEN CONCLUDING THOUGHTS **218**

    CONCLUSION..*218*
        Knowledge Gained from this Research 218
        Remaining Research to be Accomplished 223

APPENDIX A REVIEWS OF WRITERS ON EVANGELISM IN A POST-MODERN WORLD **224**

    An Evaluation of C.H. Spurgeon's Message..224
    An Evaluation of Modern Approaches to Evangelism. 227
    An Evaluation of Billy Graham's Message: "Evangelism and the Intellectualism." 230
    Which Gospel Record Gives the Best Approach to Evangelism?...................233
    An Evaluation of Adrian Roger's Message "Apostasy of a Dead Faith." 237
    Is the Terminology "Receive Christ" Proper to Use in Presenting the Gospel?...241
    An Evaluation of Ron Comfort's Message 243
    Do You Believe in Lordship Salvation, Easy-Believeism, or Something Else? 246
    An Evaluation of Ken Ham's Video. 249
    Explain and Defend the Doctrine of Eternal Security. 251
        The Biblical Basis for Eternal Security. 252
        Theological Reasons for Eternal Security. 253
    What Instruction Does the Book of Acts Give for Witnessing in Today's Culture? 254
    Message One and Two from Ewin Lutzer: "How You Can Be Sure." 257

APPENDIX B AN APOLOGETIC PRACTITIONER'S STRATEGY............................**261**

    INTRODUCTION..*261*
        Apologetics on Social Media. 262
        Research and Published Apologetics Books. 264
        Teach Doctrines and Apologetics on a National Broadcast..........................265
        Hold Worldview Forums at Secular Universities Campuses.......................267
        Teach One-week Module Classes at Local Churches. 268

    Local Church Seminary Focus on Apologetics and Leadership. 269

    Launch Church Planting and World Missions Initiatives. 270

CONCLUSION..271

APPENDIX C A REVIEW OF JOHN FRAME'S BOOK *APOLOGETICS: A JUSTIFICATION OF CHRISTIAN BELIEF*..273

INTRODUCTION..273

CONCLUSION..277

APPENDIX D A CRITICAL BOOK REVIEW OF *IS YOUR CHURCH READY?: MOTIVATING LEADERS TO LIVE AN APOLOGETIC LIFE* 278

INTRODUCTION..278

    Zacharias and Geisler's Stated Purposes 278

    A Positive Analysis of Ravi Zacharias and Norman Geisler's Book 279

    A Negative Analysis of Ravi Zacharias and Norman Geisler's Book.............280

CONCLUSION..281

    The Final Analysis of Ravi Zacharias and Norman Geisler's Book:................281

APPENDIX E A REVIEW OF THE BOOK *CHRISTIAN THEOLOGY* 283

    Biographical Sketch 283

    Summary Review of Verbal Plenary Inspiration 283

        Definition of Inspiration 283

        The Fact of Inspiration 284

        Issues in Formulating a Theory of Inspiration 285

        Theories of Inspiration 285

        The Method of Formulating a Theory of Inspiration..............................286

        The Extent of Inspiration..286

        The Intensiveness of Inspiration 286

        Model of Inspiration 286

    The Constitutional Nature of the Human 288

        Summary Review of the Nature of Man 288

        Basic Views of Human Constitution 288

        Biblical Considerations 290

        Philosophical Considerations 291

    An Alternative Model: Conditional Unity 292

        Implications of Conditional Unity...293

    Summary Review of the Fall of Man 293

        Evil in General 293

        Specific Evil...294

- Animal Nature 295
- Anxiety of Finiteness 295
- Existential Estrangement 296
- Economic Struggle 296
- Individualism and Competitiveness 297
- The Biblical Teaching 297
- Physical Death 298
- Spiritual Death 299
- Summary Review of Erickson's Four Aspects of Atonement 299
  - Effectual Calling 299
  - Conversion 300
  - Repentance 301
  - Faith 301
  - Regeneration 302
  - Sanctification 303
  - Glorification 304

APPENDIX F A REVIEW OF THE BOOK *THE DEATH CHRIST DIED: A BIBLICAL CASE FOR UNLIMITED ATONEMENT* 305

- *INTRODUCTION* 305
  - Biographical Sketch 305
  - Purpose 306
  - Summary of Contents 306
    - Introduction 306
    - Robert Lightner's Introduction 307
    - Chapter One 307
    - Chapter Two 310
  - Calvinist Beliefs 313
    - Chapter Three 314
    - Chapter Four 317
    - Chapter Five 318
  - Reaction to the Book 321

APPENDIX G ESCHATOLOGY, THE LAW, AND THE CHRISTIAN 322

- "Individual Eschatology, the Law and the Christian" 322

APPENDIX H ADDITIONAL TRAINING: LESSON ONE 336

- THE BIG PICTURE ACCORDING TO MATTHEW 336

APPENDIX I ADDITIONAL TRAINING: LESSON TWO 340

THE BIG PICTURE ACCORDING TO MARK 340

APPENDIX J ADDITIONAL TRAINING: LESSON THREE 344
THE BIG PRIORITY 344

APPENDIX K ADDITIONAL TRAINING: LESSON FOUR 348
THE MASTER'S PLAN 348

APPENDIX L ADDITIONAL TRAINING: LESSON FIVE 354
IDENTIFYING WITH CHRIST 354

APPENDIX M ADDITIONAL TRAINING: LESSON SIX 361
TRAINING TEACHERS 361

APPENDIX N ADDITIONAL TRAINING: LESSON SEVEN 366
JOINING THE FAMILY OF GOD 366

APPENDIX O ADDITIONAL TRAINING: ANSWERS ONE 370
THE BIG PICTURE ACCORDING TO MATTHEW 370

APPENDIX P ADDITIONAL TRAINING: ANSWERS TWO 372
THE BIG PICTURE ACCORDING TO MARK 372

APPENDIX Q ADDITIONAL TRAINING: ANSWERS THREE 374
THE BIG PRIORITY 374

APPENDIX R ADDITIONAL TRAINING: ANSWERS FOUR 377
THE MASTER'S PLAN 377

APPENDIX S ADDITIONAL TRAINING: ANSWERS FIVE 379
IDENTIFYING WITH CHRIST 379

APPENDIX T ADDITIONAL TRAINING: ANSWERS SIX 381
TRAINING TEACHERS 381

APPENDIX U ADDITIONAL TRAINING: ANSWERS SEVEN 383
JOINING THE FAMILY OF GOD 383

BIBLIOGRAPHY **385**

CHAPTER ONE

A BIBLICAL PHILOSOPHY

INTRODUCTION

The study of philosophy, relative to biblical Christianity, must go out of its way to clarify what is the nature and essence of the philosophy, which is the subject of discussion. This writer will attempt to connect each point of philosophy to a biblical verse and/ or principle as the discussion of biblical philosophy proceeds. The distinction that will be endeavored to illustrate is the wide cavern between humanistic philosophy and biblical philosophy.

As was discussed in volume one of Transformational Truth, the same divide may be seen between Classical Apologetics and Presuppositional Apologetics. The methodology that is advanced in presuppositional apologetics is strictly biblical as the argumentations employed are from biblical content. The biblical precedents, one could say, are the building blocks of one's worldview.

First, this author will lay some biblical foundation for what a biblical philosophy looks like. Secondly, the development of one's biblical philosophy will be discussed. Next, we will deal with the subject of knowledge. In a practical manner, we will deal with the philosophy of education. This chapter will conclude with a look at the philosophy of education and the philosophy of western thought.

BIBLICAL BASIS OF PHILOSOPHY

The basis for a biblical philosophy must, therefore, be marinated in biblical truths. Just like Christian leadership and biblical apologetics, philosophy must be biblical to be genuinely Christian philosophy. The Apostle Paul gave a strong warning, relative to the world's philosophy, as seen in Colossians 2:8: "Beware lest any man spoil you through philosophy and vain deceit, after the tradition of men, after the rudiments of the world, and not after Christ."[1]

Matthew Henry dealt with this passage this way: "There is a philosophy which is a noble exercise of our reasonable faculties, and highly serviceable to religion; such a study of works of God leads us to the knowledge of God and confirms our faith in Him. But there is a philosophy which is vain and deceitful, which is prejudicial to religion, and set up the wisdom of man in competition with the wisdom of God, and while it pleases men's fancies ruins their faith; as nice and curious speculations about things above us, or of no use and concern to us; or a care of winds and terms of art, which have only an empty and often a cheating appearance of knowledge."[2]

Thus, when discussing philosophy, one must clarify the philosophy which one is referring to, whether it is the philosophy of the world or the philosophy of the wisdom of God.

ACTS 17:18

---

[1] All scripture references will be taken from the King James Version unless otherwise noted.

[2] Matthew Henry, *Matthew Henry's Commentary: Acts to Revelation*, (McLean, VA: MacDonald Publishing Company, 1710), 757.

Then certain philosophers of the Epicureans, and of the Stoicks, encountered him. And some said, What will this babbler say? other some, He seemeth to be a setter forth of strange gods: because he preached unto them Jesus, and the resurrection.

ECCLESIASTES 1:2

Vanity of vanities, saith the Preacher, vanity of vanities; all is vanity.

ISAIAH 29:14

Therefore, behold, I will proceed to do a marvellous work among this people, even a marvellous work and a wonder: for the wisdom of their wise men shall perish, and the understanding of their prudent men shall be hid.

ROMANS 1:22

Professing themselves to be wise, they became fools.

I CORINTHIANS 1:19-20

For it is written, I will destroy the wisdom of the wise, and will bring to nothing the understanding of the prudent. Where is the wise? where is the scribe? where is the disputer of this world? hath not God made foolish the wisdom of this world?

I CORINTHIANS 2:6

Howbeit we speak wisdom among them that are perfect: yet not the wisdom of this world, nor of the princes of this world, that come to nought.

I CORINTHIANS 3:19-20

For the wisdom of this world is foolishness with God. For it is written, He taketh the wise in their own craftiness. And again, The Lord knoweth the thoughts of the wise, that they are vain.

I TIMOTHY 6:20

O Timothy, keep that which is committed to thy trust, avoiding profane and vain babblings, and oppositions of science falsely so called.

JOHN 8:32

And ye shall know the truth, and the truth shall make you free.

BIBLICAL PHILOSOPHY

When the term *philosophy* is employed here, it is being used more in a practical way rather than a historical definition of philosophy. One may use the word philosophy to describe his *philosophy of marriage* or *philosophy of work*. One may also state his *philosophy of education* or *philosophy of ministry*. In any of these examples, the word is not being used in its formal definition, but rather of a more generic application.

Webster's defined philosophy like this: "The study of life and what it means, how we should live."[3] Notice Webster mentioned "life" and "meaning," which would indicate a moral element. And of course, a moral element then must have a moral Giver.

Vinh Lu Akoue stated, "It is taught that philosophy was born in Greece, Asia Minor, with the School of Miletus. This

---

[3] Noah Webster, *Webster's Dictionary: A Comprehensive Guide to the English Language for the Home, Office, and School* (New York: Modern Publishing, 1999), 214.

proposal is questionable, for the simple reason that the history of human thought is a long chain which is starting in Egypt. Pythagoras of Samos, Thales of Miletus, Aristotle and others have learned for decades, Philosophy and/or Science in Egyptian Priests. Greece has just had the merit to popularize Philosophy. Philosophie was elitist in the Pharaohs."[4]

Akoue was helping us to understand the history of philosophy, that it has had a chain of events that has carried thought processes to how people and societies think, reason, and live. One could argue that all people are philosophers, but not all philosophy is biblical. This author would argue that everyone in the world is a theologian (study or knowledge of God), though most theologians are incorrect, relative to the scriptures. The broader argument being made here is that one could use the term philosophy in a secular application, a historical sense, or a generic application. In our study, we will, by default, be employing the term philosophy to a biblical application.

Garrett DeWeese discussed philosophy relative to Jesus like this, "Jesus was not a philosopher, at least not in any ordinary sense of the term. He wrote no books (but neither did Socrates), developed no grand metaphysis (but neither have most philosophers through the ages). He did not make his living by lecturing or teaching philosophy (but neither did Hume)."[5] What DeWeese was stating was that although Jesus did not look like the modern-day philosopher or professor, what is unmistakable is

---

[4]Vihn Lu Akoue. https://www.researchgate.net/application.ClientValidation.html?origP2019).ath=%2Fpost%2FThe_origin_of_philosophy_What_is_the_origin_of_philosophy (accessed January 14, 2019).

[5] Garrett DeWeese, *Doing Philosophy as a Christian* (Downers, IL: InterVarsity Press, 2011), 91.

that the philosophy or worldview that Jesus taught has impacted the world to a greater extent than those that taught in the stricter sense of philosophers.

The philosophy of Jesus was framed as truth when challenged, "Pilate therefore said unto him, Art thou a king then? Jesus answered, Thou sayest that I am a king. To this end was I born, and for this cause came I into the world, that I should bear witness unto the truth. Every one that is of the truth heareth my voice" (John 18:37).

DeWeese further discussed the philosophy of Jesus when he stated, "Here, the focus is on the sayings of Jesus that reveal a 'love of wisdom' or an intent to teach the 'skill of living,' as did the Hebrew sages as well as other ancient sages[6] as reported, for example, by Diogenes Laertius.[7] So many sayings of Jesus that convey a truth about human nature or commend a particular moral behavior or manner of life can be understood as giving rise to philosophical thought."[8] Thus, though the teachings of Jesus and His Words recorded in scripture are not usually considered philosophy, the characteristics of Christian thought do seem to parallel what is most commonly referred to in the traditional usage of the word philosophy.

---

[6] The three classes of religious teachers in the Old Testament were categorized into prophets, priests, and sages. Sages were private religious teachers. Their place was not in delivering sermons or writing books of the Old Testament. Their teaching though, highly influenced the ethics of Israel.

[7] Diogenes Laertius was a 3rd Century biographer of the Greek philosophers.

[8] DeWeese, *Doing Philosophy*, 106-107.

One could say, however, that the Lord gives wisdom through His Word, and His Word instructs His people how to walk in this world, as seen in Proverbs 2:6–7: "For the LORD giveth wisdom: out of his mouth cometh knowledge and understanding. He layeth up sound wisdom for the righteous: he is a buckler to them that walk uprightly."

Thus, a careful student of the Bible would conclude that indeed the Bible narratives, principles, and statues function as does philosophy. The Bible, however, comes to more conclusive answers to lives most pondered by questions of life and meaning.

John Frame gave a historical context of philosophy when he stated, "The method of the wisdom teachers was to gather the sayings of the wise, from many generations and locations, for the guidance of their own communities. What distinguishes wisdom in Israel from that of other cultures is the conviction that 'the fear of the LORD is the beginning of wisdom'" (Psalm 111:10).[9]

Frame further explained, "Philosophy, however, should not be understood as an extension of the tradition of wisdom literature. In many ways, as we will see, philosophy is historically a revolt against traditional wisdom."[10] As Frame stated earlier, that philosophy is not an extension of wisdom literature. The Christian ought to always keep in mind the supremacy of scripture. "For the word of God is quick, and powerful, and sharper than any twoedged sword, piercing even to the dividing asunder of soul and spirit, and of the joints and marrow, and is a discerner of the thoughts and intents of the heart" (Hebrews 4:12).

---

[9] John M. Frame, *A History of Western Philosophy and Theology* (Phillipsburg, NJ: P&R Publishing Company, 2015), 1.

[10] Ibid., 4.

The strength of the argument for a biblical philosophy and worldview leads to the question of why the study of philosophy is important to the Christian thinker. Frame answered this way, "Now, since the business of philosophy is to think clearly, cogently, and profoundly about the world, the hardest challenges to Christian thought have come from the disciple of philosophy. When Christians study philosophy, they become acquainted with the most formidable adversaries of the gospel: non-Christian thought in its most cogent form. Acquaintance with these is very beneficial for gospel witness."[11]

This logic would seem to coincide with the Great Commission. "And he said unto them, Go ye into all the world, and preach the gospel to every creature" (Mark 16:15). And Paul certainly confronted the philosophers of his day. "Then Paul stood in the midst of Mars' hill, and said, Ye men of Athens, I perceive that in all things ye are too superstitious. For as I passed by, and beheld your devotions, I found an altar with this inscription, TO THE UNKNOWN GOD. Whom therefore ye ignorantly worship, him declare I unto you" (Acts 17:22–23).

As the Apostle Paul confronted skeptics and unbiblical philosophers at Mars Hill in the first century, so must every believer in the present day. Paul knew the Greek philosophy; thus, he was able to speak to the Athenians from their worldview. Paul was also trained in theology, "I am verily a man which am a Jew, born in Tarsus, a city in Cilicia, yet brought up in this city at the feet of Gamaliel, and taught according to the perfect manner of the law of the fathers, and was zealous toward God, as ye all are this day" (Acts 22:3). Paul was then able to frame his argument from a biblical worldview. Paul is very likely the clearest example in scripture of a presuppositionist as seen in Acts 17:2: "And Paul, as

---

[11] Frame, *A History*, 4.

his manner was, went in unto them, and three sabbath days reasoned with them out of the scriptures." One might say that Paul was a biblical philosopher.

As one assembles his theological foundation, one then will develop his biblical philosophy. Once those two foundations are constructed, one's biblical worldview begins to take shape. Frame explained, "The Word of God is, among other things, the authoritative statement of the Christian's worldview. And because it describes a historical sequence, it may be called a metanarrative as well. Application in my definition of theology includes the 'formation' and 'defense' in my definition of philosophy. So we may say that Christian theology is Christian philosophy, or philosophy with a Christian worldview."[12] This author might use stronger adjectives to describe the use of the Bible in developing one's worldview. Two thoughts come to mind. First, that the Bible is declarative. This is to say, for example, in Genesis 1:1 ("In the beginning God"), God declares Himself to the world. The second thought would be to state that the Bible has supremacy in building one's biblical worldview and biblical philosophy.

For the further context of philosophies and order of philosophy Frame explained, "Until the twentieth century, when Eastern religion and philosophy began to make a major impact, Western thought had two roots: the Greek and the biblical. Some thinkers tried to synthesize these traditions in various ways. Others saw an antithesis between them and sought to be consistent with one or the other."[13] The analysis of the two different schools of thought brings clarity to this study.

Frame explained why biblical thought must be distinctly separate from Greek thought. He argued, "Although I greatly

---
[12] Frame, *A History*, 4.
[13] Frame, *A History*, 46.

admire the creative brilliance of the Greek thinkers, I believe it is a serious mistake to adopt their worldviews or to try to synthesize their thinking with the worldview of the Bible."[14] This exemplifies discernment, and then Frame explains the importance of studying Greek thought at all. Frame stated, "The chief benefit in studying Greek thought is to better understand the philosophical and cultural consequences of rejecting biblical theism."[15] The writer would further explain that as an apologist, one is not looking for common ground, as truth has no colleagues, but rather to lead one from a Greek worldview to a biblical worldview.

Relative to a biblical worldview and biblical apologetics, one cannot discuss this matter for long without mentioning Romans 1:18–32. Paul gave us an example of the need to confront those with a Greek worldview as was divinely recorded in Acts 17:16: "Now while Paul waited for them at Athens, his spirit was stirred in him, when he saw the city wholly given to idolatry." The biblical worldview and thought is one that is trained and disciplined. The Greek worldview and thought is much like raising a child as instructed in Proverbs 29:15: "The rod and reproof give wisdom: but a child left to himself bringeth his mother to shame." Said differently, a biblical worldview and thought does not happen by osmosis. Furthermore, the Greek worldview and thought leads one only to spiritual destruction and alienation from God.

Knowledge

As one is building his worldview and biblical philosophy, one must deal with the subject, and body of study, of knowledge.

---

[14] Ibid.

[15] Ibid.

The body of study where knowledge is found is in the study of epistemology, also known as the study of truth. Thus all knowledge must be predicated on truth. All truth must be predicated upon the Bible, biblical principles derived from the Bible, and biblical mandates.

Paul Moser defined knowledge this way: "Epistemology in the Western philosophical tradition has until recently offered a prominent definition of knowledge that analyzes knowledge into three essential components: justification, truth, and belief. According to this analysis, propositional knowledge is, by definition, justified true belief."[16] Now it is imperative to insert here the relationship of truth and the local church, as God's candlesticks are charged with defending and advancing God's Word. I Timothy 3:15: "But if I tarry long, that thou mayest know how thou oughtest to behave thyself in the house of God, which is the church of the living God, the pillar and ground of the truth." The local church is built upon the truth of the Word of God; thus, knowing comes from the truth.

Moser further argues the aspect of being, relative to knowledge. He stated, "For a true belief to be knowledge, it must have what philosophers call justification, warrant, or evidence."[17] He continued, "Justification is the third essential condition for knowledge in the tripartite analysis. Justification for a belief must include some good reasons for regarding the belief as truth."[18] It

---

[16] Paul K. Moser, Dwayne H. Mulder, and J.D. Trout, *The Theory of Knowledge: A Thematic Introduction* (New York: Oxford University Press, 1998), 14.

[17] Moser, Mulder, and Trout, *The Theory of Knowledge*, 15.

[18] Ibid.

is also imperative to point out that these are not extra-biblical arguments as these all tie in together with the doctrine of knowledge.

Furthermore, what one must have at the forefront of their mind when discussing knowledge is the supremacy of scripture. Hebrews 4:12: "For the word of God is quick, and powerful, and sharper than any twoedged sword, piercing even to the dividing asunder of soul and spirit, and of the joints and marrow, and is a discerner of the thoughts and intents of the heart."

When one has the supremacy of scripture as a presupposition for defining knowledge would coincide with Moser's remarks, "If you have good reasons in support of the truth of your belief, and your belief is true and is based on good reasons, then you have knowledge, according to the traditional analysis."[19] When one has the belief that the Bible is God's inerrant, infallible Word, then one truly does have knowledge.

Old Testament

PROVERBS 1:7

The fear of the LORD is the beginning of knowledge: but fools despise wisdom and instruction.

PROVERBS 2:5–6

Then shalt thou understand the fear of the LORD, and find the knowledge of God. For the LORD giveth wisdom: out of his mouth cometh knowledge and understanding.

PROVERBS 9:10

---

[19] Ibid., 16.

A Biblical Philosophy

The fear of the LORD is the beginning of wisdom: and the knowledge of the holy is understanding.

New Testament

ROMANS 11:33

O the depth of the riches both of the wisdom and knowledge of God! how unsearchable are his judgments, and his ways past finding out!

II COLOSSIANS 4:6

For God, who commanded the light to shine out of darkness, hath shined in our hearts, to give the light of the knowledge of the glory of God in the face of Jesus Christ.

EPHESIANS 1:17

That the God of our Lord Jesus Christ, the Father of glory, may give unto you the spirit of wisdom and revelation in the knowledge of him.

PHILIPPIANS 3:8

Yea doubtless, and I count all things but loss for the excellency of the knowledge of Christ Jesus my Lord: for whom I have suffered the loss of all things, and do count them but dung, that I may win Christ.

I TIMOTHY 2:4

Who will have all men to be saved, and to come unto the knowledge of the truth.

Truth

The body of study that refers to the study of truth is called *epistemology*. This is a foundational aspect within the body of the study of apologetics. Otherwise stated: how can one argue for anything without the truth, nevertheless, arguing for Christ and the Bible? John Frame explained it like this: "All our knowledge, therefore, originates in him. Thus, "The fear of the LORD is the beginning of knowledge" (Proverbs 1:7).[20] And Frame argued, "God is not only the origin of truth, but is also the supreme authority of knowledge."[21] Certainly, Jesus and the truth are one and the same as seen in John 14:6: "Jesus saith unto him, I am the way, the truth, and the life: no man cometh unto the Father, but by me."

Frame then argued what the pursuit of truth without personally knowing Christ looks like: "But when sinners try to gain knowledge without the fear of the Lord, that knowledge is suppressed, distorted (Romans 1:21-25; 1 Corinthians 1:18-25). This is not to say that every sentence they utter is false. It is to say that their basic worldview is twisted and unreliable. Their most serious epistemological mistake is, typically, to assert their own autonomy: to make themselves, or something other than the biblical God, the final standard of truth and right."[22] In biblical times there were many false prophets in Israel. It is noteworthy to mention that in the Old Testament era, one that was proven to be a false prophet would be put to death. In the current era, the church age and the age of grace, it is imperative for the Christian

---

[20] John M. Frame, *Apologetics: A Justification of Christian Belief* (Phillipsburg, NJ: P&R Publishing, 2015), 48.

[21] Ibid.

[22] Frame, *Apologetics*, 48.

today to discern truth. Fortunately, Christians have the benefit of the full canonized Word of God.

Nevertheless, believers must be discerning relative to truth as charged to in I John 4:1–3: "Beloved, believe not every spirit, but try the spirits whether they are of God: because many false prophets are gone out into the world. Hereby know ye the Spirit of God: Every spirit that confesseth that Jesus Christ is come in the flesh is of God: And every spirit that confesseth not that Jesus Christ is come in the flesh is not of God: and this is that spirit of antichrist, whereof ye have heard that it should come; and even now already is it in the world."

Frame made the argument that there are apologists for truth and those who have offered up untruths. He argued, "The apologist must not only refuse to compromise with these distorted epistemologies, but also summon unbelievers to abandon them. For such epistemologies are part of the unbeliever's sinful suppression of the truth. Like the distortions in metaphysics, they represent his desire to escape from responsibility, to avoid hearing the voice of God telling him what to do."[23]

Frame is breaking people into two categories: first are unbelievers and then those who are born-again Christians. This writer would believe that apologetics benefits both categories of people. As Frame asserted, unbelievers must reject falsehoods, relative to truth. Apologetics edifies the believer as arguments for the things of God are learned. Once the Christian has learned the arguments for the faith, the natural application of apologetics is that the Christian is more confident in advancing the truths of the Word of God to the world around him.

---

[23] Ibid., 49.

One of the most edifying principles in the Christian experience is the concept of the supremacy of scripture. John MacArthur dealt with this issue when he stated, "It indicates that scripture is so comprehensive that if carefully obeyed, it can transform a person's whole life in every regard. The truth of scripture gives full life to all aspects of the soul."[24] MacArthur argued that the truth of scripture is complete to meet every human need of the heart. Needless to say, every human being needs the truth of the Word of God in order to have the completeness that God has for every person.

MacArthur further argued for the sufficiency of the truth of scripture to meet each human need as he explained, "One of the main reasons the Word of God is sufficient for all of humanity's spiritual needs is because it leaves no doubt regarding essential truth. Life itself is confusing and chaotic. Seeking truth apart from scripture only adds to the confusion. scripture, by contrast, is remarkably clear."[25] It should go without saying, but without the Word of God in one's life, it cannot be complete, nor be the spiritual being in which God made each person to be.

The study of epistemology relative to developing a biblical worldview is imperative. Epistemology is far more than seeking knowledge for knowledge's sake. Paul Moser stated, "We seek knowledge, not in an unstructured pursuit of any random piece of information, but always within a structured overall pursuit of significant truths."[26] The pursuit of truth is without question the highest priority for the Christian. Said differently, if Christians

---

[24] John MacArthur, *Think Biblically: Recovering a Biblical Worldview* (Wheaton: Crossway Books, 2003), 30.

[25] Ibid., 31.
[26] Moser, Mulder, and Trout, *The Theory of Knowledge*, 182.

want the best for themselves and the world around them, they will, in fact, be avid pursuers of the truth. The Old Testament prophet spoke to this in Hosea 4:6, "My people are destroyed for lack of knowledge: because thou hast rejected knowledge, I will also reject thee, that thou shalt be no priest to me: seeing thou hast forgotten the law of thy God, I will also forget thy children."

Christians have a personal relationship with the Lord, and every Christian wants everyone to have a relationship with the Lord as well. Moser continued, "Explanation provides a basic motivation not only for the pursuit of knowledge, but also for the philosophical study of knowledge, which is itself the pursuit of a certain kind of knowledge."[27] The world clammers for truth, but it is the small people group in the world known as Christians that hold the ultimate truth of God's Word in their hands and in their hearts.

The local churches are the keepers of the truth. Matthew 28:20: "Teaching them to observe all things whatsoever I have commanded you: and, lo, I am with you alway, even unto the end of the world. Amen." The Greek meaning of the word *observe* has the idea to guard or protect. This is to say that the local church is commissioned to protect God's Word. One might think that the Great Commission is to spread God's Word, and that would be correct. To guard God's Word is certainly to protect it from its many critics and attacks, but furthermore, when God's Word is advanced throughout the world, it is protected because more hands and hearts are protecting the Bible.

Philosophy of Education

The philosophy of education is important to epistemology (the study of truth) as many may hold to a certain philosophy but

---

[27] Ibid., 183.

not to a biblical definition of truth, or a Christian worldview. Without a biblical philosophy or worldview, one would not hold to a Christian philosophy of education. Kenneth Gangel and Warren Benson offered this biblical philosophy of education: "The early Christian apologists took a deep and practical interest in education. Christ had commanded the church to teach and spread the good news. The followers of Jesus were to go, make disciples of all nations, baptize, and teach."[28]

Per this rationale, it seems reasonable that apologetics goes hand in glove with Christian education. Matthew 28:19: "Go ye therefore, and teach all nations, baptizing them in the name of the Father, and of the Son, and of the Holy Ghost." It is important to note that the only verb in verse nineteen is "teach," as "baptizing" is a participle. Thus, the main thrust of the Great Commission is to teach, while all the time evangelizing and baptizing are happening simultaneously.

Gangel and Benson agreed with this view when they explained, "Making disciples was the central imperative among going, baptizing, and teaching, which were descriptive of what is involved in the making of disciples."[29] The Great Commission is central to education, and it is most certainly central to the philosophy of education.

The two most prominent teachers to be referenced from scripture would be the Lord Jesus Christ and the Apostle Paul. Gangel and Benson expressed it this way: "It seems quite clear that the ministry of the Master had a much greater teaching than preaching trust to it. . . . The Apostle Paul's work was heavily of a

---

[28] Kenneth O. Gangel, and Warren S. Benson, *Christian Education: Its History & Philosophy* (Chicago: Moody Press, 1983), 77.

[29] Ibid.

teaching character as well. It is readily apparent that education was of paramount importance in the New Testament."[30]

This would seem to sync up with the commonly used scripture of Bible institute mottos, II Timothy 2:2: "And the things that thou hast heard of me among many witnesses, the same commit thou to faithful men, who shall be able to teach others also." When one considers the Great Commission and the biblical model of teaching, the compounding and multiplying effects of teaching God's Word to reach the world must be of utmost priority for any serious Christian.

Gangel and Benson continued their explanation this way: "Christ taught from an educational strategy that included a ministry to the masses of people, the seventy, the twelve disciples (Mark 3:13–15), and also to Peter, James, and John (Mark 14:33; Luke 9:28). His peripatetic teaching of the twelve constituted the greatest educational situation ever to exist. Christ recognized that the ministry He modeled with the small group and the large group would be perpetuated by the church."[31] This author would add to this sentiment that the local church is the educational institution that God has authorized to teach and is the primary educational institution. The small group model of teaching does seem to be the most effective in teaching God's Word and training men for the Gospel ministry.

The culture of any one given time seems to be the cradle which God uses in order to accomplish His work, through His people, in that particular period. In the late 1700s in England, there were no child labor laws, and so children worked in factories six days a week, and this was the culture and time that

---

[30] Gangel and Benson, *Christian Education*, 67.

[31] Ibid., 69.

the Lord used the man known as the "father of the Sunday School movement," Robert Raikes. D. Bruce Lockerbie recorded, "Thus, in 1780, he turned to helping rowdy youths and children on Sundays, their one day free from work. He established a meeting place and a time for rudimentary instruction in reading, writing, and Christian doctrine."[32] This seemed to be a classical, Hebrew approach to education. In the Hebrew home B.C., the parents would teach an academic truth alongside of a moral, Old Testament truth.

The Great Commission teaching principle proved to spread the influence of the Gospel throughout the Western hemisphere, as Lockerbie recorded, "Before his death in 1811, Robert Raikes' influence had spread to all parts of Great Britain. John Newton, the converted slave trader who wrote 'Amazing Grace'; William Wilberforce, the great crusader for the abolition of slavery; and Hannah More were all supporters of the Sunday School movement, which eventually made its way across the Atlantic."[33] The impact of the Sunday School movement is difficult to calculate but has certainly had a profound influence on education and Western thought. Lockerbie also stated, "At the heart of education in the Western world stands the Cross."[34] Thus the influence on education in Great Britain was a direct connection from the Sunday School movement. Said differently, discipling young people for the Lord has a generational and multiplying impact, even to the extent of a whole culture and hemisphere.

---

[32] D. Bruce Lockerbie, *A Passon for Learning: A History of Christian Thought on Education* (Colorado Springs: Purposeful Design Publications, 2007), 194.

[33] Ibid., 195.
[34] Lockerbie, *A Passion for Learning*, 195.

A Biblical Philosophy

Johnathan Edwards, though most famous for his sermon that sparked a great awakening—"Sinners in the Hands of an Angry God"—was also well known as an intellectual and an educator. Lockerbie described Edwards's life this way, "Edwards left a legacy of intellectual as well as evangelistic example."[35] This may very well be the best combination of applying the Great Commission to teaching the Word of God and evangelizing the lost.

George Knight discussed the connection between Christian philosophy and education this way: "Educational practices are conditioned by philosophic beliefs. Teachers, parents, and other educators develop unnecessary difficulties when their practices conflict with the worldview that they are seeking to transmit to the youth in their charge."[36] To advance this thought, one needs to be reminded that a Christian worldview comes from Christian doctrine, and a Christian philosophy is developed from both biblical doctrine a Christian worldview.

The philosophy of education, relative to a biblical philosophy of education, has much to do with one's view of scripture. In fact, an educational outcome can be drastically different based on an educator's view of the Bible. Lawrence Richards and Gary Bredfeldt explained both a low view and a high view of scripture and how they affect the outcome of their students.

Richards and Bredfeldt explained, "To the neo-orthodox educator, however, the Bible was not the Word of God, but

---

[35] Ibid., 225.

[36] George R. Knight, *Philosophy and Education: An Introduction in Christian Perspective*, 4th ed. (Berrien Springs, MI: Andrews University Press, 2006), 197.

instead, it became the Word of God as people encountered God in the scriptures. Neo-orthodox educators argued that the text itself was nothing more than a human record of God's encounters with humanity.

But when the Bible causes the reader to encounter God it becomes the Word of God to the believing person."[37] The obvious takeaway from this view of scripture is that it is not really authoritative if it is not really the Word of God. A low view of scripture elevates man while it condescends to the Word of God. In contrast, consider a high view of scripture.

Richards and Bredfeldt stated, "Because the revelation is in words, evangelicals often say that the Bible itself is God's revelation. They claim that it does not contain the Word of God; it is the Word of God. Failure of the teaching of the Bible to transform must lie somewhere other than in the Bible itself or its literal interpretation."[38] The argument for a high view of a philosophy of biblical education was further argued, "In order to teach the Bible creatively and with authority so as to change lives, we must begin with a high view of scripture.

Such a view mandates that the Bible teacher recognize the inspiration of scripture and understand something of the literary nature of the inspired text."[39] This does seem to be the major point when teaching the Bible, which is to say, who is really authoritative here? And if Bible teachers want to have high impact

---

[37] Lawrence O. Richards and Gary J. Bredfeldt, *Creative Bible Teaching* (Chicago: Moody Press, 1998), 32.

[38] Ibid., 35.

[39] Richards and Bredfeldt, *Creative Bible Teaching*, 35.

outcomes on their students, it is therefore imperative that their philosophy of biblical education takes a high view of scripture.

Western Thought

As the rise of the West came into being, so came the rise of a secular worldview, which included replacing theism with naturalism, and replacing Bible authority with human authority. Otherwise stated, explaining the world without God and the Bible. John Frame gave a historical background when he stated, "But in the seventeenth century there was a similar rebirth in non-Christian thought, in which secular thinkers renewed and pressed the claim of autonomous knowledge more consistently than anyone since the Greeks. Indeed, this rebirth echoes strikingly the beginning of philosophy itself in Greek Asia Minor. Greek philosophy was intended to be a replacement for religious and traditional ways of thinking. The philosophers sought for the first time to understand the world by reason alone."[40]

The Renaissance serves only to remind us of Genesis 3:5: "For God doth know that in the day ye eat thereof, then your eyes shall be opened, and ye shall be as gods, knowing good and evil." The idea of *knowing* is humanism, which has not changed since the Fall in the Garden of Eden; only the name has changed.

The beginning of the Renaissance period to the present time has not been favorable to the authority of the Bible relative to society. This is a case and point for the ever-growing importance of Biblical apologetics. The culture must be confronted with the truth-claims of the Bible. Furthermore, as the Apostle Paul employed biblical apologetics in order to win those at Mars Hill to Christ, it is all the more the reason for Christians

---

[40] Frame, *Apologetics*, 177.

today to employ biblical apologetics to reach those for Christ who still hold to a Renaissance worldview.

Frame painted a picture of a history of philosophies that, especially from the time of the Renaissance to present, has been in a battle for the minds and, subsequently, the souls of mankind. Paul dealt with this same battle at Mars Hill, and it could be summed up as the two worldviews of Jerusalem versus Athens. Frame stated it this way, "Thus was born the movement known as modern philosophy. Modern philosophy, in this sense, has dominated the philosophical conversation to the present day, though thinkers have arisen from time to time who have gone against the grain, trying to do philosophical work on a Christian foundation. So from a present-day perspective, the Christian dominance of philosophy of the Middle Ages and the Renaissance must be seen as a parenthesis between two periods (the ancient and the modern) in which philosophy is dominated by unbelief."[41]

What is abundantly clear from this study is that the Devil never changes his playbook. They are the same lies that date back to the Garden of Eden. With the understanding of this reality, it is all the more imperative that Christians are on the offensive to debunk the lies of the Devil and aggressively advance the truth-claims of Christ and His world-changing Gospel.

Frame summed up this age-old battle for the mind and soul this way: "To review the story so far: God revealed in scripture not only a way of salvation, but a worldview capable philosophical articulation. The way of salvation presupposes the worldview. In that worldview, the Supreme-Being, distinct from all others beings, is a tri-personal absolute, who rules over His Creation.[42]

---

[41] Frame, *Apologetics*, 177.
[42] Frame, *Apologetics*, 214.

Frame continued, after offering a historical summary and then highlighting a contrast of worldviews, "The modern philosophers found it no easier than the Greeks to impose autonomous rational thought on a world of recalcitrant fact. They disagreed over many things, particularly the relative roles of reason and sense. But even then (as Hume) modern philosophers veered toward skepticism, they grasped tightly to the claim of autonomy and showed no interest in compromising that fundamental point. They did not call out to God for intellectual salvation."[43]

It seems to be appropriate here that human beings are designed by God to be spiritual beings. Thus, whether a person embraces theism and personal salvation through Christ, or completely rejects Christ, he will find an object to worship and a cause to give himself to. It is further appropriate to insert here that the tomb of Christ is empty, and that there is no salvation in any other than through faith in Jesus Christ.

One of the most instructive explanations one might find to explain philosophically and theologically the difference between mainline denominational churches and Bible-centered, independent churches are as follows: "This naturalistic view of scripture led to a total abandonment of traditional theology (both Protestant and Catholic). These thinkers did not, however, want to reject Christianity entirely.

They were moved by the ideas of God and Jesus. But the gospel of the Bible, as we have seen, presupposes a thoroughly supernaturalist worldview. The supernatural view of biblical inspiration was incredible to these thinkers; how could they accept stories of Creation, of miracles, of incarnation, virgin birth, atonement, and resurrection? They came to believe that they

---

[43] Ibid., 215.

must reject not only the authority of scripture but also its supernatural content, its gospel. But after this drastic criticism, what of biblical Christianity could remain?"[44] Frame could not have made the argument better to understand how philosophy has impacted the very basics of how one views the Bible and the gospel to advance the thought of a biblical worldview, a high view of scripture, and personal acceptance of the gospel.

As was mentioned previously, the supremacy of scripture is paramount. One may have a biblical worldview and yet hold to a low view of scripture. As Frame discussed, the denominational churches have a naturalistic view of the scriptures. The problem with holding a low view of scripture (in other words, higher criticism) is that a low view of scripture will end in a naturalistic view of scripture.

It should be noted when referencing the Enlightenment that this is a historical term. What is more accurate is that it was really a spiritual dark age. Frame explained, "The dominance of Christian thought, however, came to an end in the early seventeenth century, with a convulsion initiating 'modern' philosophy and the period of its initial dominance, otherwise known as the Enlightenment.

Again, the main body of Western philosophers cast aside the restraints of tradition and Christian theology and sought to understand the world by autonomous thinking, sometimes emphasizing reason, sometimes sense experience. And at almost the same time, the convulsion spread to theologians in liberal theology, which sought to accommodate Christian doctrine to the presuppositions of the Enlightenment."[45]

---

[44] Frame, *Apologetics*, 216.
[45] Frame, *Apologetics*, 251.

A Biblical Philosophy

The thought that a Christian thinker cannot get past is seen in John 12:42–43: "Nevertheless among the chief rulers also many believed on him; but because of the Pharisees they did not confess him, lest they should be put out of the synagogue: For they loved the praise of men more than the praise of God."

When a Christian looks at the Bible and then at humanity and its history, one cannot help but notice that the character and its flaws have been consistent throughout human history. The fleshly mind has an insatiable appetite for the applause of men, while the spiritual mind has a quiet desire to hear from their Lord, "His lord said unto him, Well done, thou good and faithful servant" (Matthew 25:21).

One could easily argue that the Christian life is very much an intellectual discipline. Paul wrote in Philippians 2:5, "Let this mind be in you, which was also in Christ Jesus." Certainly the heart must be changed and converted, but it is the mind in which the message of the gospel and the Bible flow through to get to the heart of an individual. Thoughts are where people live.

Thought comes before action. Western thought has certainly impacted how people see God, the world, and themselves. Western thought has largely shaped how people see the world. Frame gave this historical assessment like this, "But God has not abandoned the world of thought. Through all this time, faithful pastors, church teachers, evangelists, theologians, and fathers and mothers have maintained the authentic biblical gospel.

Hearts have been transformed, and Christian people have spread abroad the love of Christ."[46] The serious Christian, whatever their walk in life is, must be able to communicate the

---

[46] Frame, *Apologetics*, 512.

gospel in the context of history, science, languages, and current events. Certainly, every Christian must be able to make the case that the death, burial, and resurrection of Christ is the central theme in world history—and furthermore, that the gospel of Christ not only has relevance today but that there is no higher relevance.

The Renaissance's effect on people's worldview was certainly seen during the first century of American history. It is of great interest that even when naturalism was on the rise, the gospel of Christ prevailed and had a great impact on the early American worldview.

Hoffecker found in his research, "America exhibited both a great diversity of denominations and a remarkable revivalism that swept the colonies and the new nation into the nineteenth Century. The Enlightenment took its toll on traditional religion, as evidenced by the spread of Unitarianism, principally in New England, and the brief impact that deism had, especially among the political leadership until the War of 1812. But the underlying beliefs during the Colonial period testify to the continuing influence of traditional theism as the prevailing worldview."[47] What early American history showed is that though there were some satanic headwinds, the truth of the gospel not only got through but also had some of the more profound spiritual awakenings that America has ever experienced.

Richard Lints discussed the effect that the Renaissance had on the nineteenth Century this way, "In Europe and America belief in God was much more fragile at the end of the nineteenth Century than at its beginning. At the heart of the revolution was a

---

[47] W. Andrew Hoffecker, *Revolutions in Worldview: Understanding the Flow of Western Thought* (Phillipsburg, NJ: P&R Publishing, 2007), 272.

conflict over the foundational claims of biblical theism—belief in the existence of God who created the world, who orders history, who will bring all things to their proper consummation, and in whose image human beings are created. Idolatry was the attempt to fashion a god in our own image."[48] Thus, the devilish effects of the lies of the Garden (humanism) and the Renaissance were beginning to be seen in the worldview of society. On the contrary, the widely held beliefs in the truth-claims of the Bible were increasingly under attack.

The worldview of society was undergoing a seismic shift. Lints addressed these changes in people's worldview. Lints stated, "The burden of proof had shifted during the century. As the century wore on, atheism, earlier considered intellectually indefensible, became a much more reasonable alternative. By the end of the century, many of the significant voices we will hear in this chapter would have thought atheism on a relative par, intellectually speaking, with biblical theism. As atheism became less regnant, theism became much more precarious in Europe and America."[49]

What is noteworthy is all the while atheism was on the rise, the nineteenth century was also known as America's great missionary century, as referenced by Kaley Carpenter when she stated, "By the 19th century, Christian missions began expanding into foreign countries thanks in part to convicted college students during the Second Great Awakening."[50] College students held

---

[48] Richard Lints, *Revolutions in Worldview: Understanding the Flow of Western Thought* (Phillipsburg, NJ: P&R Publishing, 2007), 281–282.

[49] Lints, *Revolutions*, 282.
[50] Kaley M. Carpenter, "Missionary Movement," Association of Religious Archives, http://www.thearda.com/timeline/movements

prayer meetings, known as the "Haystack Revival," praying for revival and world missions to expand. Thus the Gospel expanded all the while a naturalistic worldview was coming into vogue.

CONCLUSION

The first principle to be addressed relative to philosophy was establishing a biblical framework for a biblical worldview. A narrow definition of philosophy was offered along with a broader and more casual use of the word philosophy that might be used to describe a worldview on a host of different subjects. Clarification of a biblical definition of philosophy was given as to the philosophy to be considered.

A number of scriptures were given to develop the basis for biblical philosophy, as well as to define biblical knowledge within the study of epistemology. The subject of truth was discussed, and scripture, argumentation for its significance, and other experts in this body of study were consulted. A fair bit of time was given to developing a biblical philosophy of education. Both biblical references and historical accounts of Christian education were developed. The historical account of the development of Western thought was offered, along with how Christian thought, to include revivals, was presented in order to have a better understanding and perspective of Christianity in the present time.

/movement_45.asp (accessed October 8, 2019).

A BIBLICAL PHILOSOPHY:

QUESTIONS ONE

A Biblical Philosophy

A Biblical Philosophy—Questions One

Questions:

1. Noah Webster's definition of philosophy is "The study of life and what it means, how we should live." This definition indicates a moral element in his use of "life" and "meaning." What does the inclusion of a moral element imply?

   _____

   _____

   _____

2. Paul's confrontation of the philosophers of his day at Mars Hill in Athens provides a reason why Christians should _____ in order to become a better gospel witness?

3. What takes supremacy when one is building a biblical worldview and biblical philosophy?

   _____

4. A) By what term do we refer to the study of knowledge?

   _____

   B) What must all knowledge be predicated on?

   _____

C) What must truth be predicated on?

_____

5. Frame discusses an individual's pursuit of truth without knowing Christ. How does he describe the problem with this individual's worldview (see page 16)?

_____

_____

_____

6. How does the study of apologetics benefit A) unbelievers and B) believers?

A)_____

B)_____

7. Which institution does the text point out is God's appointed keeper of the truth of the gospel and the primary educational institution for His Word?

_____

8. **Matthew 28:19:** "Go ye therefore, and teach all nations, baptizing them in the name of the Father, and of the Son, and of the Holy Ghost."

A BIBLICAL PHILOSOPHY

A) What is the main thrust of the Great Commission?

_____

B) Who are the two most prominent teachers referenced in Scripture?

_____

_____

9. What worldview is prevalent today that removes God from the equation when it comes to determining meaning and instead centers life around man himself and man's reason?

_____

10. In what way did college students aid the spread of missions in foreign countries in the nineteenth century?

_____

_____

_____

Transformational Truth Volume II

A Biblical Philosophy—Answers One

Answers:

1. Noah Webster's definition of philosophy is "The study of life and what it means, how we should live." This definition indicates a moral element in his use of "life" and "meaning." What does the inclusion of a moral element imply?

    Answer: A moral giver

2. Paul's confrontation of the philosophers of his day at Mars Hill in Athens provides a reason why Christians should _____ in order to become a better gospel witness?

    Answer: Christians should study philosophy.

3. What takes supremacy when one is building a biblical worldview and biblical philosophy?

    Answer: The Bible

4. A) By what term do we refer to the study of knowledge? B) What must all knowledge be predicated on? C) What must truth be predicated on?

    Answer:
    A. Epistemology
    B. Truth
    C. The Bible, biblical principles derived from the Bible, and biblical mandates.

5. Frame discusses an individual's pursuit of truth without knowing Christ. How does he describe the problem with this individual's worldview (see page 16)?

Answer: The unbeliever's worldview is twisted and unreliable. This individual asserts his own autonomy, making himself or something other than the biblical God the final standard of truth and right.

6. How does the study of apologetics benefit A) unbelievers and B) believers?

Answer:
   A. Unbelievers must reject falsehoods.
   B. Believers are edified as they learn the things of God.

7. Which institution does the text point out is God's appointed keeper of the truth of the gospel and the primary educational institution for His Word?

Answer: The church

8. **Matthew 28:19:** "Go ye therefore, and teach all nations, baptizing them in the name of the Father, and of the Son, and of the Holy Ghost."

A) What is the main thrust of the Great Commission? B) Who are the two most prominent teachers referenced in Scripture?

Answer:
   A. Teaching (making disciples)
   B. The Lord Jesus Christ and the Apostle Paul

9. What worldview is prevalent today that removes God from the equation when it comes to determining meaning and instead centers life around man himself and man's reason?

   Answer: Humanism or naturalism

10. In what way did college students aid the spread of missions in foreign countries in the nineteenth century?

    Answer: They held prayer meetings (known as the "Haystack Revival"), praying for revival and world missions to expand.

CHAPTER TWO

A BIBLICAL WORLDVIEW OF

EVIL, SUFFERING, AND MIRACLES

INTRODUCTION

One's worldview of evil, suffering, and miracles may have some of the widest interest and appeal to the broadest spectrum of people anywhere. To be sure, the study of evil is the subject matter of any theological institution that teaches on the subject of apologetics. When considering the problem of suffering, relative to God, it is certainly a question that demands answers to the skeptic and the Christian alike.

The skeptic would like to use any of these three—evil, suffering, and miracles—to be proof that God does not exist. When one looks at these three topics from a naturalistic worldview, it is not unrealistic to be a skeptic, which is exactly why these topics are so widely researched and communicated through broadcasts, lectures, debates, and writings from a biblical worldview. Having said that, this is exactly why a theistic worldview of evil, suffering, and miracles is so important to address and may bear the most fruit by addressing this topic for the unsaved world's consideration.

The Christian may be most concerned with finding reasonable answers for evil and suffering. The most likely question a Christian may ask himself is, "If I am living for the Lord and serving Him with my life, then why would bad things happen to me?" This is by no means a question to be dismissed or taken lightly. This is a very real question to be addressed, and one that has real-life ramifications. The Christian may have questions about miracles, relative to the biblical account of Creation, a worldwide flood, the parting of the Red Sea, and the bodily resurrection of Jesus Christ. The Christian may also want to further understand how miracles square with the laws of nature. The Christian may then be further encouraged and strengthened in his faith in Jesus Christ and better equipped to communicate these truth-claims to the lost world.

Two worldviews collide, sometimes referred to as Jerusalem and Athens. This is to say, a biblical worldview and a humanistic worldview. Otherwise stated, the naturalist versus the theist. In the midst of this seismic collision, humanity is in continual pursuit of the truth. It would be quite reasonable to disagree with this statement, except for the fact that research is the largest industry in the world. Most of humanity is looking around while Christians are looking up. This author likes to say, everyone in the world is a theologian; most just have bad theology. The whole world is searching for truth, and it is the believer's job to communicate and explain the truth-claims of the Bible and Christianity to the skeptics and those who are earnestly seeking the truth.

The Problem of Evil

The problem of evil almost seems like a riddle. The skeptics refuse to trust Christ as Savior because there is evil in the world, and God (the One they don't believe in) must be to blame. The Christian looks at the problem of evil and is perplexed by this apparent conundrum; he cannot believe that Christians should suffer as much if not more than their unbelieving counterparts. Chad Meister and James Dew addressed this issue by asking, "If it is possible that God has a good reason to allow evil, then the existence of evil is not incompatible with the existence and nature of God."[51]

When the skeptic considers the existence of God, relative to the problem of evil, the burden of proof for the existence of God falls on the skeptic, and not the believer. Whereas, when the believer considers the problem of evil, the burden is on the believer to pursue after a greater, deeper, more intimate knowledge of God. One should conclude then, that all of humanity is responsible to know the Lord.

The problem of evil cannot be answered outside a theistic worldview. Therefore, the only body of thought that will adequately and completely answer the problem of evil is a presuppositional approach to apologetics. The Apostle Paul went to the unbelieving Jews in the synagogues, and he went to Mars Hill to confront the unbelieving philosophers of his day. The way Paul approached each of these people groups was to expound the truth of what would be considered the Old Testament scriptures, as he used the scriptures to persuade them that Christ was the promised Messiah and the Creator of the universe.

Now, contrast a theistic worldview and biblical reasoning with Platonic, naturalistic reasoning relative to the problem of evil, and see how the conclusions differ from each other. A naturalistic approach to evil might be addressed this way: "A natural answer is that God must be a person who, at the very least, is very powerful, very knowledgeable, and morally very good. But if such a being exists, then it seems initially puzzling why various evils exist.

---

[51] Chad Meister and James Dew, *God and Evil: The Case for God in a World Filled With Pain* (Downers Grove: IVP, 2013), 15.

For many of the very undesirable states of affairs that the world contains are such as could be eliminated, or prevented, by a being who was only moderately powerful, while, given that humans are aware of such evils, a being only as knowledgeable as humans would be aware of their existence. Finally, even a moderately good human being, given the power to do so, would eliminate those evils. Why, then, do such undesirable states of affairs exist, if there is a being who is very powerful, very knowledgeable, and very good?"[52] First, this quoted author comes to no conclusions, only questions without having any answers to offer. Furthermore, this author then concluded that God must not be omnipotent (all-powerful) or omniscient (all-knowing), and God must not be a moral God if He allows evil to exist in His world.

A naturalistic worldview is not only incredibly flawed but only concludes with a dark existence in this life and a damnable eternity. In order to arrive at an accurate conclusion relative to a worldview, one must seek theistic answers to the problem of evil. Genesis 2:17: "But of the tree of the knowledge of good and evil, thou shalt not eat of it: for in the day that thou eatest thereof thou shalt surely die." God did not make man to obey with robotic obedience to Him, nor did God make humans to be secular beings. God made humans to be moral beings. This means that humans must have to have the ability to choose to make morally right decisions.

The alternative is also true. Humans were made as free, moral agents who can make wrong decisions. The theist must act in faith to look outside himself and look to the Creator and Savior recorded for the human race in the Bible. The theist begins with

---

[52] https://plato.stanford.edu/entries/evil/#RelConGod (accessed October 25, 2019).

the problem and concludes with credible, precise answers to evil. The conclusion is a better understanding of the essence and the character of God. And since knowing God is one of man's chief purposes in life, the knowledge to understand why God allows evil in His world will be of great benefit.

Greg Bahnsen explained the challenge of understanding the problem of evil this way: "Perhaps the most intense, pained and persistent challenge which believers hear about the truth of the Christian message comes in the form of what is called 'the problem of evil.' The suffering and evil which we see all about us seem to cry out against the existence of God—at least a God who is both benevolent and almighty."[53]

What is being described is pushback from unbelievers. An unbeliever is either knowingly or unwittingly fighting against God and is accusing God of wrongdoing for the evil in this world. Bahnsen continued, "This is thought by many to be the most difficult of all problems which apologists face, not only because of the apparent logical difficulty within the Christian outlook but because of the personal perplexity which any sensitive human being will feel when confronted with the terrible misery and wickedness that can be found in the world."[54] Bahnsen pointed out one aspect of the challenge of explaining the problem of evil and the ensuing suffering that was caused by evil. Certainly, no apologist ever wants to be indifferent to anyone's suffering.

It is of importance to note that skeptics never place blame for the problem of evil, which rightfully belongs to the Devil and free moral agents. As was referenced in Genesis chapter two,

---

[53] Greg Bahnsen, *Always Ready: Directions for Defending the Faith* (Nacogdoches, TX: Covenant Media Press, 2011), 163.

[54] Ibid.

Bahnsen explained, "Satan's strategy then (as now) was to work toward undermining man's presuppositional submission to this authoritative word from God. He began by calling the Word into question (v. 1) and then contradicting it openly (v. 4). The epistemological situation was thrown into upheaval when Eve began thinking that she could have a meaningful and proper understanding of reality apart from God's revelation. In that case she was free to examine what God had to say and autonomously determine its truth over against the conflicting hypothesis of Satan. She suspended thinking God's thoughts after Him in order to become the prime authority in the world of thought. Specifically, she abandoned loyalty to her Creator so as to make herself His equal (v. 5), determining good and evil for herself. She took her stand as a 'neutral' judge over God's hypothesis, thereby exalting her 'autonomous' reason over God's epistemologically necessary Word. By thus usurping the epistemic prerogatives of the Lord, she plunged the human race into the lawlessness we see ever about us in thought and behavior."[55]

The account of the Fall in the Garden of Eden is a major example of the principle of presuppositions for which one's doctrinal building blocks develop one's worldview. Furthermore, the presuppositions found in Genesis are examples of biblical argumentation for a biblical Creation, the supremacy of scripture, and biblical manhood and womanhood. Thus, when a skeptic is questioning (these may be overt or covert attacks on the Word of God) the source of evil, the apologist (all Christians) needs to point the skeptic to the real and responsible source of evil (Satan and free moral agents).

It is imperative that the apologist for Christ let the skeptic know that he is personally responsible for his own sinful nature.

---

[55] Bahnsen, *Always Ready*, 96.

A Biblical Worldview of Evil, Suffering, and Miracles

Romans 3:23: "For all have sinned, and come short of the glory of God." As free moral agents, we are all accountable to God's Word. John 12:48: "He that rejecteth me, and receiveth not my words, hath one that judgeth him: the word that I have spoken, the same shall judge him in the last day." The heart and motives of the skeptic are clearly revealed to not be noble or credible. This is purely a failed attempt of the skeptic to escape personal responsibility and guilt. The apologist is equally accountable to the Word of God and is responsible for advancing the Gospel of Jesus Christ to the world.

The battle between worldviews seems to focus on this area of the problem of evil. If the skeptics' perspective is right, maybe God doesn't exist. If, however, the Christians perspective is correct, then there would be strong evidence of the existence of God. The skeptic then might be honor-bound to accept the existence to God. Bahnsen addressed the issue this way, "Only when we become emotionally and intellectually intense about the existence of evil can we appreciate the depth of the problem unbelievers have with the Christian worldview—but, likewise, realize why the problem of evil ends up confirming the Christian outlook, rather than infirming it. When we talk about evil with unbelievers, it is crucial that both sides 'play for keeps.' Evil must be taken seriously 'as evil.'"[56]

- If God is responsible for evil, He must then exist.

- If the skeptic admits that God exists, then he cannot deny God's existence.

- Because the skeptic acknowledged God's existence, he will then will learn that God is a good, moral God.

---

[56] Bahnsen, *Always Ready*, 164.

- The Christian worldview sees that God is good and that He is the source of all good, and not evil.

Bahnsen explained, "God commanded Adam and Eve not to eat of a certain tree, testing them to see if they would attempt to define good and evil for themselves. Satan came along and challenged the goodness and truthfulness of God, suggesting He had base motives for keeping Adam and Eve from the delight of the tree. And at that point the whole course of human history depended upon whether Adam and Eve would trust and presuppose the goodness of God. Since they did not, the human race has been visited with torments too many and too painful to inventory. When unbelievers refuse to accept the goodness of God on the basis of His own Self-Revelation, they simply perpetuate the source of all of our human woes. Rather than solving the problem of evil, they are part of the problem."[57]

The atheist's argument against the existence of a good God is truly fighting against one's own best self-interest. If the atheist were to win the argument against the existence and love of God, what does he gain? The atheist's worldview would be a dark, pointless existence on a planet without a Creator, Divine purpose, a Savior for sins, a God that answers prayers, or a promise of eternal life. The atheist might be best described as doing "a fool's errand." To reject God's existence, creation, and love is to reject all meaning of life. It is reminiscent of our Lord's admonition to the Apostle Paul prior to his conversion. He recorded in Acts 26:14, "And when we were all fallen to the earth, I heard a voice speaking unto me, and saying in the Hebrew tongue, Saul, Saul, why persecutest thou me? it is hard for thee to kick against the pricks."

---

[57] Bahnsen, *Always Ready*, 174.

A Biblical Worldview of Evil, Suffering, and Miracles

The problem of evil also comes down to the argument of the sovereignty of God. John Frame explained, "The problem is simply that God is sovereign over all events, good and evil, and however one analyzes evil metaphorically, it is part of God's plan."[58] The naturalist has not yet come to believe that there is anything beyond the material world. What is wrong-headed about this thinking is that the naturalist also has nobody to praise for the good things in life. What good is Thanksgiving without the antecedent? Who is the atheist thankful to—the earth?

Frame then explained God's purpose of allowing evil to exist: "The philosopher G.W. Leibniz and others have argued that this world, for all its evils, is nonetheless the best world that God could have produced. The reason is not the weakness of God... but rather the very logic of creation. Certain evils are logically necessary to achieve certain good ends. For example, there must be suffering if there is to be compassion for sufferers."[59]

The logic that Frame presented here forces even believers to rethink their view of evil. Frame continued, "So the best possible world will include some evil. God necessarily, on this view, makes the best world possible; including whatever evils may be required for the best overall result. Because of the very excellence of His standards, He can do nothing less."[60]

This perspective on the problem of evil changes one's view of God's character. This perspective of evil helps the Christian to heal from the trials that have been allowed into his life. This now seems to make more sense to the Christian. As for the skeptic, he

---

[58] Frame, *Apologetics*, 162.

[59] Ibid.

[60] Ibid.

may or may not become a Christian, but the skeptic has been given a plausible reason for the problem of evil. The answer to why God would allow evil into the world gives the atheist very credible reasons that must be seriously considered.

Our Lord foretold the trials Christians would have in this world. The Apostle James gave the reason why the Lord allows Christians to go through trials in James 1:2–4: "My brethren, count it all joy when ye fall into divers temptations; Knowing this, that the trying of your faith worketh patience. But let patience have her perfect work, that ye may be perfect and entire, wanting nothing." The word *perfect* can be translated from the Greek to mean "mature," which is to say that the trials that the Lord divinely allow in our lives are to mature Christians in their faith in Him.

To the Believers:

- Trials cause the believer to seek the Lord more intensely.

- Seeking the Lord more intensely brings greater maturity to the believer.

- Christians that mature in their faith in Jesus Christ will have a greater testimony for the Lord and be a witness to the unsaved.

- Maturing Christians and new Christians to the faith bring greater glory to the Lord.

To the Unbelievers:

- Trials happen to unbelievers, and those trials have a big impact on the unbeliever.

- Many times, it is exactly the trial in an unbeliever's life that has a cause and effect, which may lead to his conversion.

- Sometimes the trials that unbelievers go through only harden their hearts to accepting Jesus Christ as their personal Savior.

- Other times, after many years of chastening, one will accept Christ as Savior.

- Whether the unbeliever accepts or rejects Jesus Christ as his personal Savior, the Lord is glorified.

The battle for the problem of evil between the atheist and the theist is communicated well, as Win Corduan explained, "Let us remind ourselves that the classic problem of evil in Christianity is rooted in a Christian theistic worldview. There could be no inconsistency between the God of theism and the reality of evil unless we began with the stark, seemingly insurmountable chasm between God and evil."[61]

What Corduan seems to be saying here is that if God did not exist, why would anyone mention evil? Or what measuring stick would one use to determine evil? And how would anyone determine good? It would seem to be an impossible question to answer without the existence of God. Corduan continued, "Only a fully biblical view of theism that upholds the purity and holiness of God and the irreparably devastating nature of evil can present the problem in all of its force. But for that reason, this 'Christian' problem of evil can also be solved only with propositions drawn from the worldview that gave rise to it, namely Christian theism."[62]

---

[61] Win Corduan, "Evil in Non-Christian Religions," in Meister and Dew, 175.

[62] Ibid.

This is to say that the problem of evil can not only prove the existence of God but also that the problem of evil cannot possibly prove the non-existence of God. The problem of evil actually confirms the existence and the goodness of God.

All biblical apologetics is based upon doctrine. Though this may seem redundant, it is imperative to understand that Bible doctrines are the baseline for what Christian apologists are seeking to advance. Corduan explained the relationship of the problem of evil with the resurrection of Jesus Christ, "However, by not minimizing evil but excepting it for all that it is, Christianity is also prepared to tell the world that Jesus Christ, in His death, burial, and resurrection, has not merely provided a method for us to avoid the consequences caused by sin but that He has defeated evil, and that we can already enjoy the benefit of Christ's defeat of evil before Satan's destruction is made visible to everyone in the future."[63] The resurrection of Jesus Christ is the cornerstone of the Christian belief system. It is also the biggest problem for atheists because the resurrection of Christ is not only the most documented event in world history but also the central event in all of world history.

Corduan continued, "But, also unlike other religions, it offers a final redemption from all evil and its consequences. By His atoning death, burial, and resurrection, Jesus Christ, God incarnate Himself, has undergone suffering for the sake of eradicating our own suffering, a status that is already confirmed for us for all eternity."[64]

---

[63] Corduan, "Evil in Non-Christian Religions," in Meister and Dew, 196.

[64] Ibid.

A Biblical Worldview of Evil, Suffering, and Miracles

By denying the love of Christ, who suffered for all humanity, the atheist denies himself of the answer to the problem of evil. The atheist, if he were to prevail in disproving the existence of God, which he cannot, would still be left with no answer to the problem of evil. The atheist is "kicking against the pricks." The only answer for the atheist, skeptic, and the world is believing in the death, burial, and resurrection of Jesus Christ. There is no other answer to evil.

- Evil and suffering do exist in the world.
- Good and evil in the world are proof of each other.
- The good in the world proves there is a moral standard.
- A moral standard comes from a good, moral God.
- God provided a divine remedy for evil.
- Therefore, Jesus Christ is the atheist's answer for evil.

The Problem of Suffering

The problem of suffering is not that suffering exists—it is to whom blame is assessed. The skeptic and atheist are quick to blame the One whom they say they do not believe in and certainly do not want anyone else to believe in either. Strangely enough, the atheists seem only to blame God, whom they say they do not believe in, rather than the more obvious choice, Satan, who is the source of much of the suffering and evil in the world.

The problem of suffering for the Christian is one that must be answered so that the believer may better understand the character and essence of God. The Christian must have answers so that his faith in the Lord might be strengthened in the face of suffering. The better understanding of why God allows suffering arms the believer to be a more effective witness for the Lord, minister to those who are suffering, and be able to answer the skeptics relative to suffering.

John Frame also explained suffering caused by evil this way: "And is God, because of His perfection able to create only perfect things? That might seem logical, but scripture teaches otherwise. Indeed, in the Bible, God creates beings who lack perfection in many ways. Adam was created good, but not perfect."[65] Genesis 2:18: "And the LORD God said, It is not good that the man should be alone; I will make him an help meet for him."

Frame further explained, "Satan himself was most likely created good, but was from the beginning capable of rebellion against God. Thus, even in the good creation there were imperfections. And so it goes throughout the historical providence of God. There is much that is imperfect that will be perfected (or destroyed) only in the new heavens and new Earth."[66] The Christian need not be caught flat-footed—or worse yet, speechless—when confronted by an atheist, relative to the problem of suffering and God's Creation in the Genesis account. Again, it is not the Christian who is without answers to difficult questions; it is the atheist that has no answers.

When Christians are pressed by atheists because of the suffering in the world, they many times are intimidated. See how Frame approached this situation: "Thus, when an unbeliever questions the consistency of God's sovereignty with His goodness in the face of evil, the apologist replies that the unbeliever has no

---

[65] Frame, *Apologetics*, 163.

[66] Ibid.

A Biblical Worldview of Evil, Suffering, and Miracles

right even to raise the question, for he cannot, on his basis, even distinguish good from evil."[67] Thus, the Christian must put the burden on the atheist to adopt a biblical worldview, because the atheist, as Frame stated, has no basis for determining between good and evil. The atheist must accept theism in order to have a basis for good and evil.

Frame continued to put the atheist in a box. He stated, "He, in a way, has a more serious problem than the believer does. If the believer faces the problem of how there can be evil (and suffering) in a theistic world, the unbeliever faces the problem of how there can be either good or evil in a nontheistic world."[68] The problem of evil and suffering in the world really does put the atheist in a box, and thus the Christian apologist must stand fast in the faith and knowledge of an omniscient, omnipotent, sovereign God.

The other problem that the atheist has is that his attempt at defining good and evil is his own moral abitur. Frame explained, "Unbelievers must surely not be allowed to take their own autonomy for granted in defining moral concepts. They must not be allowed to assume that they are the ultimate judges of what is right and wrong. Indeed, they should be warned that that sort of assumption rules out the biblical God from the outset and thus shows its character as a faith-presupposition. The unbeliever must know that we reject his presupposition altogether and insist on subjecting our moral standards to God's. And if the unbeliever insists upon his autonomy, we may have to get nasty and require him to show how an autonomous self can come to moral conclusions in a godless universe."[69]

---

[67] Ibid., 171.
[68] Frame, *Apologetics*, 172.

[69] Ibid.

The atheist began by impugning God's character over the serious matter of the problem of suffering, but then we found that he had no moral standing in himself, and no standing without a theistic worldview.

The problem of suffering is highly misunderstood by Christians, and thus it is imperative in order to help with the biblical understanding of suffering. Gary Habermas gave a surprising yet very helpful explanation as he explained, "Suffering is at the very center of the Christian gospel. There is absolutely no effort to deny it, to cover it up or to avoid Jesus' intense pain. Even before the cross, Jesus had been rejected by His family members who thought He was mentally disabled (Mark 3:20–21).

This, in itself, has often been sufficient to ruin the lives of individuals. Then in Gethsemane, even though he prayed that His Father's will be done, He pleaded that the coming events would not have to transpire (Luke 22:42) ... Luke tells us that Jesus' sweat drops appeared like blood (Luke 22:44)."[70] Many Christians mistakenly come to believe that the Christian life was intended to make their lives better, easier, or more comfortable. Though the Lord blesses faithfulness, and He loves His children, the suffering of Christ is part of His example to the world.

Habermas's explanation continued, "But the pain was nowhere near over—it simply continued, unabated. This intense emotional suffering in the garden was followed by Jesus' trial, beatings and then His crucifixion, arguably the worst death a person could undergo. But added to the excruciating physical pain was the additional, incredible emotional suffering that resulted in the Son of God's question, 'My God, my God, why hast thou forsaken me?' (Mark 15:34 KJV)."[71]

---

[70] Frame, *Apologetics*, 169.

The Christian should ask, "Shouldn't we be willing to suffer as our Savior suffered for us?" While the Atheist may ask, "How should the world respond to the central figure in human history, Jesus Christ?" The suffering of Christ cannot be ignored by the Christian nor the atheist. Both are required to respond to the suffering of Christ as the central event in human history.

One of the most painful aspects, when Christians suffer, is when they feel forgotten and abandoned. Habermas explained how Jesus must have felt and how Jesus can identify with our suffering because of the suffering He endured. Habermas stated, "The more we know about Roman crucifixion, the more we begin to fathom what was taking place. The Son of God was not exempt from such extreme suffering, even though He requested it personally of His Father. And no matter how much we gloss over Jesus' question of forsakenness, it seems plain that He felt abandon. Suffering far worse than us, He also thought that He was experiencing the silence of God!"[72]

Jesus endured the weight of the sins of the world, past, present, and future; Jesus had the entire world leave Him to suffer alone, and in maybe the most remarkable aspect of Jesus suffering, God the Father turned away from God the Son. Jesus' suffering was incalculable.

Habermas then turned to the obvious application to one's Christian life. He explained, "First, as we learn from the teachings of Jesus, Paul and others, we should actually *expect* to suffer, reminding ourselves of its inevitability. This change in thinking should allow us to face personal struggles whenever something happens, without thinking that God has zeroed in on us alone.

---

[71] Gary Habermas, "Evil, the Resurrection and the Example of Jesus," in Meister and Dew, 169.
[72] Habermas, "Evil, the Resurrection," 169.

Moreover, we should tell ourselves the sorts of truths that are consistent with this initial expectation."[73]

One of the basic verses learned in the Christian life is Acts 1:8: "But ye shall receive power, after that the Holy Ghost is come upon you: and ye shall be witnesses unto me both in Jerusalem, and in all Judaea, and in Samaria, and unto the uttermost part of the earth." When one looks deeper into this passage, he will find the Greek meaning of the word, *witness,* which is martyr, or martyrdom—this is to say, an eye witness or one that has experienced Christ. This would also be the ultimate validation of one's faith in Christ, that he would submit himself to martyrdom, even a violent death.

Some teaching from contemporary pulpits may cause more harm than good, relative to suffering. Though the blessings in the Christian life are unparalleled, the Christian life has some inherent hardships. Habermas expressed it this way, "In fact, there are many more comments in scripture as a whole about pain in general or suffering for the sake of righteousness than about us avoiding tough times.

To integrate these truths into our lives repeatedly would not only help to minimize bad teaching, but most of all would correct the false beliefs that we feed ourselves, thereby saving us a lot of hurt."[74] When a Christian apologist addresses a skeptic or atheist relative to suffering, the biblical concepts must be clearly communicated to the unbeliever in such a way that he understands the character and mind of Christ. One's worldview usually follows one's conversion; thus, it is imperative to

---

[73] Habermas, "Evil, the Resurrection," 173.

[74] Ibid., 174.

understand the plausibility of a righteous God allowing His people to suffer while the character of God is still good.

When one speaks of the benefit of suffering, he must either be crazy or speaking in terms of a biblical worldview. Habermas offered this insightful perspective, "We have seen that after Jesus suffered, His Father raised Him from the dead. Paul wanted to know Christ better, including sharing His suffering. He also wanted to share the experience of the resurrection (Philippians 3:10–11). For us too, eternity follows suffering (I Peter 5:10). This is a truth that we should always concentrate on, for it both changes our perspective on this life as well as providing motivation in the present."[75] This is the Christian life, learning and correcting one's worldview to match a biblical worldview. Christians improve their understanding of the character of Christ, and Christians are then better equipped to communicate a biblical worldview of suffering to a world that is suffering but does not yet have answers to this universal problem.

- Suffering is a universal problem that demands answers.

- Atheists do not have the answers to the problem of suffering.

- Mature Christians trust God even in their own suffering.

- A biblical approach to suffering heals Christians and convicts skeptics.

- Suffering causes Christians to seek the Lord more fervently; demonstrate compassion to those suffering; shine as a witness to the atheists, and bring greater glory to God.

---

[75] Habermas, "Evil, the Resurrection," 174.

The Morality of God

The problem of evil and the problem of suffering force the question, "If God is a moral God, how can evil and suffering exist in the world?" The glaring problem here is putting God on trial to answer for the contradiction of evil and suffering in the world. This author assessed the issue of the problem of evil in Volume I of Transformational Truth, and though it may seem unethical to change a theological position, it is most certainly reasonable to have grown in one's understanding of biblical truth. What is being referenced, relative to the morality of God, is whether a Christian needs to defend the source of evil.

Previously, this author was inclined to believe that God could not have created evil, though He has allowed evil. The conclusion was and still is that God is a moral, righteous, holy God. One must ask, "Who created Satan? Who created the tree of the knowledge of good and evil? Who created Adam and Eve?"

Yes, God created all of these, and yet He is a moral, good God. What is the change in this author's perspective? God does not need to be defended as His moral character and essence are above reproach. The skeptics are free moral agents that they alone are responsible for accepting or rejecting the truth-claims of the Bible. Believers, on the other hand, have a different responsibility. The believer is required to seek the Lord and to grow in his faith in Jesus Christ and His Word.

Basis of the Morality of God

All ethics come from outside of man because man is flawed and sinful. When one looks at the character and essence of God, one sees that God is the only One who has the moral character that can be the standard of ethics for people to live by. Thus the basis for all ethics is the Lord Jesus Christ. The following are a few scriptures that demonstrate the ethical character of God.

Psalm 119:68 "Thou art good, and doest good; teach me thy statutes."

Deuteronomy 32:4 "He is the Rock, his work is perfect: for all his ways are judgment: a God of truth and without iniquity, just and right is he."

Revelation 15:3-4 "And they sing the song of Moses the servant of God, and the song of the Lamb, saying, Great and marvellous are thy works, Lord God Almighty; just and true are thy ways, thou King of saints. Who shall not fear thee, O Lord, and glorify thy name? for thou only art holy: for all nations shall come and worship before thee; for thy judgments are made manifest."

I Timothy 1:11 "According to the glorious gospel of the blessed God, which was committed to my trust."

I Timothy 6:15 "Which in his times he shall shew, who is the blessed and only Potentate, the King of kings, and Lord of lords."

Matthew 5:48 "Be ye therefore perfect, even as your Father which is in heaven is perfect."

I John 3:2-3 "Beloved, now are we the sons of God, and it doth not yet appear what we shall be: but we know that, when he shall appear, we shall be like him; for we shall see him as he is. And every man that hath this hope in him purifieth himself, even as he is pure."

Ephesians 5:2 "And walk in love, as Christ also hath loved us, and hath given himself for us an offering and a sacrifice to God for a sweetsmelling savour."

I Peter 2:21 "For even hereunto were ye called: because Christ also suffered for us, leaving us an example, that ye should follow his steps."

The scriptures identify the character of our Lord Jesus Christ and the direct connection to morals. Wayne Grudem discussed the connection between God's character and morals this way: "In those and many other passages, the Bible emphasizes that God's moral character is good. He is a God who is good, and also loving, just, merciful, faithful, truthful, and holy. In addition, God approves of and actually delights in His own moral character."[76] Thus the beginning point of all morals and ethics is the moral character of God. When we begin to list the attributes of God, it may give more definition to who He is and how His character should be reflected in us.

Grudem explained, "Just as God is loving, just, merciful, faithful, trustful, holy, and so forth, so He also desires that we act in ways that are loving, just, merciful, faithful, truthful, holy, and so forth. These are the qualities that God approves of in Himself, and therefore these are the moral qualities that He approves of in His creatures as well."[77]

It may go without saying, but it would really be peculiar if God did not exhibit the character qualities mentioned. On the contrary, when Christians exhibit these aforementioned qualities, they are thought of to be godly. These godly characteristics are what Grudem referred to as God's moral standards. He stated, "If God's moral standards flow from His unchanging moral character, then it follows that these are the moral standards by which God

---

[76] Wayne Grudem, *Christian Ethics: An Introduction to Biblical Moral Reasoning* (Wheaton, IL: Crossway, 2018), 70.

[77] Ibid.

will hold all people everywhere accountable."[78] The skeptic cannot deny there must be some reason for the godly character of Christians.

Grudem discussed how the apostle Paul dealt with the Greek philosophers. Grudem stated, "When Paul spoke to the pagan Greek philosophers on the Areopagus in Athens, he was speaking to an audience that had no knowledge of the moral standards of the God of Israel."[79] The pagan philosophers were certainly concerned with ethics and morality but had no divine pattern to follow. Grudem continued, "These pagan Greek philosophers, Paul said, would be judged by God according to His eternal, universal moral standards."[80]

The Apostle John recorded a similar charge to all people when he penned John 12:48: "He that rejecteth me, and receiveth not my words, hath one that judgeth him: the word that I have spoken, the same shall judge him in the last day." This is why Grudem argued that all will be held to God's moral standard when he said, "The conclusion from these passages is that even people who do not believe in the God of the Bible or agree that His moral standards have divine authority on their lives will be judged by the God of all the earth. And the moral standards for which they will be held accountable are those that are found in God's 'law,' which is perfectly revealed in scripture and also written on people's hearts and consciences."[81] Everyone is without excuse since God made us, and He knows us inside and out.

---

[78] Grudem, *Christian Ethics*, 72.

[79] Ibid.

[80] Ibid.
[81] Grudem, *Christian Ethics*, 73.

The issue of the moral supremacy of God is part and parcel to the battle between naturalism and theism. This is seen in Grudem's explanation, "The Bible has a clear answer. It teaches us that when people assume that nothing exists in the world except human beings and the material Creation that we perceive with our senses, they have an incorrect assumption about what 'is' in the universe. That is because they have excluded from consideration the most important thing that exists in the universe, the most important being that 'is' namely, God Himself."[82]

This is referenced in Acts 17:24: "God that made the world and all things therein, seeing that he is Lord of heaven and earth, dwelleth not in temples made with hands." Grudem further explained, "Furthermore, this God of the Bible is not just a vague, abstract idea, an impersonal supreme being, but He is an eternal person who has a moral character. His moral character is part of what 'is' in the universe, and always has been and always will be. His approval of and delight in the excellence of His own moral character is also part of what 'is' in the universe. There can be no higher standard or moral right and wrong than God's moral character."[83]

Morals must have a moral giver. Morals have no basis other than in God. To employ a legal term, one might say morals have no standing other than from the divine moral giver, the Lord Jesus Christ.

The previous reference comparing naturalism to theism and the argument that moral standards must have a moral giver cannot be overlooked or minimized. The naturalist sees the

---

[82] Ibid., 74.

[83] Ibid.

universe in a single-dimensional worldview. This is to say, all the naturalist sees is the physical dimension in this universe.

Sometimes when referring to answered prayer or God simply moving in the affairs of men, it is referred to as the "unseen hand of God." This is to say that God is acting, moving, responding, and intervening in the affairs of men in the world. Grudem addressed the matter this way, "Therefore, in studying Christian ethics, we are not limited to our own observations of human conduct, instinct, and reasoning, for God also is part of what exists, and so are His Words.

In those words, He has given us moral laws that define what 'ought' and 'ought not' to be, what is morally right and wrong. What ought to be is 'God's moral character and also whatever He approves of in His creatures as consistent with His moral character."[84] God's moral character and His moral laws dictate Christian morality and ethics, which are to be applied in the Christian life in this world.

Gregory Ganssle argued for the goodness and morality of God from a different angle; he stated, "Most people will be surprised by the idea that evil points to the existence of a good God. Nearly everyone who considers the question thinks that evil points only away from His existence."[85] The naturalist has a wrong-headed worldview, to begin with, and most certainly has an incorrect view of evil.

In an American culture that celebrates Halloween—almost a nine billion dollar industry—it is easy to see the biggest lie told is not that Satan exists but rather that he does not exist. Thus, it is

---

[84] Grudem, *Christian Ethics*, 75.
[85] Gregory E. Ganssle, "Evil Pointing to the Existence of a Good God," in Meister and Dew, 217.

more plausible for the skeptic or critic of Christianity to automatically blame God for evil. It is noteworthy that most people would rather blame shift than take personal accountability for themselves.

Ganssle continued his argument for a moral God, "Most people are not merely expressing personal preferences in their use of moral terms. They take themselves to be ascribing something objectively true of the evil action. It is not merely that I dislike the way a person acts but I take it to be true that people ought not to act this way. When we call something evil, we are saying that there is something really wrong with it."[86]

The inference is if someone does evil, there must be a standard. Furthermore, when good is done, it must be in contrast to evil. Also, as Ganssle stated, when evil is done, people invariably know that something is wrong. Therefore, there must be a contrast between good and evil, and there must be a standard to determine good from evil.

Ganssle then argued for a good God in another surprising direction when he stated, "Things ought to be good, but evil twists that good reality away from its purpose or end. This picture presupposes that goodness is primary, and evil is a distortion. The primacy of goodness is another fact that points in the direction of a good God. If a good God exists and He created the universe and human beings for His good purposes, we would expect reality to be good. We would be surprised if it turned out that theism is true yet goodness is not primary. If atheism is true, we would have no expectation regarding goodness being primary or more fundamental than evil."[87]

---

[86] Ibid.
[87] Ganssle, "Evil Pointing," in Meister and Dew, 218–219.

One could easily see that all people, in every culture and time, have this expectation of good. Thus, Ganssle's argument from good or evil proves the existence of our Lord and Creator. Furthermore, both good and evil point to the fact that God is good. One's worldview ought to be shaped by this principle. In other words, when one sees evil in the world, he should instinctively see the evil as wrong and not a normal event, relative to the goodness of God. When one sees goodness, one should instinctively see that event as good and true reality relative to the goodness of God.

Skeptics can misunderstand good and evil, relative to a good and moral God. An atheist may attempt to use the object of evil to attempt to discredit Christianity. When hearts and minds are open to the truth, hearts and minds can be changed and pointed to the truth that our Lord and Creator are good. God is good.

Ganssle continued his apologetic argument by stating, "If God does exist, our expectation that reality is good rests on solid ground. God is the most fundamental reality, and He is good. Thus we would expect reality to be good. Goodness should be what is primary. Any evil that enters the universe will be a distortion of the original goodness. This scenario is exactly what we find. That our concepts of goodness and of evil lead us to expect that goodness is primary, then, points to the existence of a good God."[88]

- The fact that there is evil in the world demonstrates a distortion of reality.

- The fact that there is good in the world is proof of reality.

---

[88] Ganssle, "Evil Pointing," in Meister and Dew, 219.

- Both good and evil point to the ultimate reality that is in Jesus Christ.

- The ultimate reality develops one's worldview to believe that God is good.

- The goodness of God meets every need of the human heart, which is what the skeptic and atheist need.

The task of proving the goodness of God, after dealing with the problem of evil and suffering, is imperative. These subjects are complicated, but the spiritual healing and changed hearts are of the most importance. To better sum up these issues, Ganssle explained, "In Christianity, God is ultimately the one who overcomes evil. He has overcome evil at its root in the work of Jesus Christ on the cross. Furthermore, He will overcome evil in its entirety when He judges the world. In the meanwhile, He enlists His followers to be His agents of moral change and of divine healing in the world. We are placed into the world as His change agents. Our calling is to be citizens of His kingdom and to live out His counterculture values. As His followers embody and express love, sacrifice, justice and peace, divine goodness gains a foothold."[89]

As a believer, one should be encouraged by this topic of the morality of God. As a skeptic, one should be enlightened and encouraged to seek to know the Lord and His goodness through a personal relationship with Jesus Christ. As an atheist, one should be encouraged to reevaluate one's worldview, and strongly consider the claims of Christ and the fruit of godly Christian people giving their lives to share the goodness of God in this world.

---

[89] Ibid., 222.

A Biblical Worldview of Evil, Suffering, and Miracles

Atheists get hung up on this matter of the morality of God, relative to evil and suffering in the world. The atheists are by all accounts "kicking against the pricks," which is to say they are fighting against the truth. The problem for the atheists is that one cannot argue, negotiate, or reach a middle ground with the truth. The truth is non-negotiable. The atheists have a problem with the morality of God because they cannot disprove God, and it ruins their own explanation of evil.

Richard Dawkins surmised, "Many religious people find it hard to imagine how, without religion, one can be good, or would even want to be good."[90] What Dawkins was trying to do was to separate the goodness that is seen in Christians' lives and the One that the Christians are emulating. If one can be good without God or bad behavior in a Christian's life can be observed, then the reality and existence of God can be discredited. Dawkins' motives are blatantly obvious for all to see.

The real source of goodness is seen in Galatians 5:22–23: "But the fruit of the Spirit is love, joy, peace, longsuffering, gentleness, goodness, faith, Meekness, temperance: against such there is no law." Christians doing good in this world are being influenced by the Holy Spirit and led by Jesus Christ.

Dawkins went on to attempt to give what could be referred to as a metaphysical explanation for a spiritual problem. He argued his theory this way: "The whole idea of the selfish gene, with the stress properly applied to the last word, is that the unit of natural selection (i.e., the unit of self-interest) is not the selfish organism, nor the selfish group or selfish species or selfish ecosystem, but the selfish gene."[91] As a theist, one must, in part,

[90] Richard Dawkins, *The God Delusion* (Boston: Houghton Mifflin Company, 2006), 211.
[91] Dawkins, *The God Delusion*, 215.

believe that the Creator was and is the first scientist. God did create all that we see and all that we know about heaven from the scriptures.

The Bible does, however, have a warning about fake science in I Timothy 6:20: "O Timothy, keep that which is committed to thy trust, avoiding profane and vain babblings, and oppositions of science falsely so called."

Webster's Dictionary also has terminology for Dawkins' theory. The definition of fake science is referred to as pseudoscience and defined as "a system of theories, assumptions, and methods erroneously regarded as scientific."[92] Dawkins continued, "It is the gene that, in the form of information, either survives for many generations or does not. Unlike the gene (and arguably the meme), the organism, the group and the species are not the right kind of entity to serve as a unit in this sense, because they do not make exact copies of themselves, and do not compete in a pool of such self-replicating entities. That is precisely what genes do, and that is the—essentially logical—justification for singling the gene out as the unit of 'selfishness' in the special Darwinian sense of selfish."[93]

This author is not sure if Dawkins' contemporaries respect his work or not, relative to the "selfish gene." Because this author is not a biologist, but rather a theologian, this disclaimer is made, so that this argument does not come across as hypocritical. It is wonderful for any biologist also to be a Christian, and it would seem that a Christian who is a biologist would be far more

---

[92] Merriam-Webster, "Merriam-Webster Dictionary," https://www.merriam-webster.com/dictionary/pseudoscience (accessed December 7, 2019).
[93] Dawkins, *The God Delusion*, 215–216.

credible than an atheist biologist. Needless to say, the origins of life just go together with the biblical account of Creation.

This author asserts that the argument for a "selfish gene" is a complete fabrication, and the tactic of run, hide, and divert accountability is as old as the Garden of Eden. One may ask, how can a non-biologist make this assertion? Very easily, because blame-shifting, and offering a "biological explanation" for the sinful and selfishness of the unregenerate human condition, intended to deceive, does not pass the sniff test!

Consider the argument that Dawkins has put forth. He argued that a gene controls behavior. Where else has this argument been made? Many in the gay and lesbian community have claimed for years that they were born gay and lesbian. Well, it seems as though modern science has continued its march in trying to keep up with the science of the Bible. A biologist affiliated with MIT and Harvard University discussed his research, as reported in the American Family Association: "Ben Neale, an associate professor in the Analytic and Translational Genetics Unit at Massachusetts General Hospital, said, 'There is no single gay gene, and a genetic test for if you're going to have a same-sex relationship is not going to work. It's effectively impossible to predict an individual's sexual behavior from their genome."[94]

Dawkins could not contest this recent biological research if he wanted to. This author's position is theological; therefore, scripture has supremacy over all other extra-biblical sources. When an atheist argues from pseudoscience in an attempt to disprove the Bible and slander the character and essence of the

---

[94] Bryan Fischer, "Harvard and MIT Scientists: There Is No Gay Gene," American Family Association, https://www.afa.net/the-stand/culture/2019/08/harvard-and-mit-scientists-there-is-no-gay-gene/ (accessed December 8, 2019).

Creator, the atheist goes further into the indefensible area. If the atheist will accept Christ as his personal Savior, he will avoid the wrath of God. God is a good God and should be trusted to save everyone from his sins and provide eternal life in heaven one day very soon.

The point about referencing the fallacy of the "gay gene" is to point out the mutual fallacy of the "selfish gene." This tactic is purely an attempt at mass deception but has no credibility. The real answer to people's values and behavior is rather attributed to a spiritual factor, which is attributed to theology. One is no godlier than when he is charitable. When Christians show kindness to their neighbors, when Christians serve in a homeless shelter, when Christians travel halfway around the world to share the Gospel and stay for a lifetime, it is behavior that is learned and motivated by knowing the love of God.

Paul Copan took on this issue of the morality of God; he argued, "If science alone gives knowledge, as Dawkins claims, then how can he consider God's actions immoral or religion the root of all evil? As we'll see, Dawkins is helping himself to the metaphysical resources of a worldview he repudiates."[95] Copan has clearly put Dawkins in a theological box that he cannot escape. Copan continued, "Like theists, atheists have been made in God's image, and they can recognize the same sorts of virtues and behaviors, as atheists themselves like to point out. Having been made in the divine image, we've been designed to function properly by living morally."[96]

---

[95] Paul Copan, *Is God a Moral Monster: Making Sense of The Old Testament God* (Grand Rapids, MI: Baker Books, 2011), 210.

[96] Ibid.

A Biblical Worldview of Evil, Suffering, and Miracles

This is one of many reasons an atheistic zoologist is ill-equipped to comment on the Creators' design for humans to be moral, ethical beings. If one really wants to learn about the human condition (anthropology=the study of man), it is imperative that one study theology (the study of God). It is the Divine who knows us best because the Lord made us. It is the Lord who best knows the motives of our hearts. As one studies theology, one begins to understand anthropology better.

- God created man in His image and likeness.
- Human beings are sinful by nature.
- Jesus Christ atoned for the sins of humanity.
- Regenerated people exemplify the goodness of God.
- All of humanity has an innate understanding of morality.
- God is moral and good and is the moral giver of humanity.

The Problem of Miracles

Critics of the Bible and Christianity have been part of the human experience since the Garden of Eden when Satan questioned Eve (Genesis 3:1b: "Yea, hath God said...."). What Satan was doing is acting like a defense attorney, punching holes in God's instructions. Then in Gen. 3:4b ("Ye shall not surely die."), Satan used a sleight of hand to deceive. Correct, Adam and Eve did not die physically; yet they most certainly died spiritually. These types of attacks in the Garden of Eden are no different from the attacks today on Christians, the Bible, and the institution of the local church.

Attacks, relative to the problem of miracles, are a major target for demonic forces, in order to discredit the Bible and Christianity. If miracles are able to be dismissed, then every other aspect of Christianity may also be dismissed. The resurrection of Jesus Christ is the cornerstone of the Gospels and Christianity.

Apologetics has been a necessary aspect of the Christian witness since the first-century church, employed heavily by the Apostle Paul. Even the Old Testament patriarchs employed apologetics to persuade those of the coming Messiah. The culture in the current era is continuing to become more secular; thus, Christians must become better equipped to be a witness for Christ in this world.

William Lane Craig is one of the leading Christian evidential apologists in the world today. He discussed the connection between the problem of miracles and the existence of God when he stated, "The Christian argued that given the existence of God, miracles are possible because of God's omnipotence, because of His conservation of the world in being, and because of His sovereign freedom to act as He wills."[97] Craig was arguing for the existence of miracles presupposing the existence of God. This is to say, since God does exist, He can do miracles in nature and in the affairs of men.

Craig also argued from a position of historical accounts of experience. He stated, "A miracle is a matter of sense perception like any other event, and is therefore capable of being supported by historical testimony. A miracle is not contrary to experience as such, and therefore, the testimony to a miracle cannot be nullified by the testimony to the regular order of other experiences. The improbability that a miracle should occur in the past is equal to

---

[97] William Lane Craig, *Reasonable Faith: Christian Truth and Apologetics* (Wheaton: IL: Crossway Books, 2008), 258.

the probability that we should experience such events today, a probability that is slight or non-existent."[98]

Craig continued, "The Christian apologists simply sought to prove that in the case of Jesus' miracles and resurrection, the factual evidence was strong enough to establish the credibility of these events, in contrast to other stories of purported miracles. In short, miracles are neither impossible nor unidentifiable."[99] Paul documented some of the most overwhelming accounts of Christ's post-resurrection ministry in I Corinthians 15:3–6: "For I delivered unto you first of all that which I also received, how that Christ died for our sins according to the scriptures; And that he was buried, and that he rose again the third day according to the scriptures: And that he was seen of Cephas, then of the twelve: After that, he was seen of above five hundred brethren at once; of whom the greater part remain unto this present, but some are fallen asleep."

Craig also talked about the charge that miracles are an affront to the natural laws. He explained, "This would appear to bring some comfort to the modern defender of miracles, for he may now argue that it is illegitimate to exclude a priori a certain event that does not conform to known natural law, since that law cannot be rigidly applied to individual cases.

Given quantum indeterminacy, there is at least some chance of an event's occurring, regardless of how bizarre it might be."[100] What Craig is saying is that what we normally refer to as "natural laws" are not so much laws as they are the norms of what

---

[98] Ibid.

[99] Ibid., 259.
[100] Craig, *Reasonable Faith*, 260.

our general experience has been. In other words, for a miracle to happen, it does not necessarily break a natural law, but rather it may be a variation of the norms in nature.

Craig further elaborated on the natural law, relative to miracles. He explained, "According to the regularity theory, the 'laws' of nature are not really laws at all, but just descriptions of the way things happen in the world. They describe the regularities which we observe in nature. Now since on such a theory, natural law is just a generalized description of whatever occurs in nature, it just becomes part of the description. The law cannot be violated, because it just describes in a certain generalized form everything that does happen in nature."[101]

When a skeptic considers miracles against terminology and concepts that re perceived as truth, it may not be surprising that the real problem with miracles is not with the miracles but rather the way one may have previously come to know and identify nature.

After dealing with correcting the incorrect perceptions of the skeptics regarding miracles, Craig moved on with the presupposition that miracles have happened, and thus, this must lead to another affirmation of a theistic worldview. He argued, "Now the question is, what could conceivably transform an event that is naturally impossible into a real historical event? Clearly, the answer is the personal God of theism. For if a transcendent, personal God exists, then He could cause events in the universe that could not be produced by causes within the universe. It is precisely to such a God that the Christian apologists appealed. Given a God who is omnipotent, who conserves the world in being, and who is capable of acting freely, Christian thinkers seem to be entirely justified in maintaining that miracles are possible.

---

[101] Ibid., 262.

Indeed, only if atheism were proved to be true could one rationally deny the epistemic possibility of miracles."[102]

The apostles made truth-claims in the first century that people required proof of in order to believe in Christ as their Messiah. Peter wrote in II Peter 1:16: "For we have not followed cunningly devised fables, when we made known unto you the power and coming of our Lord Jesus Christ, but were eyewitnesses of his majesty." One of the most powerful proofs to believe in Christ were eyewitnesses, and the apostles provided eye witness accounts of Christ's life, death, burial, resurrection, post-resurrection ministry, and ascension.

Greg Bahnsen explained, "Peter knew it would be easy for people to 'write off' the claims of Christians as just so much more idle chatter and story-telling; he knew that people in his own generation had dismissed the church's proclamation about Jesus because they would not believe such claims regarding miracles. Far from being stupid and gullible, Peter's contemporaries had to be assured that apostolic accounts of Jesus were not cunningly devised fables, but eyewitness truth."[103]

In the Old Testament era and the first century, false prophets were a cottage industry. The penalty for being found a false witness was death by stoning, but nonetheless, false prophets were common. What immediately gave credibility to a claim was an eye witness. Relative to miracles, an eye witness brought strength to accounts of divine interventions in nature, healings, and the affairs of men.

One of the greatest proofs of miracles and all other divine truth-claims are fulfilled prophecies. One fulfilled prophecy of

---

[102] Craig, *Reasonable Faith*, 263.
[103] Bahnsen, *Always Ready*, 224.

correctly predicting the promised Messiah about seven hundred years in advance was recorded by the prophet Isaiah in Isaiah 53:3-6: "He is despised and rejected of men; a man of sorrows, and acquainted with grief: and we hid as it were our faces from him; he was despised, and we esteemed him not. Surely he hath borne our griefs, and carried our sorrows: yet we did esteem him stricken, smitten of God, and afflicted. But he was wounded for our transgressions, he was bruised for our iniquities: the chastisement of our peace was upon him; and with his stripes we are healed. All we like sheep have gone astray; we have turned every one to his own way; and the LORD hath laid on him the iniquity of us all."

    The skeptic and the atheist make their statements of denial as "'truth-claims," but in reality they are just making statements of unbelief. Bahnsen argued, "The denial of the very possibility of miracles is not a piece of evidence for rejecting the Christian worldview, but simply a specific manifestation of that very rejection."[104] Bahnsen continued his counter-argument to the skeptic, "Only if the Christian worldview happens to be false could the possibility of miracles be cogently precluded. According to scripture's account, God is the transcendent and almighty Creator of heaven and earth."[105] Bahnsen referenced Colossians 1:16-17 "For by him were all things created, that are in heaven, and that are in earth, visible and invisible, whether they be thrones, or dominions, or principalities, or powers: all things were created by him, and for him: And he is before all things, and by him all things consist."

---

[104]Bahnsen, *Always Ready*, 225.

[105] Ibid.

The believer looks at Creation and sees the handiwork of God. The believer sees the answers to prayers and sees the mercy of God. The believer sees the miraculous and sees the awesome power of God. What do you see?

One of the most important aspects of the accounts of miracles in the Bible is that it reveals God's character and His love and concern for mankind. J.P. Moreland discussed God's intervention with man by way of miracles. He explained, "If we set aside human history (especially salvation history), then a consistent picture of divine action in the natural world emerges. God is not to be seen as a direct causal factor in the sense of suspending or overriding the laws of nature and acting as a primary causal agent who creates a gap in the fabric by acting in it in a way other than normal, regular activity. Rather, God is constantly active in each and every event that happens.[106]

Note that Craig argued that "natural laws" are simply man's perception of what is normal in nature, rather than suggesting that miracles cause a suspension or break the laws of nature for a miracle to take place. The latter part of Moreland's argument is of interest to point out. The larger importance is that God is closely involved in the affairs of men, and it is important to note that God is sovereign over the affairs of man and of nature. Furthermore, it could not be overstated that the earth is the focal point of God. John 3:16: "For God so loved the world, that he gave his only begotten Son, that whosoever believeth in him should not perish, but have everlasting life." Every human being is the apple of God's eyes. His attention is focused on you!

---

[106] R. Douglas Geivett and Gary R. Habermas, *In Defense of Miracles: A Comprehensive Case For God's Action in History* (Downers Grove, IL: InterVarsity Press, 1997), 135.

Miracles are a surprisingly large part of what we know about God in the Old and New Testaments. Miracles teach us about the characteristics of God and what moves Him to work to move in a supernatural way in our world and lives. Miracles attracted and endeared people to the awesome and creative powers of the Creator and Savior of the world. The following is a list of miracles, people, and locations where the miracles took place in the Old Testament.

Miracles in Egypt

- The rod of Aaron turned into a serpent: Exodus 7:10–12.

The Ten Plagues

- Water Turned into Blood: Exodus 7:20–25.

- Frogs: Exodus 8:5–14.

- Lice: Exodus 8:16–18.

- Flies: Exodus 8:20–24.

- Murrain: Exodus 9:3–6.

- Boils: Exodus 9:8–11.

- Thunder and Hail: Exodus 9:22–26.

- Locusts: Exodus 10:12–19.

A Biblical worldview of Evil, Suffering, and Miracles

- Darkness: Exodus 10:21–23.

- The Firstborn Are Slain: Exodus 12:29–30.

- Parting of the Red Sea: Exodus 14:6, 21–31.

The Wilderness

- The waters of Marah: Exodus 15:23–25.

- Quails and Manna Sent: Exodus 16:14–35.

- Water from the Rock: Exodus 17:5–7.

- Nadab and Abihu Burnt: Leviticus 10:1–2.

- The Fire Quenched at Taberah: Numbers 11:1–3.

- The Earth and Fire Consumed Korah and 250 people: Numbers 16:31–35.

- Aaron at Kadesh; Almond Blossoms Budded: Numbers 17:8.

- Water from the Rock at Meribah: Numbers 20:7–11.

- Moses Lifted Up the Brazen Serpent: Numbers 21:8–9.

- The Jordan River Divided: Joshua 3:14–17.

The Land of Canaan—Joshua

- The City of Jericho Fallen: Joshua 6:6–25.

- The Sun and Moon Stood Still: Joshua 10:12–14.

The Land of the Philistines

- The Fall of Dagon and the Curse of the Philistines: I Samuel 5:4–6.

The Land of Israel—The Kings

- The Death of Uzzah by the Ark of God: II Samuel 6:7.
- The Withered Hand of Jeroboam: I Kings 13:4.
- The Restored Hand of Jeroboam: I Kings 13:5–6.
- Uzziah's Leprosy: II Chronicles 26:16–21.

The Land of Israel—Elijah

- Elijah Sent to the Widow; Oil Replenished: I Kings 17:14–16.
- The Son of the Widow Revived: I Kings 17:17–24.
- Elijah's Prayer Proved the Power of God: I Kings 18:30–38.
- Fire Called Down by Elijah: II Kings 1:10–12.
- Elijah's Parting of the Jordan River: II Kings 2:7–8.

The Land of Israel—Elisha

- The Parting of the River Jordan: II Kings 2:14.
- Elisha Healing Waters at Jericho: II Kings 2:21–22.
- The Destruction of Children at Bethel: II Kings 2:24.
- Water Supplied to Armies in Moab: II Kings 3:16–20.
- The Widow's Oil Multiplied: II Kings 4:2–7.
- Shunammite's Son Raised to Life: II Kings 4:32–37.
- Bringing Meat for the Pottage: II Kings 4:28–41.

- The Lord Provided for 100 Men with 20 Loaves: II Kings 4:42–44.

- Naaman, the Syrian, Healed of Leprosy: II Kings 5:10–14.

- Naaman's Leprosy Went to Gehazi: II Kings 5:20–27.

- Elisha and the Floating Axe Head: II Kings 6:5–7.

- The Syrians Attacked Israel and Were Blinded: II Kings 6:18–20.

- A Dead Man Revived After Touching Elisha's Bones: II Kings 13:21.

THE MEDITERRANEAN SEA—JONAH

- Jonah and the Great Fish: Jonah 2:1–10.

THE LAND OF ISRAEL—ISAIAH

- The Angel of the Lord Destroyed Sennacherib's Army: II Kings 19:35.

- The Sun's Shadow Went Back Ten Degrees: II Kings 20:9–11.

BABYLON, THE CAPTIVITY OF JUDAH

- Three Jewish Men in the Fiery Furnace: Daniel 3:19–27.

- Daniel Delivered from the Lion's Den: Daniel 6:16–23.

- The Writing on the Wall: Daniel 5:22–31.[107]

---

[107] Unknown, "Bible History Online," https://www.biblehistory

Miracles in the New Testament are equally important to our understanding of the characteristics and attributes of Jesus Christ. The miracles that color the earthly ministry of Jesus show His compassion for people. His miracles demonstrate His authority of the universe, as well as the concern for one of the smallest details of a person's life. As with all of the Word of God, Jesus declares Himself to be the Savior to the world. The miracles of Jesus go beyond the comprehension of the human mind. Miracles command authority, which is Jesus'. Miracles cause His followers to stand in awe of His greatness. The miracles of Jesus compel believers to love Him more. The following are miracles recorded in the New Testament.

- The Marriage in Cana; Jesus Turned Water into Wine (freshly squeezed grapes): John 2:1–11.

- A Nobleman at Capernaum was Healed: John 4:46–54.

- A Great Multitude of Fishes Caught: Luke 5:1–11.

- Jesus Healed a Man at The Synagogue with an Unclean Spirit: Mark 1:23–28.

- Jesus Healed Peter's Mother-In-Law of a Fever: Mark 1:30–31.

- Jesus Cleansed the Leper: Mark 1:40–45.

- Jesus Healed the Centurion's Servant: Matthew 8:8–13.

- Jesus Raised the Widow's Son from Nain Up: Luke 7:11–18.

- Jesus Commanded the Storm to be Calm: Matthew 8:23–27.

.com/old-testament/miracles.html (accessed December 11, 2019).

- Jesus Cast Out Devils from Two Men: Matthew 8:28–34.

- Jesus Healed a Man with Palsy: Matthew 9:1–8.

- Jairus' Daughter Raised from the Dead: Matthew 9:18–26.

- A Woman with an Issue of Blood for Twelve Years was Healed: Luke 8:43–48.

- Jesus Healed Two Blind Men: Matthew 9:27–31.

- Jesus Healed a Dumb Man Possessed with a Devil: Matthew 9:32–33.

- Jesus Healed Man at Bethesda on the Sabbath: John 5:1–9.

- Jesus Healed a Man's Withered Hand on The Sabbath: Matthew 12:10–13.

- Jesus Healed a Man That had a Devil, was Blind, and Dumb: Matthew 12:22.

- Jesus' Feeding of the Five Thousand: Matthew 14:15–21.

- Jesus Healed the Woman from Canaan's Daughter from a Devil: Matthew 15:22–28.

- Jesus Healed a Man by the Sea of Galilee Who was Both Deaf and Could Not Speak: Mark 7:31–37.

- Jesus Fed Four Thousand with Seven Loves and Three Fish: Matthew 15:32–39.

- Jesus Healed a Blind Man at Bethsaida: Mark 8:22–26.

- Jesus Healed a Boy with a Devil: Matthew 17:14–21.

- Jesus Healed a Man Born Blind: John 9:1–38.

- A Woman Healed of an Infirmity After Eighteen Years, on the Sabbath Day: Luke 13:10–17.

- Jesus Healed a Man with Dropsy on the Sabbath: Luke 14:1–4.

- Ten Men Were Cleansed by Jesus: Luke 17:11–19.

- Jesus Raised Lazarus to Life Again: John 11:1–46.

- Jesus Gave Sight Back to Two Men: Matthew 20:30–34.

- Jesus Cursed the Withering Fig Tree: Matthew 21:18–22.

- Jesus Healed the Ear That Peter Chopped Off the High Priest: Luke 22:50–51.

- Jesus Rose Victorious Over the Cross: Luke 24:5–12.

- Jesus Directed the Disciples Who Caught a Hundred and Fifty-Three Fish: John 21:1–14.[108]

An atheist or skeptic may attempt to discredit the testimony of one or a few eyewitnesses to the miracles recorded in the Old and New Testaments, but the problem remains for the atheist to disprove thousands of eyewitnesses to the eighty-seven recorded miracles listed. An eyewitness is a powerful proof of the miracles done by the Lord; furthermore, there are millions of secondary witnesses to the miracles. This is to say, this author was not present during Christ's post-resurrection forty-day ministry, but the persuading evidence of those 515 (I Corinthians 15:3–8) eyewitnesses at one time, who gave testimony to seeing Christ, is overwhelmingly convincing.

---

[108] Unknown, "Bible History Online," https://www.biblehistory.com/old-testament/miracles.html (accessed December 11, 2019).

CONCLUSION

This chapter has covered some of the deepest and richest issues in the Christian experience. The problem of evil offered what may be considered an unexpected outcome. This is to say that it may have been a surprise to find that, in fact, God did plan to have evil in the world so that His plans might come to pass, and He would receive greater glory. We also found that the atheist should not be allowed to put the Christian in a box, relative to evil. Furthermore, the Christian needs to point out that the atheist is the one in the box, as the atheist has no reference of good and evil without God in the universe.

In this chapter, the problem of suffering was also discussed. The practicality for the Christian is vital to hold to a proper biblical worldview relative to suffering. The idea was discussed that without suffering, compassion could not be demonstrated by God's people. The two issues of evil and suffering force the question about morality, which was addressed. The conclusion relative to the morality of God is, in fact, that God is a good God. He is moral, just, holy, and righteous.

The phrase that science is catching up to the Bible was appropriate as we discussed the potential of the human "selfish gene" to be the culprit for the atheist to escape responsibility for their sins. This study uncovered a recent biological admission that there is no "gay gene." The result is that humans are free, moral agents that have a sinful nature. God is a moral and just God, whom we can trust.

The problem of miracles was addressed in this chapter and offered a refreshing understanding of God's awesome powers. One noteworthy mention was how Christians and atheists may look at miracles in a similar way and how Christians should reconsider their views. The correction to this view may be that the laws of nature do not need to be suspended or broken for miracles to occur. The correct Christian view of natural laws is that they are not laws at all, but rather perceptions of how nature has often worked in the world.

    The Christian worldview should be that God can make unusual things happen in the world. He can obviously answer prayers, the universe is His, and He can move in the world as He wishes. The understanding of answered prayers, fulfilled prophecies, and miracles coming to pass are all affirmations to the believer. It is the atheists who have a real problem with miracles. The list of Old and New Testament miracles listed should be a cause to rejoice. Miracles demonstrate the compassion that the Lord has for His people. These same miracles demand that the atheists trust Christ as their personal Savior. There can be no other reasonable response.

A BIBLICAL WORLDVIEW OF EVIL, SUFFERING, AND MIRACLES: QUESTIONS TWO

Transformational Truth Volume II

A Biblical Worldview of Evil, Suffering, and Miracles—

Questions Two

Questions:

1. **Genesis 2:17:** "But of the tree of the knowledge of good and evil, thou shalt not eat of it: for in the day that thou eatest thereof thou shalt surely die."

   God did not make men to obey with robotic obedience, nor did God make human beings to be secular. Rather, what did God make men to be?

   _____

   _____

2. When a skeptic questions the source of evil, the apologist (all Christians) needs to point to the real and responsible source of evil:

   A)_____

   B)_____

3. How is an atheist "in a box," as it were, relative to the existence of evil?

   _____

   _____

A Biblical Worldview of Evil, Suffering, and Miracles

James 1:2-4: "My brethren, count it all joy when ye fall into divers temptations; Knowing this, that the trying of your faith worketh patience. But let patience have her perfect work, that ye may be perfect and entire, wanting nothing."

The word, "perfect" can be translated from the Greek to mean, "mature." What does this verse show us about trials in the life of Christians?

_____

_____

_____

4. While many Christians come to believe that the Christian life was intended to make their lives better, easier, or more comfortable, they are mistaken. The problem of suffering exists in the lives of all believers and can be largely understood through Christ himself. Explain the connection between Christ's life and Christians' suffering.

_____

_____

5. Upon what foundation should we develop our understanding of morals and ethics?

_____

_____

Galatians 5:22-23: "But the fruit of the Spirit is love, joy, peace, longsuffering, gentleness, goodness, faith, Meekness, temperance: against such there is no law."

God has enlisted Christians to be agents of moral change and divine healing in the world. What enables and empowers Christians to follow God's will by doing good in this world?

_____

6. **II Peter 1:16**: "For we have not followed cunningly devised fables, when we made known unto you the power and coming of our Lord Jesus Christ, but were eyewitnesses of his majesty."

   II Peter 1:16 lays out one of the most compelling proofs for Christ's miracles. What is this proof?

   _____

7. Why are miracles important to our understanding of God?

   _____

8. The laws of nature do not need to be suspended or broken for miracles to occur. Rather, how should the Christian understand natural laws?

   _____

   _____

A Biblical Worldview of Evil, Suffering, and Miracles

A Biblical Worldview of Evil, Suffering, and Miracles—Answers Two

Answers:

1. **Genesis 2:17:** "But of the tree of the knowledge of good and evil, thou shalt not eat of it: for in the day that thou eatest thereof thou shalt surely die."

   God did not make men to obey with robotic obedience, nor did God make human beings to be secular. Rather, what did God make men to be?

   Answer: God made humans to be moral beings, to be free, moral agents, which can make wrong decisions.

2. When a skeptic questions the source of evil, the apologist (all Christians) needs to point to the real and responsible source of evil:

   Answer:
   A. Satan
   B. Human beings as free moral agents

3. How is an atheist "in a box," as it were, relative to the existence of evil?

   Answer: He has no reference of good and evil without God's existence.

   James 1:2-4: "My brethren, count it all joy when ye fall into divers temptations; Knowing this, that the trying of your faith worketh patience. But let patience have her perfect work, that ye may be perfect and entire, wanting nothing."

The word "perfect" can be translated from the Greek to mean "mature." What does this verse show us about trials in the life of Christians?

Answer: The trials that the Lord divinely allow in our lives are to mature Christians in their faith in Him.

4. While many Christians come to believe that the Christian life was intended to make their lives better, easier, or more comfortable, they are mistaken. The problem of suffering exists in the lives of all believers and can be largely understood through Christ himself. Explain the connection between Christ's life and Christians' suffering.

Answer: The suffering of Christ is an example for Christians; we suffer as Christ Himself suffered.

5. Upon what foundation should we develop our understanding of morals and ethics?

Answer: The moral character of Jesus Christ and God the Father

Galatians 5:22-23: "But the fruit of the Spirit is love, joy, peace, longsuffering, gentleness, goodness, faith, Meekness, temperance: against such there is no law."

God has enlisted Christians to be agents of moral change and divine healing in the world. What enables and empowers Christians to follow God's will by doing good in this world?

Answer: The Holy Spirit's influence and Christ's leading

6. **II Peter 1:16**: "For we have not followed cunningly devised fables, when we made known unto you the power and coming of our Lord Jesus Christ, but were eyewitnesses of his majesty."

   II Peter 1:16 lays out one of the most compelling proofs for Christ's miracles. What is this proof?

   Answer: Eyewitnesses

7. Why are miracles important to our understanding of God?

   Answer: They show his character and attributes.

8. The laws of nature do not need to be suspended or broken for miracles to occur. Rather, how should the Christian understand natural laws?

   Answer: They are not laws at all but rather perceptions of how nature has often worked in the world.

CHAPTER THREE

CALVINISM, ARMINIANISM, AND PRESUPPOSITIONAL APOLOGETICS

INTRODUCTION

Calvinist beliefs will be the first of the beliefs to be researched and evaluated. This study discusses the definition, meaning, author, and applications of this belief. This writer will investigate dictionaries, Bible handbooks, systematic theology books, commentaries, and topical books that have dealt with this subject matter, and books that review the history of Calvinism. Secondly, the beliefs of Arminianism, its history, its author, its followers, and its applications will be reviewed.

Once the beliefs of Calvinism and Arminianism have been researched and reviewed, they will then be compared with each other for their similarities and differences, and then they will each be contrasted to a biblical approach of soteriology. This then will lead the reader to the Biblicist approach of soteriology. This writer will research theologians that have a viewpoint of Calvinism as well as theologians that have stood against this doctrine. In the conclusion, this writer will give final arguments for the strength and weaknesses of Calvinism, Arminianism, and the Biblicist approach to Soteriology.

Calvinism, Arminianism, and Presuppositional Apologetics

Calvinist Beliefs

Predestination

The Calvinist's belief focuses on the concept of predestination. This is in relation to the sovereignty of God and man's ability, or the inability of man's will to accept God's offer of salvation. The belief system then takes into account the sovereignty of God, including whom He predestinated, the nature of man, and the doctrine of soteriology. Romans 8:30: "Moreover whom he did predestinate, them he also called: and whom he called, them he also justified: and whom he justified, them he also glorified."

A definition for the word *predestinate* is defined by W.E. Vine, "This verb is to be distinguished from proginosko, to foreknow; the latter has special reference to the person's foreknown by God; proorizo has special reference to that to which the subjects of His foreknowledge are predestinated."[109]

Predestination is based upon what God foreknew, according to the Calvinist viewpoint of soteriology. Clarke gave the same definition to verse 30 as he wrote, "The Gentiles, whom He determined to call into His church with the Jewish people, He called—He invited by the preaching of the Gospel, to believe on His Son Jesus Christ."[110]

Clarke puts in context this word, predestination, with regard to what else is happening in this passage in Romans. Predestination has the idea that God purposed to invite Jews and

---

[109] W.E. Vine, *Vine's Expository Dictionary of Old and New Testament Words* (Grand Rapids: Baker Book House, 1971), 203.

[110] Adam Clarke, *Clarke's Commentary, Vol. VI., Romans–Revelation* (New York: Abingdon Press, 1832), 102.

Gentiles both to the cross of Jesus Christ by the preaching of the Gospel. Clarke indicated that all that would, through true faith and hearty repentance, would be pardoned from their sins. Wayne Grudem also discussed Romans 8:28-30 when he stated, "We know that in everything God works for good with those who love him, who are called according to his purpose."[111]

Clarke and Grudem both are respected theologians, yet they hold two very different points of view on this matter of who can be saved and who is chosen to be saved—or can all be saved that respond favorably? Clarke seems to believe that all that call upon the name of Christ in faith can be saved, while Grudem seems to believe that while some are chosen to be saved from before the foundations of the world, many have been chosen by God to be eternally separated from Him. This decision, Grudem believes, apparently took place even before the price for the sins of the world was even paid for by God's Son Jesus on the cross.

Albert Barnes assessed this passage, Romans 8:30, bluntly when referring to the apostles preaching this new gospel and he stated, "For how would it be a source of consolation to say to them that whom God foreknew he predestinated, and whom he predestinated he called, and whom he called he justified, and whom he justified might fall away, and be lost for ever?"[112]

Barnes approaches the passage as a grammarian to explain the contextual meaning of this passage. He suggested that these clauses, which each had a benefit attached to them, were contingent upon the first and the previous clause. As a result, he

---

[111] Wayne Grudem, *Systematic Theology* (Leicester: InterVarsity Press, 1994), 671.

[112] Albert Barnes, *Barnes' Notes, Acts–Romans* (Grand Rapids: Baker Book House, 1884), 192.

explained, that predestination was directly connected continuously to glorification. Barnes' position did not so much deal with who would or would not be saved but rather eternal security. Romans 8:35a: "Who shall separate us from the love of Christ?" Barnes' point, he stated, was that no one could separate you from Christ.

George Bryson, in his book, *The Dark Side of Calvinism*, used strong words. "According to Calvinism, it is futile to try to convert the lost who are not predestined to be saved.... Calvinists want other Christians to believe in their convoluted theology, which, if fully understood, destroys the gospel to every creature."[113]

Bryson continued his strong rebuke of Calvinism. In his introduction, he reported, "According to Calvin, it is all happening according to the perfect plan and purpose of God.... Can we trace moral evil back to God in the same way we can good things? Even the first sin and its terrible consequences were orchestrated by God."[114]

What Bryson has done is put Calvinism in terms of its character. When Calvinism, Bryson argued, is blaming God for the original sins, he seems to be describing Calvinism as faithless and humanistic in its character. Bryson does seem to add some balance to his approach to Calvinism. He stated, "While I am clearly opposed to Calvinism as a theological system, I do not consider Calvinists to be the enemy. In fact, I view Calvinists as the victims of Calvinism."[115] Bryson's view is significant as he

---

[113] George Bryson, *The Dark Side of Calvinism: The Calvinists Caste System* (Santa Ana: Calvary Chapel Publishing, 2004), 9.

[114] Ibid., 15.
[115] Bryson, *The Dark Side*, 16.

demonstrated human compassion, not theological, partisan arguments to defend or advance his position only. As a Christian apologist, he demonstrated that one could differ without destroying another with differing theological perspectives.

These ideas of God's sovereignty and predestination are widely contested and deeply embedded within different sects of Christendom. Jerry Walls and Joseph Dongell address this belief system, mostly within Reformed or Wesleyan churches. They referenced the Westminster Confession: "Here is what the Westminster divines insisted on. God's sovereign decrees do not in any way hinge on his foreknowledge of what his creatures will do or of their choices. God's knowledge of the future is not logically prior to his sovereign decrees, nor are his decrees based on foreknowledge. Rather, the other way around. God knew the future because of his sovereign decrees."[116]

Wells and Dongell analyzed this teaching on predestination that their readers might better understand the sovereignty of God. What they had explained is that God's foreknowledge was based upon His divine character and statues rather than on the character and actions of mankind. Thus, these authors have pointed out that the whole doctrine of redemption rests upon God's character, not man's.

Lawrence Berkhof reported that one of the early church fathers, Saint Augustine, was once persuaded and then rejected the doctrine of predestination. Berkhof's research demonstrated this. "At first, Augustine himself was inclined to this view, but deeper reflection on the sovereign character of the good pleasure of God led him to see that predestination was in no way

---

[116] Joseph R. Dongell and Jerry L. Wells, *Why I Am Not A Calvinist* (Downers Grove: InterVarsity Press, 2004), 122.

dependent on God's foreknowledge of human actions, but was rather the basis of the divine knowledge."[117]

Augustine's reaction to Calvinism would seem to be a reflection of one that knew the character of God and found that Calvinism did not mirror that same character that scripture depicts. Lewis Chafer discussed this conflict of the nature of God that Calvinism portrays and the nature of God that is seen through a father-son relationship. Chafer wrote, "Having secured for the believer a perfect union with Christ, a perfect standing, and a perfect acceptance in Christ, and on the ground of such infinite equality that God remains just when He justifies the ungodly, there remains only the problem of communion, fellowship, and a walk which is well-pleasing to God. As a son may be in fellowship or out of fellowship with his earthly father without affecting the immutable fact of Sonship, the child of God may be in fellowship and communion or out of fellowship and communion with his heavenly Father without disturbing the immutable fact of a sonship relation to God."[118]

What Augustine, as well as Chafer, was saying is that the philosophy of Calvinism and the doctrine of soteriology and the character of Christ should be in line with each other if Calvinism were to be consistent with the Bible. Since Calvinism does not align with the Bible doctrine of soteriology, in that it holds to a low view of the character of Christ, Augustine and Chafer ultimately rejected the philosophy of Calvinism.

Election

---

[117] Lawrence Berkof, *Systematic Theology* (Grand Rapids: William B. Eerdmans Publishing Company, 1939), 9.

[118] Lewis Sperry Chafer, "The Saving Work of the Triune God," Bibliotheca Sacra (July 1950): 264.

Charles Ryrie gave his understanding of election and broke it down into three areas. First, Ryrie discussed the idea of God's foresight as it relates to soteriology. He explained, "God looked down the corridor of time and in His foreknowledge saw who would accept Christ and then elected them to salvation. This makes foreknowledge foresight without any pre-temporal elective action on God's part."[119] What Ryrie has done is to lay out different perspectives of this controversial Philosophy. This first aspect, it would seem, lends itself to the belief of Calvinist.

The next view of election that Ryrie gives is what he called "Corporate election." This view focused on the assembly of believers rather than the individual believer. The corporate idea would coincide with Ephesians 1:1: "Paul, an apostle of Jesus Christ by the will of God, to the saints which are at Ephesus, and to the faithful in Christ Jesus." Ryrie explained, "An evangelical form of this same concept views election as the choosing of the group, the church, in Christ, but not of individuals until after they became members of the group by faith."[120] The controversy of election revolves around a number of scriptures, one being Ephesians 1:4: "According as he hath chosen us in him before the foundation of the world, that we should be holy and without blame before him in love." As mentioned, it is likely that Ryrie laid out several different positions and then the serious Bible student would dig deeper until the truth was found. As one that takes the position of the supremacy of scripture, there can only be one correct interpretation of scripture. The answer to this study is more grammatical than theological. The antecedent of "us" in

---

[119] Charles C. Ryrie, *Basic Theology: A Popular Systematic Guide To Understanding Biblical Truth* (Wheaton: Victor Books, 1986), 310.

[120] Ibid.

Ephesians 1:4 is a clear reference to the believers in the church of Ephesus.

Ryrie discussed the view of election as individual and pre-temporal. He explained, "Thus election is unconditional, pre-temporal, unmerited, and the basis of salvation. Those who hold this view also acknowledge that election is in Christ, but they mean that He is the ground and cause and guarantee of the election of individuals."[121]

William Shedd elaborated on the doctrine of soteriology and dealt with the use of the word elect in the Old Testament and giving his explanation. Shedd stated, "The covenant of grace and that of redemption are two modes or phases of the one evangelical covenant of mercy. The distinction is only a secondary or sub-distinction."[122] Shedd was dealing with the Isaiah 42:1 passage, "Behold my servant, whom I uphold; mine elect, in whom my soul delighteth; I have put my spirit upon him: he shall bring forth judgment to the Gentiles." Shedd explained first what the covenant was and then to whom the covenant was to. He stated, "The covenant is not made with them as alone and apart from Christ....And in like manner, when Christ, as in Isaiah 42:1-6, is spoken of as the party with whom the Father covenants, the elect are to be viewed as in Him."[123] Shedd nowhere in this passage stated that the Gentiles could not be saved, though primarily this passage dealt with the believing Jews. Shedd's reference was that the elect were those that, in the Old Testament setting, were believers. Shedd's discussion about covenants was significant as it

---

[121] Ryrie, *Basic Theology*, 311.

[122] William G.T. Shedd, *Dogmatic Theology, Vol. II* (Nashville: Thomas Nelson Publishers, 1980), 360.

[123] Ibid., 361.

demonstrated the bilateral relationship between God and His people.

Delitzsch gave further definition and explanation of this special relationship between God and Israel, which Isaiah referred to as the "elect." Delitzsch described Israel this way: "Israel's true nature as a servant of God, which had its roots in the election and calling of Jehovah, and manifested itself in conduct and action in harmony with this calling, is all concentrated in Him, the One, as its ripest fruit. The gracious purposes of God towards the whole human race, which were manifested even in the election of Israel, are brought by Him to their full completion."[124] Delitzsch detailed this relationship between God and His people, Israel, in a way that demonstrates a divine relationship that shows the purpose of God and His covenant relationship to Israel.

Ralph Smith took note of this covenant relationship between Jehovah-God and 'Israel His people.' Smith looked at this passage historically. Isaiah 45:4: "For Jacob my servant's sake, and Israel mine elect, I have even called thee by thy name: I have surnamed thee, though thou hast not known me." Smith explained the passage this way: "Nicholson noted that F. Giesebrecht first challenged Wellhausen's view that Israel's early relationship to Yahweh was a natural relationship—like that of son and father. This made Israel similar to other gods.... From the beginning, it was the belief in divine election that shaped the peculiar direction. It brought with it an aggressive exclusivism and 'a belief in the incomparability of Yahweh.'"[125] This covenant relationship

[124] F. Delitzsch and C.F.Keil, *Commentary on the Old Testament, Vol. VII, Isaiah* (Grand Rapids: William B. Eerdmans Publishing Company, 1986), 175.
[125] Ralph L. Smith, *Old Testament Theology: It's History, Method, And Message* (Nashville: Broadman & Holman Publishers, 1993), 132.

was not like those of the pagan gods. The exclusivity of this relationship demonstrated the holiness of God and the divine intervention that Jehovah-God worked in the Israelites.

Infralapsarian Election

Chad Brand began his explanation of infralapsarian election with his running definition. He stated that "Infralapsarian election to salvation may be defined as God's gracious choice, made in eternity past, of those whom he would save by faith through the atoning death of his Son, a choice which considered all of humanity as fallen, sinful, and guilty in Adam, fully deserving of eternal condemnation while fully undeserving of the bestowal of any favor or kindness, according to which God elected out of the whole of this fallen and guilty humanity some particular sinners to be granted eternal life in Christ, by grace, and through faith."[126]

What Brand has said is that before God the Father sent God the Son to die on the cross for the sins of the world, He decided who would be saved and who would not be saved. Since, as Brand stated, "some particular sinners" would be saved, the inference could only be that God decided not to grant salvation to most of humanity. The deeper and darker inference is that God must have made most of humanity in order to be then separated from that humanity for all eternity.

Paul Copan's viewpoint of God and His relationship to man was much different from the Calvinist viewpoint. Copan expressed, "Our being made in God's image is simply God's 'spreading the wealth.' God's rich goodness overflows to his creation, which lives, moves, and has its being in him. Though God

---

[126] Chad Owens Brand, *Perspectives on Election: Five Views* (Nashville: B & H Publishing Group, 2006), 47–48.

created freely and without constraint, God is bursting with joy and love to share His goodness with His creatures. He allows us, His image-bearers, to share in His characteristics."[127]

Copan described for his readers the heart that God has for His Creation, including mankind, which is unmistakably the divine love that can only be from God Himself. Contrary to Calvinism, the love that Copan describes God demonstrating is for everyone in His Creation. The idea that Copan was communicating, as it might apply to Calvinism, was there was no parsing out of who would be saved down through the corridors of time and whom God would decide before time even began would not get saved.

Millard Erickson has given a technical definition for the term infralapsarianism. Erickson stated, "The terminology relates to whether logically the decree to save comes before or after the decree permitted the fall. The positions also differ on whether the atonement was for all or only for those chosen to be saved."[128] Erickson listed the steps in the Calvinist's order of God's decrees as "the decree to create human beings; to permit the fall; to save some and condemn others, and to provide salvation only for the elect."[129]

Erickson, while defining this belief system, would seem to believe several inconsistencies that are cause to consider what the mind of God is in the totality of Creation and humanity. Since God is One of order, He has the preeminence, and all things exist and consist because and in Him. Colossians 1:16–18 gives some

---

[127] Copan, *Is God a Moral Monster*, 29.

[128] Millard J. Erickson, *Christian Theology*, 2nd ed. (Grand Rapids: Baker Books, 1983), 931.

[129] Ibid.

context to the mind of God as it relates to Creation and mankind. "For by him were all things created, that are in heaven, and that are in earth, visible and invisible, whether they be thrones, or dominions, or principalities, or powers: all things were created by him, and for him: And he is before all things, and by him all things consist. And he is the head of the body, the church: who is the beginning, the firstborn from the dead; that in all things he might have the preeminence." This matter of God's preeminence is that He is in control of all His Creation and all of mankind.

Every person was created for God's enjoyment, and He created each one for fellowship with Him. Matthew Henry stated, "He has the pre-eminence in the hearts of His people above the world and the flesh."[130] What Henry was describing was the God of Creation that was and continues to be involved in His Creation. Matthew further stated, "It pleased the Father that all fullness should dwell in Him; and we may have free resort to Him for all that grace for which we have occasion. He not only intercedes for it, but is the trustee in whose hands it is lodged to dispense to us: Of His fullness we receive, and grace for grace, grace in us answering to that grace which is in Him, and He fills all in all."[131] Henry was saying that God is the keeper, giver of His grace, and is the Intercessor for the people that He created.

Brand made his argument for infralapsarian election this way, "First, many passages of scripture that speak of God's election indicate that it is an election to salvation. It stands to reason, if this is the case, that God must have in view persons needing to be saved who are consequently chosen by Him for that gracious saving work. But of course, if God's elect is of persons

---

[130] Henry, *Matthew Henry's Commentary*, 753.

[131] Ibid.

needing to be saved, then it follows that those persons elected are viewed as sinners.... Put differently, in eternity past and before the creation of the world, God must have had in mind that the fall into sin had already occurred when He contemplated the totality of humanity out of which He elected some to be saved. Divine election to salvation, then, is infralapsarian."[132]

Brand exposed his real philosophy that he has relied upon human reason as he stated, "It stands to reason." Then Brand supposes to know the thoughts of God: "God must have had in mind." Brand then referenced Acts 13:48, "And when the Gentiles heard this, they were glad, and glorified the word of the Lord: and as many as were ordained to eternal life believed." Though Brand may not have referenced Isaiah 42:1, "Behold my servant, whom I uphold; mine elect, in whom my soul delighteth; I have put my spirit upon him: he shall bring forth judgment to the Gentiles." Though this writer has referenced this passage previously, the Calvinists teach in the later verse that the Gentiles are not God's elect while the former verse teaches that these Gentiles were God's elect.

Fred Brown dealt with this issue of election in the Bible. He discussed election this way: "Nothing in the Word of God requires a belief in the Unconditional Election of saved and lost. The philosophy of John Calvin requires belief in both. If for no other reason than his personally crafted definition of the sovereignty of God, there are no alternatives. For those of us who are Biblicists, as opposed to being Calvinists, other possibilities do exist. First, it should be restated that no man speaks infallibly on that which has not been detailed in the Bible."[133]

---

[132] Brand, *Perspectives on Election*, 50–51.
[133] Fred Brown, *Inside The Tulip Controversy: Calvinism Rebuked and Revisited* (Southern Pines: Calvary Press, 1986), 74.

Brown made a simple but profound argument as to the validity of Calvinism. Brown's question, which goes unanswered by the proponents of Calvinism, is "Why the Bible does not have the same requirements for salvation as does the philosophy of Calvinism?" Brown stated, "The great thinkers among men pale into insignificance as we meditate upon this declaration of the Eternal Sovereign of the universe."[134] And then he referenced Matthew 11:25: "At that time Jesus answered and said, I thank thee, O Father, Lord of heaven and earth, because thou hast hid these things from the wise and prudent, and hast revealed them unto babes." Brown is arguing for a simple gospel that even a young child could understand. With all the intellectual complexities of Calvinism, one would find great difficulty explaining Calvin's theory to children. Children will respond the love of Jesus to without question.

Limited Atonement

Another point of Calvin's philosophy was limited atonement. Samuel Telloyan first parsed out the difference between the Calvinists and the Arminians, which was that the Arminians did not believe in the unlimited atonement. Telloyan wrote with the intent to answer the question, "For whom did Christ die?" "Arminians hold that Christ's death was for all men alike, and that it secured for everyone a measure of common grace whereby all are able to believe if they will."[135] Telloyan than identified those that hold to a limited atonement position this way, "Those who consider that Christ died only for the elect can for convenience be referred to as limited redemptionists."[136]

---

[134] Ibid.
[135] Samuel Telloyan, "Did Christ Die For All?" Central Bible Quarterly (Winter 1967):16.

[136] Ibid.

Telloyen also discussed a more moderate position to the Calvinist or limited redemptionist. Telloyen stated, "Those who feel that this position is not true to scripture, the unlimited redemptionists, say that Christ Jesus died for all, but only those who trust Him receive eternal life."[137]

After Telloyen clarified terms that would be discussed regarding limited atonement, he made a number of arguments for the limited atonement position, followed by numerous scriptures in favor of the unlimited atonement position. Telloyen began with his list of arguments for limited atonement. "The first argument for the limited redemption rests on the tenet of election."[138]

Telloyen then referenced the second argument. "A second argument for limited atonement, quite similar to the first, is from the covenant of redemption. In this covenant, a relation supposedly was established between the Father and the Son and those for whom Christ would lay down His life. Since the covenant of redemption did not include all, it follows that Christ did not die for all.... A third argument for the limited atonement is the argument from the special love of God. It is stated that God had a peculiar love to His people, to His church, to the elect, and that this love prompted Him to send Christ."[139]

In the fourth argument, from the Old Testament, Telloyen argued that the Aaronic priesthood was a type of Christ, and he only interceded for his own tribe and not for any other. It stood to reason then that Christ died only for His elect. Telloyan concludes

---

[137] Ibid.

[138] Ibid., 17
[139] Telloyen,"Did Christ Die," 17.

the list of humanistic arguments for limited atonement with a Calvinistic viewpoint of Isaiah 53:12: "Therefore will I divide him a portion with the great, and he shall divide the spoil with the strong; because he hath poured out his soul unto death: and he was numbered with the transgressors; and he bare the sin of many, and made intercession for the transgressors."

Consider the difference in Matthew Henry's understanding. "In the foregoing verses, the prophet had testified very particularly of the sufferings of Christ, yet mixing some hints of the happy issue of them; here he again mentions his sufferings, but largely foretells the glory that should follow."[140] The One that Isaiah was referring to in this passage was Christ and the sufferings that were foretold. Nowhere does this passage exclude anyone from the benefit of Christ's propitiation of sins. Matthew Henry, in the commentary on this passage, never makes any reference to those chosen to eternal life or dammed to hell.

Unlimited Atonement

Ron Rhodes discussed clear Scriptural references and biblical thinking as he explained the viewpoint of unlimited atonement. The strength of his argument is the scriptural references put forth, such as John 1:29, "The next day John seeth Jesus coming unto him, and saith, Behold the Lamb of God, which taketh away the sin of the world." Rhodes then explained, "Though Calvin is often cited in favor of limited atonement, here is a clear statement in which unlimited atonement is in view."[141] The credibility aspect regarding Rhodes is his command of the

---

[140] Henry, *Matthew Henry's Commentary*, 306.
[141] Ron Rhodes, "The Extent of the Atonement: Limited Atonement Versus Unlimited Atonement," Chafer Theological Seminary Journal (Fall 1996): 6.

biblical languages, thus giving confidence that his use of scripture is based on sound exegesis.

Rhodes then referenced John 3:16: "For God so loved the world, that he gave his only begotten Son, that whosoever believeth in him should not perish, but have everlasting life." He then stated, "Christ applied the story spiritually when He says that 'whosoever' believes on the uplifted Son of Man shall experience spiritual deliverance."[142] Rhodes again references a powerful account from John 4:42 to demonstrate the biblical persuasion of God's unlimited atonement. "And said unto the woman, Now we believe, not because of thy saying: for we have heard him ourselves, and know that this is indeed the Christ, the Saviour of the world."[143]

Rhodes made a good argument that Jesus is the Savior of the world, and that would include everyone. He then wrote, "It is quite certain that when the Samaritans called Jesus 'the Saviour of the world,' they were not thinking of the world of the elect. To read such a meaning into this text would be sheer eisegesis."[144] Rhodes continued his argument for unlimited atonement as he referenced I Timothy 4:10, "For therefore we both labour and suffer reproach, because we trust in the living God, who is the Saviour of all men, specially of those that believe." He explained, "Christ has made a provision of salvation for all men, though it only becomes effective for those who exercise faith in Christ."[145]

---

[142] Ibid.

[143] Ibid.
[144] Rhodes, "The Extent," 6.

[145] Ibid.

Again Telloyan appropriately referenced I John 2:1, 2: "My little children, these things write I unto you, that ye sin not. And if any man sin, we have an advocate with the Father, Jesus Christ the righteous: And he is the propitiation for our sins: and not for ours only, but also for the sins of the whole world." He then stated, "The elect people of God are encouraged not to sin, but if they would sin Jesus Christ is an advocate at God's right hand to plead His blood on their behalf. The apostle continues by stating that the blood of Christ was not only shed for the elect but for the sins of the whole world. This strongly asserts not unlimited salvation, but unlimited atonement."[146]

Paul Martin Henebury gave a strong pro-unlimited atonement position when he referenced I Timothy 1:15: "This is a faithful saying, and worthy of all acceptation, that Christ Jesus came into the world to save sinners; of whom I am chief." And then he referenced II Peter 3:9: "The Lord is not slack concerning his promise, as some men count slackness; but is longsuffering to us-ward, not willing that any should perish, but that all should come to repentance."

Henebury approached the scriptures—in particular, those that dealt with the unlimited atonement doctrine as plenary, verbal, grammatical, and historical in its hermeneutics. He demonstrated this when he stated, "The Bible plainly says that Christ died for 'sinners,' 'the lost,' 'the ungodly,' 'the world,' etc.

Unless only the elect qualify as belonging to this group, these verses ought to be taken to mean that Christ died for all lost sinners. After all, Adam plunged the whole of his posterity into sin and judgment."[147]

---

[146] Telloyan, "Did Christ Die," 20.
[147] Paul Martin Henebury, "Christ's Atonement: Its Purpose and Extent, Part 1," Conservative Theological Journal (March 2005): 105.

Arminian Beliefs

Historical Background

J. D. Douglas took the time to explain in general terms some history of Arminianism. He gave the church history approach to defining Arminianism as it was a manufactured system of beliefs. Because this belief system was not found in the Bible, Douglas explained the history from which the Arminian philosophy was established and taught. "A theological system named after Jacobus Arminius, a Dutch theologian (1560–1609) who was educated at Leyden, Basle, and Geneva. After studying under Beza, he went to Amsterdam to serve as minister of a Reformed congregation (1588). Holland had become the center of Calvinism during the sixteenth century, but during his fifteen years as a pastor, Arminius came to question some of the teachings of Calvinism. Disputes arose, and he left the pastorate and became a professor of theology at the University of Leyden. Here he gave a series of lectures on the doctrine of predestination."[148]

Beliefs Defined

Douglas, after giving a brief historical overview, gave a brief outline of the beliefs that separated Arminianism from Calvinism. Again, the reason for the need of an explanation, as opposed to the systematic theologies that define Christian orthodoxy, is that the Arminian system of beliefs is not laid out in scripture. Rather this belief system would be defined as a man-made philosophy.

---

[148] J.D.Douglas, *The New International Dictionary of the Christian Church* (Grand Rapids: Zondervan Publishing House,1978), 70.

Douglas then outlined the belief system of Arminianism this way: "After the death of Arminius, his followers issued the Remonstrance of 1610, which outlines the system known as Arminianism. The major points of departure from strict Calvinism are that (1) the decree of salvation applies to all who believe on Christ and who persevere in obedience and faith; (2) Christ died for all men; (3) the Holy Spirit must help men to do things that are truly good (such as having faith in Christ for salvation); (4) God's saving grace is not irresistible; (5) it is possible for those who are Christians to fall from grace."[149]

Robert Picirilli discussed the matter of foreknowledge. It would appear that he came at it from an Arminian perspective as he compared it to the Calvinistic view of foreknowledge, "The certainty of a future event means, simply, the fact that it will occur.... If God is omniscient, it follows that all things that occur are certainly foreknown by God. Everything that happens is certain and known as such by God from all eternity."[150]

Picirilli then described the Calvinistic view of foreknowledge. "Calvinists affirm that all events, including future ones, are certain and foreknown because God has foreordained all events: In that case, there is no problem with absolute foreknowledge, or with divine control; the question is whether there is any real freedom and moral responsibility for humans."[151] Picirilli began his humanistic reasoning, trying desperately to get into the mind of God, almost in a Nixonian hearing kind of way ("What did the president know and when did he know it?").[152]

---

[149] Douglas, *The New International Dictionary*, 70.
[150] Robert E. Picirilli, "Foreknowlege, Freedom, And the Future," Journal of the Evangelical Theological Society (June 2000): 262.

[151] Picirilli, "Foreknowledge," 265.

Picirilli then contrasted the Calvinist approach with Arminius; and though they seem to be in agreement on the foreknowledge aspect, the focus of the Calvinist seemed to be on the response by mankind, and whether humans had free will to choose correctly.

Lewis Sperry Chafer discussed eternal security as understood by Arminius. And then, he quickly communicated the biblical approach to eternal security. Chafer stated, "Eternal security, by which term it is meant that those chosen of God and saved by grace are, of necessity, preserved unto the realization of the design of God. Since sovereign election purposes this and sovereign grace accomplishes it, the scriptures could not—being infinitely true—do other than to declare the Christian's security without reservation or complication. This the scriptures assuredly declare."[153] Chafer was decisive and forceful in his choice of words as he communicated this biblical position. In contrast, he gave no space to the Arminian position.

Chafer continued by stating the Armenian's non-security position and contrasted it with the biblical, eternal security position. He argued, "It may be restated that, as for human experience which the Arminian believes is at times a proof that one once saved can be lost again, it cannot be proved that such a case ever existed. On the contrary, revelation so defines the saving and keeping power of God that it can be said with all assurance that not one of those who have been truly regenerated has ever been lost, nor could such a one be lost. As for human reason, which the Arminian employs against the doctrine of

---

[152] Michael McKinney, "What Did He Know and When Did He Know It?" (Leadership Now, November 2011) available from http://www.leadershipnow.com/leadingblog/2011/11/what_did_he_know_and_when_did.html, (accessed Mar. 12, 2012).

[153] Lewis Sperry Chafer, "The Eternal Security of the Believer," Bibliotheca Sacra (July 1949): 261.

security, it need only be pointed out that no human is able to trace the divine undertaking which provides both salvation and safekeeping on the ground of the sacrificial and imputed merit of the Son of God, and with no other requirement resting on the sinner than that he believes on Christ as his Savior." [154]

Chafer again made the contrast between Calvinist and Arminian beliefs on eternal security. He put forth the facts of the Arminian and made the strong, biblical case and arguments for the eternal security position. He finished by stating the totality of the requirements for salvation and eternal security by placing simple faith in Jesus Christ.

Conflicted Beliefs

Armenians are many times, Roger Olson stated, compared to Calvinists. Olson argued that these two philosophes were not compatible with one another. Olson then listed numerous points of difference between Armenians and Calvinists.

He explained, "While they accept a form of limited atonement, they reject the idea that God sent Christ to die only for a portion of humanity. The atonement's limited nature is grounded not in God's intention but in human response. Only those who accept the grace of the cross are saved by God; those who reject it and seek salvation elsewhere fail to be included in it by their own choice, much to God's dismay. While Arminians embrace the necessity of supernatural grace for salvation, they deny that God irresistibly bends human wills so that they are effectually saved apart from their own spontaneous response."[155]

---

[154] Chafer, "The Eternal Security," 290.
[155] Roger E. Olson, *Arminian Theology: Myths and Realities* (Downers Grove: Inner Varsity Press, 2006), 63.

By pointing out inconsistencies with the two philosophies, Olson has, rightly so, brought doubt to these belief systems. Olson, later in his book, corrected a falsehood regarding Arminianism. There have been a number of myths, he explained, about Arminianism, such as the myth that this belief is humanistic, and also that it is not a theology of grace. Olson clarified this misconception when he stated, "Arminius went out of his way to elevate grace as the sole efficient cause of salvation and even of the first exercise of a good will toward God, including the desire to receive the good news and respond positively to it."[156]

Olson seems to have clarified, at least on this point, that Arminius believed the grace that is seen in Ephesians 2:8, 9: "For by grace are ye saved through faith; and that not of yourselves: it is the gift of God: Not of works, lest any man should boast." At least Olson found the basis of faith and salvation written within the belief system of Armenians' view of Christianity.

Beliefs Debated

Alan Sell documented both Arminius' contentions as well as Calvin's contentions as it related to the depravity of man and the free will of man. Sell put forth the Arminius' position this way: "Arminius, as we have seen, was equally concerned to emphasize that God was not the author of sin."[157]

The Calvinists' position was not acceptable to Arminius. As it relates to total depravity, Sell stated, "Further, the Remonstrant points did not mention, and certainly did not deny, the doctrine of total depravity. There was, however, a gradual drift from this doctrine on the part of many Armenians, especially when they

---

[156] Ibid., 161.
[157] Alan P.F. Sell, *The Great Debate: Calvinism, Arminianism, and Salvation* (Grand Rapids: Baker Book House, 1982), 16.

came to deny the imputation of Adam's first sin to his descendants, and when they elaborated their view of man's freedom in such a way as to threaten the notion of man's total inability. Here we approach the crux of the Calvinist-Arminian dispute."[158]

Sell that stated the Calvinist's position rests on man's depravity and man's will. Sell explained, "Calvin wishes to argue that man's will is bound, but that he is still responsible. His freedom consists in his being able to act freely in a manner consistent with his will; but fallen man's will is depraved, and from this depravity he can be rescued only by the grace of God in Christ."[159]

BIBLICIST BELIEFS

Predestination

The final arbiter for any theological question or debate is the Bible. This writer sometimes refers to the Bible and the debates that ensue as the great finalizer. Robert Peterson and Michael Williams gave their final answers on the belief system of Arminianism. Their first conclusion was on the doctrine of predestination. They wrote, "First, although the Armenians hold to corporate rather than individual election, the Bible teaches both.... Arminians, then, make a false distinction between individual and corporate election."[160]

They then referenced, John 6:37–40 to make their point. "All that the Father giveth me shall come to me; and him that

---

[158] Ibid.
[159] Sell, *The Great Debate*, 17.

[160] Robert A. Peterson and Michael D. Williams, *Why I Am Not An Arminian* (Downers Grove: InterVarsity Press, 2004), 64.

cometh to me I will in no wise cast out. For I came down from heaven, not to do mine own will, but the will of him that sent me. And this is the Father's will which hath sent me, that of all which he hath given me I should lose nothing, but should raise it up again at the last day. And this is the will of him that sent me, that every one which seeth the Son, and believeth on him, may have everlasting life: and I will raise him up at the last day."

Laurence Vance used the ridicules to demonstrate the absurdity of an unbiblical view of election and predestination. Vance stated it this way, "Consider the implications of this teaching: (1) The 'elect' were 'in Christ' before the foundation of the world. (2) The 'elect' fell out of Christ and became lost 'in Adam.' (3) The 'elect' got back 'in Christ' at the cross. (4) The 'elect' fell out of Christ again so they could be born 'in sin.'(5) The 'elect' got back 'in Christ' when God applied Irresistible Grace to them and they got saved. But if the 'elect' fell out of Christ even once, what is to prevent them from falling again?"[161]

Two of the verses Vance used to make his biblical case that anyone can be saved were Romans 5:12 ("Wherefore, as by one man sin entered into the world, and death by sin; and so death passed upon all men, for that all have sinned") and I Corinthians 15:22 ("For as in Adam all die, even so in Christ shall all be made alive").

Peterson, Williams, and Vance all made simple yet profound cases for an unlimited atonement position. Furthermore, the simplicity of their arguments all pointed to the authoritativeness of scripture as the final authority that salvation was provided for everyone at the cross.

---

[161] Laurence M. Vance, *The Other Side of Calvinism* (Pensacola: Vance Publications, 1991), 362.

Perseverance

Erickson came to an appropriate conclusion regarding the preservation of the saints. He gave consideration to both Armenian and Calvinist views before arriving at the biblical view. He concluded, "The practical implication of our understanding of the doctrine of perseverance is that believers can rest secure in the assurance that their salvation is permanent; nothing can separate them from the love of God. Thus, they can rejoice in the prospect of eternal life. There need be no anxiety that something or someone will keep them from attaining the final blessedness that they have been promised and have come to expect."[162] Here he alluded to this quote in Romans 8:28: "And we know that all things work together for good to them that love God, to them who are the called according to his purpose."

Peterson and Williams make a compelling case for the biblical view of the perseverance of the saints. Their conclusion was expressed this way: "First, we sampled the abundant biblical testimony to God's preservation of the saints. Preservation relates to perseverance as cause to effect. Because God preserves His saints, they will persevere and not fall from grace. God's power and faithfulness preclude true believers from committing final apostasy."[163] Peterson and Williams then argued from scripture that believers do not work for their salvation but rather work out their salvation when they referenced Philippians 2:12, 13, "Wherefore, my beloved, as ye have always obeyed, not as in my presence only, but now much more in my absence, work out your

---

[162] Erickson, *Christian Theology*, 1007.

[163] Peterson and Williams, *Why I Am Not*, 89.

own salvation with fear and trembling. For it is God which worketh in you both to will and to do of his good pleasure."

Their final argument with regard to the warning against apostasy in Hebrews was not in reference to the believers but rather to the unbelievers. They explained, "Further evidence of the impossibility of believers committing apostasy is provided by the presence of preservation texts in Hebrews. In the very book where the sternest warnings against apostasy appear are some of the sweetest affirmations of believer's security in Christ."[164] They had referenced Hebrews 6:4–6: "For it is impossible for those who were once enlightened, and have tasted of the heavenly gift, and were made partakers of the Holy Ghost, And have tasted the good word of God, and the powers of the world to come, If they shall fall away, to renew them again unto repentance; seeing they crucify to themselves the Son of God afresh, and put him to an open shame."

Election

Vance gave a comprehensive biblical reasoning and biblical references from throughout the scriptures that backed up his position. He explained, "This fallacy is the whole idea that mankind is divided into two groups: the 'elect' and the 'reprobate.'"[165] He then referenced Psalms 33:13–15, "The LORD looketh from heaven; he beholdeth all the sons of men. From the place of his habitation he looketh upon all the inhabitants of the earth. He fashioneth their hearts alike; he considereth all their works." Vance also referenced I John 5:1, "Whosoever believeth that Jesus is the Christ is born of God: and every one that loveth him that begat loveth him also that is begotten of him."

---

[164] Ibid., 91.
[165] Vance, *The Other Side*, 333.

Limited Atonement

With regard to the limited atonement position of the Calvinists, Vance dismantles it and unconditional election in one sentence when he stated, "Limited Atonement is simply adding insult to the injury of Unconditional Election. For if certain men are not of those elected to salvation, then what does it matter whether Christ died for them or not?"[166] Most importantly, he referenced I Timothy 4:10: "For therefore we both labour and suffer reproach, because we trust in the living God, who is the Saviour of all men, specially of those that believe."

He also used as a proof text II Corinthians 5:19: "To wit, that God was in Christ, reconciling the world unto himself, not imputing their trespasses unto them; and hath committed unto us the word of reconciliation." Vance argued that "all men" and "the world" constitute that every person has the opportunity by virtue of God's provision to be saved. Vance exposed the fallacy of human philosophy. The clear contradiction within the false teaching of unconditional election and limited atonement was thought through by Vance in a way that would make any Spirit-led believer reconsider the unbiblical philosophy of Calvinism and Arminianism strongly.

CONCLUSION

This research began with a discussion as to the meaning and application of predestination. The battle line was drawn between the foreknowledge of God and the purpose of God. With the aid of Clarke's research, the outcome, without diminishing God's foreknowledge, was that His purpose for both Jews and Gentiles was to call both to salvation, through grace, by faith in Jesus Christ. Dongell and Wells put straight the concepts of

---

[166] Ibid., 470.

foreknowledge and clarified that God's foreknowledge was the basis for God's sovereign decrees. The Calvinists, they stated, had this order reversed.

This research on the matter of election uncovered the term Ryrie used ("corporate election"[167]) to clarify his position on election. It would seem that a proper understanding of the grammatical structure would solve this controversy, namely finding the proper antecedent. His explanation of election was that those that were elect were elect once they got into the church by way of salvation.

The explanation found for infralapsarian election showed that God would have had to predetermine not to make salvation possible for most of humanity for this philosophy to be consistent with God's thought process. The most consistent thought is that as God's image-bearers, He created us all to accept Him and fellowship with Him.

The matter of limited atonement was found to be inconsistent with scripture and the major theme of the Bible: the redemption of sinful man back to a holy, righteous God. This research leads to a belief and conviction in an unlimited atonement.

A review of the Arminian beliefs was found to be works-salvation, the emphasis being on what man can do rather than what Christ did (It is finished). The conclusion of this research is the biblical promise of salvation, freely offered to all, eternally secure in Jesus Christ.

---

[167] Ryrie, *Basic Theology*, 310.

CALVINISM, ARMINIANISM, AND PRESUPPOSITIONAL APOLOGETICS: QUESTIONS THREE

Calvinism, Arminianism, and Presuppositional Apologetics—

Questions Three

Questions:

1. What is the Calvinist belief that relates to the sovereignty of God and his foreknowledge of the salvation of souls?

   _____

2. How do Calvinists refer to their belief that Christ died for the elect?

   _____

3. List three Scripture references given in this chapter that support unlimited atonement.

   A)_____

   B)_____

   C)_____

4. **1 Timothy 4:10:** ""For therefore we both labour and suffer reproach, because we trust in the living God, who is the Savior of all men, specially of those that believe."

   How does this passage contradict the doctrine of limited atonement?

   _____

5. Clarify which of the two groups discussed believes in the doctrine of total depravity (all men are sinners as a result of the fall and original sin) and which group denies it.

   A)_____

   B)_____

6. What biblical case does Vance make when he cites Romans 5:12 ("Wherefore, as by one man sin entered into the world, and death by sin; and so death passed upon all men, for that all have sinned") and 1 Corinthians 15:22 ("For as in Adam all die, even so in Christ shall all be made alive")?

   _____

7. Peterson and Williams discuss the biblical view of perseverance of the saints. What is their conclusion?

   _____

   _____

8. Our status as God's image-bearers shows that God created us all to accept Him and have fellowship with Him. What doctrinal position of Calvinism does this contradict?

   _____

Calvinism, Arminianism, and Presuppositional Apologetics—Answers Three

Answers:

1. What is the Calvinist belief that relates to the sovereignty of God and his foreknowledge of the salvation of souls?

    Answer: Predestination

2. How do Calvinists refer to their belief that Christ died for the elect?

    Answer: Limited atonement

3. List three Scripture references given in this chapter that support unlimited atonement.

    Answer:
    - John 1:29
    - John 3:16
    - John 4:42
    - 1 Timothy 4:10
    - 1 John 2: 1-2
    - 1 Timothy 1:15
    - 2 Peter 3:9

4. **1 Timothy 4:10:** ""For therefore we both labour and suffer reproach, because we trust in the living God, who is the Savior of all men, specially of those that believe."

    How does this passage contradict the doctrine of limited atonement?

Answer: The verse says that God is the Savior of all men.

5. Clarify which of the two groups discussed believes in the doctrine of total depravity (all men are sinners as a result of the fall and original sin) and which group denies it.

   Answer:
   - Calvinists believe in total depravity.
   - Armenians deny total depravity.

6. What biblical case does Vance make when he cites Romans 5:12 ("Wherefore, as by one man sin entered into the world, and death by sin; and so death passed upon all men, for that all have sinned") and 1 Corinthians 15:22 ("For as in Adam all die, even so in Christ shall all be made alive")?

   Answer: Anyone can be saved

7. Peterson and Williams discuss the biblical view of perseverance of the saints. What is their conclusion?

   Answer: "Because God preserves His saints, they will persevere and not fall from grace."

8. Our status as God's image-bearers shows that God created us all to accept Him and have fellowship with Him. What doctrinal position of Calvinism does this contradict?

   Answer: Limited election

CHAPTER FOUR

A BIBLICAL WORLDVIEW OF MANHOOD AND WOMANHOOD

INTRODUCTION

PERCEPTION OF THE PROBLEM

The perception of the problem with biblical manhood and womanhood is that as the culture moves further from its biblical roots, men and women drift further and further from their identity as men and women. God has made normal, godly sexuality and identity to have a high significance and consequence for lack of adherence. I Corinthians 6:9: "Know ye not that the unrighteous shall not inherit the kingdom of God? Be not deceived: neither fornicators, nor idolaters, nor adulterers, nor effeminate, nor abusers of themselves with mankind."

Human sexuality involves all humans, but this author is specifically addressing Christians in this writing. The problem is that as the culture moves, Christianity generally moves along with the culture. These cultural problems were discussed in the Danvers Statement: relative to confusion of the sexes, (1.) "The widespread uncertainty and confusion in our culture regarding the complementary differences between masculinity and femininity,"[168] and the devaluation of children and motherhood,

---

[168] The Counsel on Biblical Manhood and Womanhood, "The Danvers Statement, 1987," http://www.churchcouncil.org/iccp

(4.) "the widespread ambivalence regarding the values of motherhood, vocational homemaking, and many ministries historically performed by women."[169] The cultural shift relative to manhood and womanhood has adversely affected the local church, (7.) "the emergence of roles for men and women in church leadership that do not conform to Biblical teaching but backfire in the crippling of Biblical faithful witness."[170] These cultural shifts discussed have significantly harmed the biblical blueprints for human sexuality, the Christian home, and the testimony of the local church.

Description of the Problem

The problem happens when God is removed from the human experience, which is to say that men and women live as if God did not exist. When the worldview of men and women eliminates God from their hearts and minds, their worldview, relative to their sexuality, identity, and their station in life, changes. All these changes are counterproductive to the Divine Designer's plan.

Romans 1:25–28: "Who changed the truth of God into a lie, and worshipped and served the creature more than the Creator, who is blessed for ever. Amen. For this cause God gave them up unto vile affections: for even their women did change the natural use into that which is against nature: And likewise also the men, leaving the natural use of the woman, burned in their lust one toward another; men with men working that which is unseemly,

---

_org/Documents_ICCP/English/17_Male_Female_Distinctives_A&D .pdf (accessed April 14, 2017).

[169] Ibid.

[170] Ibid.

and receiving in themselves that recompence of their error which was meet. And even as they did not like to retain God in their knowledge, God gave them over to a reprobate mind, to do those things which are not convenient." Thus, the problem moves from not retaining God in their minds to changing their worldview of their own sexuality, to God giving them over to their reprobate minds.

The Problem in Biblical Perspective

The description of the problem begins with the Divine design. Genesis 2:21–23: "And the LORD God caused a deep sleep to fall upon Adam, and he slept: and he took one of his ribs, and closed up the flesh instead thereof; And the rib, which the LORD God had taken from man, made he a woman, and brought her unto the man. And Adam said, This is now bone of my bones, and flesh of my flesh: she shall be called Woman, because she was taken out of Man." God was not only the Designer, but He also made Woman for the purpose of companionship for the Man. Genesis 2:18: "And the LORD God said, It is not good that the man should be alone; I will make him an help meet for him." God also made Man and Woman distinctly different from each other. Genesis 1:27–28a: "So God created man in his own image, in the image of God created he him; male and female created he them. And God blessed them, and God said unto them, Be fruitful, and multiply, and replenish the earth." This is the Divine design for men and women.

I Kings 2:2-4

The biblical foundation and model for biblical manhood are those who have given themselves to spiritual matters. "I go the way of all the earth: be thou strong therefore, and shew thyself a man; And keep the charge of the LORD thy God, to walk in his ways, to keep his statutes, and his commandments, and his judgments, and his testimonies, as it is written in the law of Moses, that thou mayest prosper in all that thou doest, and whithersoever thou turnest thyself: That the LORD may continue his word which he spake concerning me, saying, If thy children take heed to their way, to walk before me in truth with all their heart and with all their soul, there shall not fail thee (said he) a man on the throne of Israel." The promises made by the Lord to men committing to being spiritual are extraordinary promises. Those who are wise do well to follow this biblical pattern for biblical manhood.

Micah 6:8

The call of the prophet Micah was for manhood to resemble the Lord. "He hath shewed thee, O man, what is good; and what doth the LORD require of thee, but to do justly, and to love mercy, and to walk humbly with thy God?" The attributes of God can only be employed as men commit themselves to follow the Lord.

Proverbs 6:9

The spiritual man understands that although he may make his own plans, the Lord has a plan for him. "A man's heart deviseth his way: but the LORD directeth his steps." The spiritual man will then stay open to the Lord's leading and be sensitive to the Holy Spirit nudging him one direction or another along life's path.

A Biblical Worldview of Manhood and Womanhood

Psalm 1:1–6

The psalmist gave the spiritual man superb counsel, relative to associations, and the fruit of this advice pays great dividends. "Blessed is the man that walketh not in the counsel of the ungodly, nor standeth in the way of sinners, nor sitteth in the seat of the scornful. But his delight is in the law of the LORD; and in his law doth he meditate day and night. And he shall be like a tree planted by the rivers of water, that bringeth forth his fruit in his season; his leaf also shall not wither; and whatsoever he doeth shall prosper. The ungodly are not so: but are like the chaff which the wind driveth away. Therefore the ungodly shall not stand in the judgment, nor sinners in the congregation of the righteous. For the LORD knoweth the way of the righteous: but the way of the ungodly shall perish."

The spiritual man has a heart for the Lord and His Word. The Spirit of God leads the spiritual man away from danger, while the carnal man runs headlong into trouble and destruction. The spiritual man is blessed in his life as he follows the instruction from the Lord.

New Testament

I Corinthians 16:13–14

Knowing the ways of the Lord and being taught to be generous makes the spiritual man a better man as he follows the Lord. "Watch ye, stand fast in the faith, quit you like men, be strong. Let all your things be done with charity. I beseech you, brethren, (ye know the house of Stephanas, that it is the firstfruits of Achaia, and that they have addicted themselves to the ministry of the saints,) That ye submit yourselves unto such, and to every one that helpeth with us, and laboureth." The spiritual man develops a submissive spirit within himself. He, of course, is submissive to the Lord but is also submissive to other Christians. He is sensitive to the needs of others and seeks to serve them.

I Peter 3:7

The effect on men that the Lord has had is that the Lord makes men better husbands and dads. "Likewise, ye husbands, dwell with them according to knowledge, giving honour unto the wife, as unto the weaker vessel, and as being heirs together of the grace of life; that your prayers be not hindered." The man is no dummy; if he treats his wife and children right, that benefits him, too, and he also gets his prayers answered!

I Corinthians 13:11

A mature Christian man matures spiritually, emotionally, and intellectually. He then can be better used of the Lord. "When I was a child, I spake as a child, I understood as a child, I thought as a child: but when I became a man, I put away childish things." A spiritual man makes progress in his life. He moves on to other things that the Lord has for him.

II Timothy 2:15

A spiritual man is a student of God's Word. "Study to shew thyself approved unto God, a workman that needeth not to be ashamed, rightly dividing the word of truth." He learns how to understand the Bible properly. He learns how to listen to the Spirit of the Lord as He speaks to him through His Word.

Biblical Manhood

Masculine Identity

A biblical masculine identity is something the Lord wants man to be conscientious of and for him to carry himself in such a way as to honor the Lord and be the man God has designed him to be. John Piper explained it this way, "The tendency today is to stress the equality of men and women by minimizing the unique significance of our maleness or femaleness. But this depreciation of male and female personhood is a great loss. It is taking a tremendous toll on generations of young men and women who do not know what it means to be a man or a woman. Confusion over the meaning of sexual personhood today is epidemic. The consequence of this confusion is not a free and happy harmony among gender-free persons relating on the basis of abstract competencies. The consequence rather is more divorce, more homosexuality, more sexual abuse, more promiscuity, more social awkwardness, and more emotional distress and suicide that comes with the loss of God-given identity." [171]

The biblical manhood and womanhood identities are God's divine plan for humanity. Whenever men and women try to alter those identities, everything in our culture that can go wrong does go wrong. This cultural and theological equation could be likened to the apologetic argument of the clay and the potter or the watch and the watchmaker. When one comes to the dark place where he thinks he knows more about his own identity than the One who gave him his identity, one can be sure that a destructive outcome will be the result.

In her book, *Radical Womanhood*, Carolyn McCulley described her conversion to feminism while taking women's studies classes for her minor and her subsequent struggles with her identity leading up to her conversion to Christianity. McCulley

---

[171] John Piper, and Wayne Grudem, *Recovering Biblical Manhood & Womanhood: A Response to Evangelical Feminism* (Wheaton: IL: Crossway Books, 1991), 33.

said, "I really didn't know what to do with my feminist identity, but I knew how to spar with men."[172]

McCulley's testimony about her transformation into an angry feminist at Iowa State University before coming to Christ and then struggling with her feminism is very real in our culture today. Her willingness to receive biblical teaching on manhood and womanhood was to her credit. Through subsequent biblical teaching after her conversion, she was able to rethink her view of manhood and womanhood. This story reveals how devastating unbiblical teaching can be on people's worldview of manhood and womanhood.

The men, meanwhile, to have a proper worldview of manhood and womanhood must have sound biblical teaching. When men hold to a biblical worldview of manhood and womanhood, men produce biblical responses and actions. John Piper also stated, "At the heart of mature masculinity is a sense of benevolent responsibility to lead, provide and protect women in ways appropriate to a man's deferring relationships. At the heart of mature femininity is a feeling of disposition to affirm, receive and nurture strength and leadership from worthy men in ways appropriate to a woman's differing relationships."[173] Thus, Piper described the conduct of both men and women toward each other who have a biblical worldview of manhood and womanhood's identities.

One of the major places Satan attacks is at the identities of manhood and womanhood. These attacks on manhood and

---

[172] Carolyn McCulley, *Radical Womanhood: Feminine Faith in a Feminist World* (Chicago: Moody Publishers, 2008), 23.

[173] Piper and Grudem, *Recovering Biblical Manhood*, 35–36.

womanhood are the same attacks on marriages. John Piper and Wayne Grudem discussed this issue, saying, "We believe the Bible teaches that God means the relationship between husband and wife to portray the relationship between Christ and His church. The husband is to model the loving, sacrificial leadership of Christ, and the wife is to model the glad submission offered freely by the church."[174] Thus, if the institutions of the family and the local church are to remain strong, vibrant, and operate as divinely intended, they must hold to and implement a biblical worldview.

Piper and Grudem continued relative to the married woman, "Submission refers to a wife's divine calling to honor and affirm her husband's leadership and help carry it through according to her gifts. It is not an absolute surrender of her will. Rather, we speak of her disposition to yield to her husband's guidance and her inclination to follow his leadership. Christ is her absolute authority, not the husband. She submits 'out of reverence for Christ' (Ephesians 5:21). The supreme authority of Christ qualifies the authority of her husband. She should never follow her husband into sin. Nevertheless, even when she may have to stand with Christ against the sinful will of her husband (1 Peter 3:1, where she does not yield to her husband's unbelief), she can still have a spirit of submission—a disposition to yield. She can show by her attitude and behavior that she does not like resisting his will and that she longs for him to forsake sin and lead in righteousness so that her disposition to honor him as head can again produce harmony."[175]

This one paragraph might very well send blood out of the eyes of radical liberal women in our culture today, but what about

---

[174] Piper and Grudem, *Recovering Biblical Manhood*, 61.

[175] Ibid.

how Christian women conduct themselves today in even the most conservative of churches? Relative to the men in the culture today, it is paramount that men lead spiritual, personal lives, and that they conduct themselves as the spiritual leader in the home. The best church and the best pastor in the world cannot take the place of a spiritual husband and dad in the home. Only the spiritual man can accomplish in the home what God wants to be accomplished in the lives of wives and children.

Masculine Leadership

Masculine leadership in the home demonstrates itself in the spiritual, emotional, and physical wellbeing of his wife and children. I Timothy 3:4 says, "One that ruleth well his own house, having his children in subjection with all gravity." Considering this passage is from the "pastoral epistles," this writer does not consider it taking hermeneutical liberty to consider a running definition of a *bishop* to mean "overseer: a spiritual manager." A spiritual leader in the home is a man that is sensitive and proactive in meeting the needs of his wife and children. Charles Swindoll stated, "Knowing your wife includes those things about her that others don't know and won't know. Her deep fears and cares. Her disappointments, as well as her expectations. Her scars and secrets; and, also her thoughts, and dreams. That's knowing your wife. It calls for a sensitive spirit, a willingness to be involved, to listen, to communicate, to care. Husbands—if your marriage is encoded, this is one of the most important issues you can give yourself to."[176]

Masculine leadership comes from having right perspectives of life. Jesus taught the right priorities in Matthew 6:33, "But seek ye first the kingdom of God, and his righteousness;

---

[176] Charles R. Swindoll, *Man to Man* (Grand Rapids: Zondervan Publishers, 1996), 33.

and all these things shall be added unto you." John Ashcroft learned this lesson as a spiritual man and stated it like this: "Dad's devotion to the spiritual over the material, and the eternal over the temporal, required great sacrifice."[177]

Biblical Womanhood

Feminist Mind

The historical perspective of feminism helps one to understand how the culture has moved away from biblical womanhood. Carolyn McCulley explained, "Liberal theology denies the authority of the Bible, the atoning work of Jesus Christ, and many other core doctrines of Christianity even as it embraces the popular philosophies of the time. The rise of liberalism eventually led to the twentieth-century division of American Christianity into liberal mainline churches and conservative evangelical and fundamentalist churches.[178]

This history actually depicts how Satan has gotten a toehold in the culture, especially in the Western hemisphere. Liberal churches have invited feminism in, not only to the pew but also to the pulpits. The response has been a weakening of the institution of the local church and a devastating result of innumerable marriages. The destruction to the following generations and the confusion in the culture relative to womanhood can largely be attributed to feminism.

McCulley also addressed the empowerment of a spiritual woman when she stated, "It takes a strong woman to selflessly

---

[177] John Ashcroft, *Lessons from a Father* (Nashville: Thomas Nelson, 1998), 166.

[178] McCulley, *Radical Womanhood*, 192.

nurture four children into adulthood. It takes a spiritually mature woman to follow her husband in his calling and support him in his gifting, traveling to the other side of the world to help him carry out his plans. It takes a bold woman to live counter to her culture, choosing the glory of Christ above any personal honor."[179]

If one really considers how God (scripture) looks at womanhood and what the culture (Hollywood, public education, secular media) teaches about womanhood, no reasonably minded person would argue that they are not polar opposites. For secular women, this secular view of womanhood is a sin of commission as secular women have deliberately chosen to view womanhood without a biblical worldview. Romans 1:20: "For the invisible things of him from the creation of the world are clearly seen, being understood by the things that are made, even his eternal power and Godhead; so that they are without excuse."

The Christian woman who holds to an unscriptural view of womanhood is at least guilty of sin by omission, which is to say, Christian women who may not have completely thought through, or needless to say, have not been very well discipled, have been deceived into embracing an ungodly worldview of womanhood.

Adam's Helper

Nancy DeMoss put forth some research concerning wives being submissive to their husbands. She stated, "The fact is, successful relationships and healthy cultures are not built on the claiming of rights but on yielding of rights."[180] DeMoss also gave a historical context: "The turmoil and rebellion of the 1960's was birthed out of a philosophy that promoted rights. This philosophy

---

[179] McCulley, *Radical Womanhood*, 198.
[180] Nancy DeMoss, *Lies Women Believe: And the Truth That Sets Them Free* (Chicago: Moody Publishers, 2001), 74.

has permeated our Christian culture. It creeps into our conversations. It helped shape the way we view all of life."[181] It is easy to argue that all sin is rebellion against God, and DeMoss has certainly made a clear connection to the vehicle that sin rode into the culture, the feminist movement, which was shamelessly built on rebellion.

DeMoss also mentioned the biblical characteristics of a mother. At the end of this list, she pointed out the destructive impact an ungodly worldview has had on children. She explained, "They redefined what it means to be a woman and tossed out widely held views of a woman's priorities and mission in life. Concepts such as virtue, chastity, submission, and modesty were largely eliminated from our vocabulary, and replaced with choice, divorce, infidelity, and unisex lifestyles. The daughters and granddaughters of that generation have never known any other way of thinking."[182]

What has happened in the culture is that virtually all biblical attributes of a biblical worldview of womanhood have been removed from the culture. This removal of biblical virtues has to much degree happened in the Christian community as well. The New-Evangelical movement has exasperated the problem further by not holding to any standards of dress, music, or conduct, and by adopting the Hollywood philosophy of dating rather than biblical courtship.

The Bible discusses order in the family, and DeMoss elaborated on that order: "The Truth is that God did not make man to be a 'helper' to the woman. He made the woman to be a

---

[181] Demoss, *Lies Women Believe*, 74

[182] Ibid., 124.

'helper' to the man. Of course this does not mean that men are not to serve their wives and children."[183] The first time God said, "It is not good" was in reference to man's not having a mate. Genesis 2:18: "And the LORD God said, It is not good that the man should be alone; I will make him an help meet for him."

Godly Examples

Scripture gives us wonderful examples of godly women recording their love for the Lord, their husbands, their children, and others. Edith Deen captured examples of some of the women of the Bible and their godly womanhood. She wrote about Eve, stating, "All of the great epochs in a woman's life, her marriage, mating, and motherhood, unfold in all of their completeness in the Genesis account of Eve. The family, too, with all its joys and headaches, comes into being, with Eve as the center of it. In Eve all the elemental questions of life, birth, and death, even sin and temptation, are shown in their human dimension."[184]

The life of Eve was and is instrumental in understanding God's plan for marriage and family. Eve was not perfect, but she did present a model of a woman who was godly and has now had countless numbers of women model their lives, marriages, and families after her.

Deen also discussed the life of Sarah and pointed out how Sarah conducted herself in a godly manner with her husband, Abraham. Their lives together were tested by God, but Sarah showed herself to be strong personally, in her faith in God, and in trusting her husband. Deen explained, "Sarah's life became

---

[183] Demoss, *Lies Women Believe*, 142–143.

[184] Edith Deen, *All The Women of The Bible* (New York: Harper Collins Publishers, 1983), 5.

Abraham's. Where he went she went, not as his shadow but as a strong influence. Together they experienced the vicissitudes of nomatic life and found in them great spiritual significance. Abraham, man of God, was willing to forsake home and country for the unknown, with Sarah ever at his side. Her love and loyalty were blessed by Abraham's devotion to her."[185]

Sarah's life did not paint a picture of ease and comfort, but rather a picture of many twists, turns, and ups and downs. Her life also exemplified not only personal faith and courage but also dignity and graciousness. Her and other women's biblical profiles exemplify the principle, more is caught than taught. Sarah's life profile is one that is admired by all that see her on the pages of biblical history.

Miriam was mentioned in Exodus 15:21, "And Miriam answered them, Sing ye to the LORD, for he hath triumphed gloriously; the horse and his rider hath he thrown into the sea." Miriam is referred to as the first woman singing unto the Lord. Singing unto the Lord truly is worship, and Miriam certainly exemplified worship and love for the Lord.

Deen took a look at the godly life of Miriam and discussed her dedicated life to the Lord. She stated, "Miriam is the first woman singer on record. The wonder of it is that she sang unto the Lord, using her great gift for the elevation of her people. With her they exulted over their escape from their enemies. And with freedom came a newly discovered faith and confidence in God. This was Miriam's great hour. She was the new Israel's most renowned woman, and her people held her in high regard. She had filled an important role in the founding of the Hebrew commonwealth."[186]

---

[185] Deen, *All the Women*, 9.
[186] Deen, *All the Women*, 59.

Miriam holds a significant place and legacy in biblical history. This is one that men and women alike should take notice of and praise God for as Christian women make an application to their own walk with the Lord. Miriam's life story is one that demonstrates how much influence one may have as she uses her life as an instrument for the Lord's glory. Her life was mentioned not only because of her life of worship but for the byproduct, which was the influence she had on the Hebrews.

The final woman from the Bible that will be profiled is perhaps the most famous one, described in Proverbs 31:10: "Who can find a virtuous woman? for her price is far above rubies." The virtuous woman has been taught and preached on possibly every Mother's Day. Deen explained, "Her chastity, her diligence, her efficiency, her earnestness, her love for her husband and children, even her business foresight, are brilliantly illustrated in words that rise up majestically from the page. But the light in all its effulgence shines upon her godliness. This quality, the Bible seems to say, is what gives meaning, purpose, and direction to her life."[187]

Deen described this virtuous woman with great terminology, and each word was merited by this woman recorded for us in the book of Proverbs. In the description of this virtuous woman in verses 10–30, her virtues are many. The grocery-list of virtues is one to be studied and considered. These virtues are timeless and applicable to all cultures in all time periods, and they will serve all women well, blessing those in their lives.

CONCLUSION

The perception of the problem in this research relative to sexuality within Christianity is the shifting culture that was stated

---

[187] Ibid., 152.

and defined. One specific problem addressed was feminism and the confusion that has been brought into the culture—more specifically, the challenges that feminism brings into the marriage relationship. Another stated problem is how feminism has brought additional problems into churches and church leadership. Though space did not allow addressing this more fully, one can conclude that if there is trouble in the marriages of church leadership, it will hinder or disqualify men from the pastorate or holding the office of deacon.

The description of the problem was stated as the biblical worldview losing its central place in the institutions of the family and the local church and in the culture at large. The theological problem with the culture and with Christians is the departure from sound doctrine.

The problem of biblical perspective was stated with Genesis chapters one and two as foundational to the culture. The worldview of manhood and womanhood has its foundational principles in the Genesis account, including the issues of identity, sexuality, masculinity, and femininity. The biblical perspective includes both Old and New Testament references to establish a biblical worldview of manhood and womanhood.

Masculine identity was addressed in the context of a biblical worldview. The devastating fallout in the culture and within Christianity was addressed, including the unbiblical deviations from biblical principles. The cultural problems associated with this changing worldview were listed. The connection between having a biblical worldview of manhood and womanhood was made with having a proper, healthy, happy, and godly identity of oneself as a man or woman.

Masculine leadership in the local church and home were addressed. The Pastoral Epistles were referenced, giving a sound biblical basis for the leadership in the local church. Masculine leadership was dealt with relative to home life as a husband and a dad.

Biblical womanhood was discussed. The authors that were sourced were a great help in identifying the feminist mindset within the culture and within Christianity. Some historical context of the feminist movement was discussed, along with the areas within the culture that Satan has been able to get a toe-hold in, such as the mainline churches and other institutions in the culture where liberalism has flourished.

Biblical womanhood was very well communicated by Nancy DeMoss. She identified Genesis chapters one and two and explained how God made woman to be a helper to man.

This research concluded with the most beautiful examples of godly womanhood: the character and life of Eve were discussed, the life and faith of Sarah were highlighted, and the wonderful testimony of Miriam was brought to light. And finally, this study of manhood and womanhood came to a beautiful close with a discussion of the list of virtues that the Lord has given to us in the virtuous woman recorded in Proverbs 31.

A BIBLICAL WORLDVIEW OF MANHOOD AND WOMANHOOD: QUESTIONS FOUR

Transformational Truth Volume II

A Biblical Worldview of Manhood and Womanhood—Questions

Four

Questions:

1. Romans 1:25-28 demonstrates what happens when people do not retain God in their minds and serve "the creature more than the Creator": they change their worldview of their own sexuality. What is the consequence of this behavior?

   _____

2. **Micah 6:8:** "He hath shewed thee, O man, what is good; and what doth the LORD require of thee, but to do justly, and to love mercy, and to walk humbly with thy God?"

   What does Micah say that Biblical manhood looks like?

   _____

   _____

3. **1 Corinthians 16:13-14:** "Watch ye, stand fast in the faith, quit you like men, be strong. Let all your things be done with charity. I beseech you, brethren, (ye know the house of Stephanas, that it is the firstfruits of Achaia, and that they have addicted themselves to the ministry of the saints,) That ye submit yourselves unto such, and to every one that helpeth with us, and laboureth."

   How does being a spiritual man and following the ways of the Lord affect one's relationships with other people?

A Biblical worldview of Manhood and Womanhood

_____

_____

4. John Piper points out the consequences of today's cultural tendency to stress the quality of men and women and minimize their unique significance. Identify 1 or 2 of those consequences.

   A)_____

   B)_____

5. What relationship is the marriage relationship between husband and wife to portray?

   _____

   _____

6. How does godly masculine leadership demonstrate itself in the home?

   _____

   _____

7. The modern feminist movement is built on what sin?

   _____

8. Nancy DeMoss points out that God made woman to be a _____ to the man.

Transformational Truth Volume II

A Biblical Worldview of Manhood and Womanhood—Answers

Four

Answers:

1. Romans 1:25-28 demonstrates what happens when people do not retain God in their minds and serve "the creature more than the Creator": they change their worldview of their own sexuality. What is the consequence of this behavior?

   Answer: God gives them over to their reprobate minds.

2. **Micah 6:8:** "He hath shewed thee, O man, what is good; and what doth the LORD require of thee, but to do justly, and to love mercy, and to walk humbly with thy God?"

   What does Micah say that Biblical manhood looks like?

   Answer: Biblical men resemble the Lord, and therefore employ the attributes of God.

3. **1 Corinthians 16:13-14:** "Watch ye, stand fast in the faith, quit you like men, be strong. Let all your things be done with charity. I beseech you, brethren, (ye know the house of Stephanas, that it is the firstfruits of Achaia, and that they have addicted themselves to the ministry of the saints,) That ye submit yourselves unto such, and to every one that helpeth with us, and laboureth."

   How does being a spiritual man and following the ways of the Lord affect one's relationships with other people?

Answer: A spiritual man will be sensitive to the needs of others and seek to serve them.

4. John Piper points out the consequences of today's cultural tendency to stress the quality of men and women and minimize their unique significance. Identify 1 or 2 of those consequences.

Answer:
- More divorce
- More homosexuality
- More sexual abuse
- More promiscuity
- More social awkwardness
- More emotional distress and suicide

5. What relationship is the marriage relationship between husband and wife to portray?

Answer: The relationship between Christ and His church

6. How does godly masculine leadership demonstrate itself in the home?

Answer: The spiritual, emotional, and physical wellbeing of a man's wife and children.

7. The modern feminist movement is built on what sin?

Answer: Rebellion

8. Nancy DeMoss points out that God made woman to be a _____ to the man.

Answer: Helper

CHAPTER FIVE

A BIBLICAL WORLDVIEW OF SEX AND MARRIAGE

INTRODUCTION

PERCEPTION OF THE PROBLEM

Sex is part of the human experience to be sure, but the question might be, "Is the proper expression of human sexuality for the Christian to be driven by theology or by culture?" Scripture and cultural studies seem to indicate a divergence. Malachi 3:6a says, "For I am the LORD, I change not." Scripture seems to indicate consistency, while the culture seems to be shifting and shifting dramatically. George Barna's research found that "there are disparities, for instance, between generational cohorts. Overall, Elders and Boomers tend to share a stronger consensus about the purpose of sex. That is, clear majorities among the older generations say sex is for procreation (79% Elders; 71% Boomers), expressing intimacy between two people who love each other (68% Elders; 73% Boomers) or uniting a man and woman in marriage (62% Elders; 50% Boomers)."[188]

One can see that the attitudes shift from one generation to the next, as shown in the next reference from the Barna Group's

---

[188] George Barna, "What Americans Believe About Sex," The Barna Group. https://www.barna.com/research/what-americans-believe-about-sex/ (accessed April 3, 2017).

research. Barna stated, "The two younger adult generations are much less likely to embrace these traditional views of sex. Most Gen-Xers and Millennials continue to believe conventional ideas of sex: that it is to express intimacy between two people who love each other (57% Gen-Xers; 56% Millennials) or to procreate (52% Gen-Xers; 51% Millennials). However, the notion that it should unite a man and woman in marriage is endorsed by just one-third of Xers and Millennials."[189]

It appears that there is a drifting of thought relative to human sexuality between one generation and the next. In fact, the maternity rate has dropped by over 20% in just one generation. The rationale for sex to unite a man and a woman in marriage dropped over 20% and 30% respectively in just one generation. Thus, there must be and is a reason for this seismic shift in people's thinking and behavior regarding human sexuality. When one analyzes the two possibilities of causations of this problem—either the culture or the biblical principles that govern human sexuality—one would have to conclude that it is the culture that changed.

Description of the Problem

Chip Ingram addressed this problem of the non-biblical worldview of sex and relationships. He stated, "We've made the point that love, sex, and lasting relationships are among the most passionate desires of people's hearts. We've also noted that most people are simply not experiencing love and sexual intimacy to the degree or to the extent that they desire."[190] Ingram talks in very real terms about human relationships and sexuality.

---

[189] Barna, "What Americans Believe About Sex."

[190] Chip Ingram, *Love, Sex & Lasting Relationships: God's Prescription for Enhancing Your Love Life* (Grand Rapids: Baker

Then he later stated that, in large part, it is the unbiblical philosophy which has permeated the culture. Ingram said "that the culture is saturated with Hollywood's formula. We sing along with the formula hits. We read about it, and unconsciously almost all of us have bought into it to one degree or another. I find the Hollywood formula just as prevalent among Christians as among non-Christians. And the results are equally disastrous."[191] Thus, the description of the problem is both spiritual and cultural. The Hollywood philosophy that Ingram describes is a dating model versus a biblical courtship model of moving from singlehood to married life.

The Problem in Biblical Perspective

The philosophy, worldview, and culture of men and women changed when Adam and Eve were divinely removed from the perfect environment of the Garden of Eden. The culture in the Garden of Eden was relatively easy study as there were only two of them! Prior to the Fall, the culture, which is to say, the philosophy of sex and marriage, and their whole worldview was different. Prior to the Fall, and just after the Creator had met the need of the man for a helpmate, marriage was heaven on earth. The first couple went from being "one flesh" (Genesis 2:24c) to "knowing good and evil" (Genesis 3:5d) to "they knew they were naked" (Genesis 3:7b). Their entire philosophy, culture, and worldview shifted from paradise to peril in one moment of time. All this, and Adam didn't have a mother-in-law. When the new philosophy, culture, and worldview changed, it brought many devastating challenges to human sexuality and marriage.

Old Testament

Books, 2003), 17.

[191] Ibid.,, 30.

Genesis 1:28

God laid out a plan for mankind for marriage and procreation as found in Genesis 1:28: "And God blessed them, and God said unto them, Be fruitful, and multiply, and replenish the earth, and subdue it: and have dominion over the fish of the sea, and over the fowl of the air, and over every living thing that moveth upon the earth." God's plan was for marriage to produce children and fill the earth with God's image-bearers. In other words, it is biblical for the husband to go out for surf and turf and romance his wife.

Genesis 2:18

Genesis points out God's plan for fulfilling the man's need for companionship and a helpmate, as stated in Genesis 2:18: "And the LORD God said, It is not good that the man should be alone; I will make him an help meet for him." The Lord was pleased with all He had made up until He made man, who did not yet have a mate. When He made man and had not yet made woman, He said, "It is not good." So then by inference, God could say, "It is good," too!

Genesis 2:24

God's instructions for the home life and marriage continued with Genesis 2:24: "Therefore shall a man leave his father and his mother, and shall cleave unto his wife: and they shall be one flesh." This passage is sometimes referred to as "leave, cleave, and weave." The divine instructions indicate that each new family unit should have its own dwelling for nesting and rearing children. One could also conclude that there can only be one head of a home and, specifically, one man in a household. Furthermore, a young couple can get counsel for their new life together, but ultimately, they must work things out for themselves, and thus, they need their own space to live and grow together.

Proverbs 5:15–19

The Lord also gave instructions relative to human sexuality within the marriage relationship. The Lord explained in Proverbs 5:15–19, "Drink waters out of thine own cistern, and running waters out of thine own well. Let thy fountains be dispersed abroad, and rivers of waters in the streets. Let them be only thine own, and not strangers' with thee. Let thy fountain be blessed: and rejoice with the wife of thy youth. Let her be as the loving hind and pleasant roe; let her breasts satisfy thee at all times; and be thou ravished always with her love."

There are a few implications to this passage regarding intimacy with one's spouse. First, the divine instruction is to have your intimacy needs met with your spouse and not anyone else's spouse. The instruction from the Lord is to marry young, stay married, and stay excited about and with one's wife. Furthermore, beyond staying in love with one's wife, one should stay in a life pattern of intimacy with her.

Song of Solomon 7:6–12

The Lord uses metaphoric language here to discuss the sexual life between husband and wife. He recorded this for His people in Song of Solomon 7:6–12: "How fair and how pleasant art thou, O love, for delights! This thy stature is like to a palm tree, and thy breasts to clusters of grapes. I said, I will go up to the palm tree, I will take hold of the boughs thereof: now also thy breasts shall be as clusters of the vine, and the smell of thy nose like apples; And the roof of thy mouth like the best wine for my beloved, that goeth down sweetly, causing the lips of those that are asleep to speak. I am my beloved's, and his desire is toward me. Come, my beloved, let us go forth into the field; let us lodge in the villages. Let us get up early to the vineyards; let us see if the vine flourish, whether the tender grape appear, and the pomegranates bud forth: there will I give thee my loves."

What the Lord seems to be conveying is an ongoing, passionate relationship between husband and wife. Furthermore, it appears that the sexual relationship between husband and wife, beyond procreation, is for the mutual pleasure and enjoyment that each brings to one another. This is one of God's greatest gifts to each marriage partner.

New Testament

I Corinthians 6:13-20

The Apostle Paul, while dealing with the church at Corinth about their sexual immorality, instructed the Corinthian believers on the sacredness of the marriage relationship and the body. Paul, under inspiration, wrote in I Corinthians 6:13-20, "Meats for the belly, and the belly for meats: but God shall destroy both it and them. Now the body is not for fornication, but for the Lord; and the Lord for the body. And God hath both raised up the Lord, and will also raise up us by his own power. Know ye not that your bodies are the members of Christ? shall I then take the members of Christ, and make them the members of an harlot? God forbid. What? know ye not that he which is joined to an harlot is one body? for two, saith he, shall be one flesh. But he that is joined unto the Lord is one spirit. Flee fornication. Every sin that a man doeth is without the body; but he that committeth fornication sinneth against his own body. What? know ye not that your body is the temple of the Holy Ghost which is in you, which ye have of God, and ye are not your own? For ye are bought with a price: therefore glorify God in your body, and in your spirit, which are God's."

A Biblical Worldview of Sex and Marriage

Prior to their salvation, the Corinthians had no understanding of a biblical view of sex and marriage. When they became Christians, their worldview changed, but only after Paul taught them the biblical view of their bodies and sex within marriage. Prior to their discipling by Paul, they had continued to live in an immoral lifestyle.

Ephesians 5:33

Paul addressed the church at Ephesus regarding the relationship between husbands and wives and how they should conduct themselves as those having a Christian worldview of marriage and sex. Under inspiration, Paul penned the words in Ephesians 5:33, "Nevertheless let every one of you in particular so love his wife even as himself; and the wife see that she reverence her husband."

The marriage relationship is a special one that depicts Christ and His Church. The biblical worldview of marriage and sex is counter to the vast majority of the world's cultures. The treatment of women in most cultures of the world is shameful. The biblical way that women are treated stands out from all other cultures and sub-cultures. The result is a relationship that is heaven on earth, where husband and wife see Christ in each other.

Hebrews 13:4

The Lord contrasted the way He views immoral sex, outside of marriage, and the way He views sex that is blessed by Him in marriage, as referenced in Hebrews 13:4: "Marriage is honourable in all, and the bed undefiled: but whoremongers and adulterers God will judge." Sex is a good and pleasing thing in the Lord's sight and is the Lord's divine plan to bless the husband and wife through the institution of marriage.

The worldview of sex and marriage for most of our culture is that sex before marriage is acceptable because the couple is in love, and they intend to marry anyhow. But "the road to hell is paved with good intentions."[192] The culture of the Bible-believing couple, who is serious about living for the Lord, has a much different worldview of sex and marriage. The Christian couple has a worldview that they want to live right and be blessed both in their marriage and while they are on the path leading to marriage.

A Biblical Husband

A biblical husband conducts himself with his wife far differently than do unsaved men. The Apostle Paul stated in Ephesians 5:25-26, "Husbands, love your wives, even as Christ also loved the church, and gave himself for it; That he might sanctify and cleanse it with the washing of water by the word." This is the implementation of biblical principles into the institution of marriage. Marriage is the first institution that the Lord created and is the most basic of relationships within society. John Piper and Wayne Grudem addressed the conduct of a Christian man toward his wife this way: "First, the loving husband gives himself. In his leadership role as head, he seeks to lead by giving of himself to his wife in ways analogous to how Christ gave Himself to His bride. Christ's giving of himself was personal and sacrificial."[193] Sometimes this form of leadership is referred to as servant leadership and other times as follower-first leadership.

The matter of leadership within the biblical worldview of sex and marriage was also addressed in scripture. Ephesians 5:22-24 says, "Wives, submit yourselves unto your own

---

[192] Saint Bernard, https://en.m.wikipedia.org/wiki/The_road_to_hell_is_paved_with_good_intentions (accessed April 7, 2017).

[193] Piper, and Grudem, *Recovering Biblical Manhood*, 172.

husbands, as unto the Lord. For the husband is the head of the wife, even as Christ is the head of the church: and he is the saviour of the body. Therefore as the church is subject unto Christ, so let the wives be to their own husbands in every thing."

This view of leadership is opposed to popular culture, but it is the divine plan for marriages to be blessed. Piper and Grudem stated, "Since by God's decree marriage partners are 'one flesh,' God wants them to function together under one head, not as two autonomous individuals living together. Since Paul is concerned about that unity, we should be concerned about it too."[194] God by His nature is One of order. He has structured the husband and wife relationship with the man as head of the home, but with careful instruction to love his wife.

A Biblical Wife

Proverbs 31 maybe the most referenced passage about godly women mentioned in the Bible. Certainly, this woman is a superb Christian example for women who want to pattern their marriage relationship after a godly example. Proverbs 13:10–12: "Who can find a virtuous woman? for her price is far above rubies. The heart of her husband doth safely trust in her, so that he shall have no need of spoil. She will do him good and not evil all the days of her life." This passage depicts the heart of a Christian woman who has dedicated her heart, life, and marriage to the Lord. Relative to Sarah and Abraham Gien Karssen stated, "Abraham had obeyed immediately. And Sarah had adjusted to the decision. They had suddenly become seminomads, instead of citizens of a wealthy, comfortable city. As with most women, she hadn't found it easy to leave her home and loved ones behind to

---

[194] Piper and Grudem, *Recovering Biblical Manhood*, 170.

face an unknown future. But she had obeyed he husband and trusted God who had spoken to him."[195]

Sarah was not a perfect Old Testament believer, but when one looks upon the horizon of her life, it is reasonable to conclude that she was a God-fearing woman and one that had the faith to follow the Lord and submit to her husband, Abraham. Their life together was not without its challenges, and yet their life together is one to be admired and modeled.

Carolyn McCulley, shortly after her conversion to Christ, had a crash collision with her worldview of how marital relationships should work. When she was first confronted with the "submission" and "love" dynamic found in Ephesians 5:22–25, she pretty much lost it! But the Lord did a work in her heart, and this passage taught her the biblical worldview of husband-wife relationships. She wrote, "Submission! Surely that was an ancient concept that no one practiced anymore! There was no way on God's green earth that I would ever concede that women are inferior and must live as second-class to men. That passage was just wrong, wrong, wrong. All my feminist offences roused themselves in objection."[196] What happened after McCulley's salvation conversion was that her unbiblical, feminist worldview had to convert to a biblical worldview.

McCulley continued, "Once again, I read the rest of the offending passage. Though the first part was for wives, the verses that followed for husbands were far more challenging and provided a definition of leadership that was not for self-glory but for the benefit of another."[197] McCulley offered a great service to

---

[195] Gien Karssen, *Her Name is Woman* (Colorado Springs: CO: NavPress, 1975), 31.

[196] McCulley, *Radical Womanhood*, 25.

women by sharing the testimony of her worldview conversion towards a biblical view of womanhood and a biblical mandate for submission of the woman and the husband to love his wife!

Biblical Intimacy

The biblical worldview of intimacy, contrary to the ungodly, is that the godly view of sex is for one's marital partner and not one's self. J. Budziszewski wrote, "Mutual and total self-giving, strong feelings of attachment, intense pleasure, and the procreation of new life are linked by human nature in simple complex of meanings and purpose."[198] The Lord did give a command to procreate, but in the process, He gave pleasure and a means of bonding the marital relationship.

Budziszewski continued, "All those things about a woman that arise from this difference, such as warmth, tender mildness, and sensitivity to the emotions of other, are signs of this potentiality. The more fully they are developed, the more intense and beautiful her womanhood, and the deeper its complement to manhood."[199] The Lord uses our opposites to complete and develop each other into the person Christ wants us to be.

Timothy Clinton and George Ohlschlager explained, "Viewing sex as God's good creation. We are often asked, 'Why did God create sex?' The answer is that he wanted to teach us about intimate relationships, which are so dear to His heart. He wanted us to understand His very makeup and image. It's no surprise that a God who calls us to reflect Him in characteristics such as

---

[197] McCulley, *Radical Womanhood*, 25

[198] J. Budziszewski, *On the Meaning of Sex* (Wilmington:DE: ISI Books, 2012), 29.

[199] Ibid., 97.

holiness, love, and forgiveness would also call us to reflect Him in intimacy and oneness. As the doctrine of the Trinity demonstrates, God is an intimate one. He created us male and female—distinctly different—and He called us to be one. Sexuality is the Almighty's grand metaphor, providing special insight into Himself."[200]

Clinton and Ohlschlager's explanation of oneness continued, "Clearly, God designed sex for physical pleasure. Our bodies are wonderfully made to respond to sexual stimulation with great delight. Denying this reality is not any more true to God's design for sex than acting as if sex is only about physical pleasure and not also about deeply connecting with one's spouse. Sex with one's husband or wife provides a unique opportunity to explore each other physically, emotionally, mentally, and spiritually."[201]

Clinton and Ohlschlager help Christians to understand the difference between an ungodly worldview of sex and a biblical worldview of sex within marriage. It is significant that in marriage, couples reveal the image of God, especially His goodness. The connection between physical, emotional, and spiritual aspects of sex within marriage, and the parallel with the Trinity, is helpful to understand the spiritual connection.

CONCLUSION

This writing on the subject of the Biblical view of sex and marriage began with discussing the perception of the problem. A

---

[200] Timothy Clinton and George Ohlschlager, *Competent Christian Counseling* (Colorado Springs: WaterBrook Press, 1984), 501.

[201] Ibid.

few statistics of sexuality in our current culture were offered by George Barna. The statistics relative to the culture of the recent generations were given to point out the shift in our society. This writing also gave a description of the problem of an ungodly worldview of sex and marriage, which identified at least some of the causes of the ungodly worldview of sex and marriage.

The contrast came by offering the problem from a biblical perspective. Some foundational scripture from Genesis was offered, which built a biblical worldview of sex and marriage. Both Old Testament and New Testament scriptures were given, which continued to build a biblical worldview. Next, a biblical worldview for husbands was offered with an emphasis on Ephesians chapter five.

A biblical worldview of women was discussed with a look at Proverbs, Ephesians, and a couple of female Christian authors. Finally, a biblical worldview of sex was discussed, along with a couple of authors who are experts in the fields of ethics and Christian counseling. The intent of this writing was to make clear how a Christian ought to view marriage and sex and to demonstrate the purpose, heart, and love that God has for His people and how His plan is to bless marriages.

A BIBLICAL WORLDVIEW OF SEX AND MARRIAGE:

QUESTIONS FIVE

A Biblical Worldview of Sex and Marriage

A Biblical Worldview of Sex and Marriage—Questions Five

Questions:

1. Proverbs 5:15-19 presents what teaching on sex and intimacy in a marriage relationship?

    _____

    _____

    _____

2. In 1 Corinthians 6:13-20, Paul taught the Corinthians the biblical view of their bodies and sex within marriage. He asserts that one who commits fornication sins against his own body—how is this true?

    _____

    _____

    _____

3. **Ephesians 5:25-26**: "Husbands, love your wives, even as Christ also loved the church, and gave himself for it; That he might sanctify and cleanse it with the washing of water by the word."

    In his role as husband, not only is the man to love his wife, but he's also commanded to take on what role?

    _____

    _____

4. As the life of Sarah demonstrates, biblical submission by a wife entails what two things?

   A) _____

   B) _____

5. What are three purposes for sex within the marriage relationship?

   A) _____

   B) _____

   C) _____

6. Timothy Clinton and George Ohlschlager explained sexuality as "the Almighty's grand metaphor." Briefly explain this metaphor.

   _____

   _____

   _____

   _____

A Biblical Worldview of Sex and Marriage

A Biblical Worldview of Sex and Marriage—Answers Five

Answers:

1. Proverbs 5:15-19 presents what teaching on sex and intimacy in a marriage relationship?

   Answer: A married couple should stay in love and in a pattern of intimacy; this relationship should exist only with each other.

2. In 1 Corinthians 6:13-20, Paul taught the Corinthians the biblical view of their bodies and sex within marriage. He asserts that one who commits fornication sins against his own body—how is this true?

   Answer: A Christian's body is the temple of the Holy Ghost, who lives in us. Our bodies no longer belong to ourselves but to God.

3. **Ephesians 5:25-26**: "Husbands, love your wives, even as Christ also loved the church, and gave himself for it; That he might sanctify and cleanse it with the washing of water by the word."

   In his role as husband, not only is the man to love his wife, but he's also commanded to take on what role?

   Answer: He is to take on the role of leadership; he is the head of the household.

4. As the life of Sarah demonstrates, biblical submission by a wife entails what two things?

Answer:

    a. Trust in God
    b. Obedience to one's husband

5. What are three purposes for sex within the marriage relationship?

Answer:

    a. Procreation
    b. Pleasure
    c. A means of bonding the marital relationship

6. Timothy Clinton and George Ohlschlager explained sexuality as "the Almighty's grand metaphor." Briefly explain this metaphor.

Answer: God is an intimate God, and he wanted us to learn about intimate relationships. The intimate relationship between husband and wife is a metaphor for a Christian's relationship to God.

CHAPTER SIX

A BIBLICAL WORLDVIEW OF COUNSELING IN THE LOCAL CHURCH

INTRODUCTION

WHERE SHOULD BIBLICAL COUNSELING HAPPEN?

The Local Church

The purpose of biblical counseling is to do the greatest good for men and women and bring the greatest glory to God. Throughout the study of the psychological counseling model and the biblical counseling model, the prevailing questions seem to be, "Which model works, and which model is correct?" A similar comparison could be made between numerous Christian service endeavors, and yet, the locations of the efforts bring varying levels of success.

Biblical counseling needs to happen in the God-ordained place where God will bless to the greatest extent, and the greatest fruitfulness will be realized. Jim Gent explained, "The local church has a critical and significant responsibility in the world. Simply stated, the local church is the focal point of God's truth; it is the citadel of truth; it is through the church that God promulgates and disseminates His truth. The local church is God's ordained means to propagate the truth and to preserve truth."[202]

---

[202] Jim Gent, *The Local Church: God's Plan for Planet Earth* (Old

What is being offered here is that the local assembly of believers is the place in which God promised His presence. Matthew 28:20b says, "And, lo, I am with you alway, even unto the end of the world. Amen." Gent's larger point was that truth is dispensed in and through the local assemblies. I Timothy 3:15: "But if I tarry long, that thou mayest know how thou oughtest to behave thyself in the house of God, which is the church of the living God, the pillar and ground of the truth."

That is not to say that the Word of God does not work elsewhere, but that God has ordained His assemblies to reach the world with the Gospel message. To expand this point, while still focusing on the message of the local church, Kenneth Good discussed the autonomy of the local church. "Baptists insist upon that form of government under which each local church is entirely autonomous. As such, the individual, organized assembly is independent of outside control by any other human agency. It is directly responsible to Jesus Christ alone."[203] Again the reference to church government speaks to the protection and the purity of the message. If truth is communicated to and received by the counselee, then the truth will do its work to bring hope and heal hurting people.

What is Biblical Counseling?

In order to define biblical counseling, one needs first to state the obvious that the main tool used in counseling is the

---

Bridge: Smyrna Publications, 1994), 77.

[203] Kenneth H. Good, *God's Blueprint for a Church* (Rochester, NY: Backus Book Publications, 1987), 102.

Bible. Furthermore the biblical counselor must have a full and complete faith in the Bible and that all that the human heart and mind need for healing, wisdom, peace, and direction are found within its pages. John MacArthur explained biblical counseling this way: "God is the center of counseling. God is sovereign, active, speaking, merciful, commanding and powerful. The Lord and Savior, Jesus Christ, is the central focus of counseling and the exemplar of the Wonderful Counselor. The Word of God and the work of the Holy Spirit are the foundation to all significant and lasting change. The Word of God is about counseling, giving both understanding of people and methods of ministering to people."[204]

MacArthur places the Lord Jesus Christ right in the center of both the counselee and the counselor. The nonverbal from MacArthur is that the counselor does not fix people; Jesus Christ fixes people. He made clear that the Holy Spirit is working on the inside to make changes in the lives of the counselees. Counseling is meant to point people God-ward and to encourage people to give God the glory in and through their relationships as expressed in Psalms 57:5, "Be thou exalted, O God, above the heavens; let thy glory be above all the earth."

In addition to MacArthur's biblical perspective on counseling, it is important to note an observation made by James Beck and Bruce Demarest in their point to contrast evolutionary psychology with biblical counseling. They stated, "Self-denial is putting Christ first, putting our own personal agendas second, and following Christ even if it means following Him to our deaths."[205] Thus, a major cavern exists between the biblical philosophy of

---

[204] John MacArthur, *Counseling: How to Counsel Biblically* (Nashville: Thomas Nelson Publishers, 2005), 27.

[205] James R. Beck and Bruce Demarest, *The Human Person in the Theology and Psychology: A Biblical Anthropology for the Twenty-First Century* (Grand Rapids, MI: Kregal Publications, 2005), 188.

that the Christian counselor teaches his counselees and the secular counselor, especially in marriage relationships, as the Christian counselor shifts one's relational worldview from self to Savior.

    This view goes beyond changing "me first" to "you first" to putting Christ first in one's marriage and other relationships. With regard to marital relationships, no one gets divorced because they have the other one's best interest in mind. Christian relationships are not self-serving but rather for God's glory and the other's highest good. Matthew 16:24: "Then said Jesus unto his disciples, If any man will come after me, let him deny himself, and take up his cross, and follow me." Thus, the counselor for any relationship needs to point out to the counselee that the standard Christ gave to his followers was to deny one's self. Biblical counseling involves edification. MacArthur explained this way, "How will biblical counselors develop greater skill in the care of souls? How will we become wiser practitioners, thinkers, apologists, and Christian men and women? The task of edifying biblical counselors demands advances that are both exegetically sound and case-tried. It demands that we think well about many issues."[206]

    The case was made for the care of souls as the counselor edifies the counselee in and through the issues that are being dealt with. The argument was advanced that the way to be a greater help in the edification of counselees is to better prepare oneself in the areas of apologetics, hermeneutics, and case study on applying biblical truths to people and their challenges.

    MacArthur made the argument for the supremacy of scripture as the source for the care of the soul. His argument was for counselors to direct the counselees to the scriptures for their

---

[206] MacArthur, *Counseling*, 29.

greatest good and God's greatest glory. His robust language expressed it like this: "Far greater than all the universe of general revelation is the glory of God revealed in His Word, because it alone transforms the heart of man!"[207]

He further argued that the Bible has the effectiveness to teach and help counselees in their need. He said, "Only the Word of God can effectively instruct believers concerning how to glorify Him."[208] His position is that of pointing the counselees toward Christ rather than pointing them toward self. The focal point of biblical counseling is to see Christ, not man, and also to see problems and priorities as God sees them. The biblical counselor helps those in need to look to the Wonderful Counselor for the answers and challenges of life.

The foundation for biblical counseling is, plainly, theology. Timothy Clinton and George Ohlschlager believed that theology was the foundation for counseling and stated it this way: "Theology is primarily the articulation of a specific religious belief system itself (doctrine). But it also includes reflection on the nature of believing, as well as declaring concerning the integration of commitment with personal and community life. The Christian theologian seeks to set forth a coherent presentation of the themes of the Christian faith."[209]

The biblical counselor will employ the use of theology in the counseling curriculum. The counselee will be directed to know God in a more intimate way as answers to life are sought. Douglas Bookman offered an elaborate explanation of biblical

---

[207] MacArthur, *Counseling*, 46.

[208] Ibid.

[209] Clinton and Ohlschlager, *Competent Christian Counseling*, 96.

counseling. The theme of the book that he helped write along with John MacArthur is biblical counseling. The main point of this book was to contrast biblical counseling with evolutionary psychology. The authors' position was that because the supremacy of scripture is paramount, the evolutionary psychology approach should be dismissed and not seen as authoritative in counseling.

MacArthur argued for a biblical worldview of counseling, "By definition, the biblical counselor is one who is persuaded of and allegiant to a Christian worldview, that is, one that functions within a frame of reference that consciously sees all of the realities and relationships of life from a perspective that is biblically coherent and consistent, and thus honors the God of scriptures. The one element of such a worldview that most dramatically distinguishes it from all pretenders is the commitment to a theocentric perspective on all of life and thought. Thus any model of counseling that is authentically biblical will be framed, designed, and executed in happy submission to the biblical demand that our lives be lived out entirely for the glory of God! In short, biblical counseling is animated by a Godward focus."[210]

Bookman's definition certainly expanded other aspects that biblical counseling touch on. Within his definition, one's worldview was referenced. Certainly, one's worldview is influenced and possibly strengthened toward a more biblical worldview by biblical counseling. He mentioned the alignment between biblical counseling and the scriptures. Finally, he brought into his definition of biblical counseling the theological term *theocentric perspective of life*. In other words, Bookman was saying that a goal of biblical counseling is to cause people to live their lives in such a way as to bring honor to Christ. Thus when

---

[210] MacArthur, *Counseling*, 51.

A Biblical Worldview of Counseling in the Local Church

Christ is the focus of your life, relational problems are greatly diminished.

Who should do Biblical Counseling?

The ministry of biblical counseling ought to be the goal of every mature believer. The local church is a place for worship and fellowship, but it is also a place for healing and service. I Thessalonians 5:11: "Wherefore comfort yourselves together, and edify one another, even as also ye do." Paul instructed the church members in Thessalonica to encourage and build up one another in the faith. William Goode discussed this mandate for believers to be involved in counseling others. He explained, "Counseling is the responsibility of each believer and its only rightful arena is the church. These truths carry a strong implication: the pastor's involvement and leadership is critical."[211] This idea that all believers have some responsibility to be a counselor diminishes the idea, rightly so, of the caste system within a biblical church.

There are no clergy or laity just members. I Peter 2:9: "But ye are a chosen generation, a royal priesthood, an holy nation, a peculiar people; that ye should shew forth the praises of him who hath called you out of darkness into his marvellous light." The "priesthood of the believer" was coined by Martin Luther and, although a protestant term, is a good term. The idea is that all believers have the truth of the Word of God and the Holy Spirit and thus have the major spiritual tools needed to care for the soul of another. The Apostle Paul taught the church at Ephesus in Ephesians 4:11, 12: "And he gave some, apostles; and some, prophets; and some, evangelists; and some, pastors and teachers; For the perfecting of the saints, for the work of the ministry, for the edifying of the body of Christ."

---

[211] MacArthur, *Counseling*, 223.

Good restated it this way: "God wants these problems solved, and He has raised up pastor-teachers to equip the saints to do just that."[212] Pastors must teach and train more members to do all the counseling and ministering that needs to be done. Adding more on the place of counseling, Good said, "For the biblical counselor, the training ground must be the local church."[213] The local church is the primary place for training other believers to be biblical counselors. For one reason, it is where the believers are on a weekly basis. Furthermore, the local church is the primary place of service, as it is the focal place for Christians to worship. Therefore, biblical counseling can be taught in the church regularly.

Clinton and Ohleschlager discussed the challenge pastors face while counseling people with a wide variety of needs and a plethora of worldviews that collide with godly admonition. They explained, "Most pastors are not negative regarding the advisability of such care, but they're fearful because so few in the church are prepared to undertake the challenge. It was Paul who told the Roman believers of his great confidence in their ability to handle such a ministry of transitional care."[214] Paul expressed this confidence in Romans 15:14: "And I myself also am persuaded of you, my brethren, that ye also are full of goodness, filled with all knowledge, able also to admonish one another." The idea of admonishment is both positive and negative. The first aspect is to warn another believer of potential oncoming danger. Certainly, any parent would warn a child about being too close to a hot stove or would pull a child out of the way of a moving car. Equally

---

[212] MacArthur, *Counseling*, 223.

[213] Ibid., 229.

[214] Clinton and Ohlschlager, *Competent Christian Counseling*, 420.

so, any Christian—especially older Christians to younger Christians— would warn against spiritual or practical dangers. The positive counsel is to exhort—that is, to encourage—other Christians. Every believer has the ability to encourage others.

Clinton and Ohlschlager further made the argument that all believers are equipped for ministry. They explained, "All believers are gifted by the Holy Spirit for ministry. The church cannot be effective unless all believers utilize their gifts to serve the body of Christ"[215] (local assembly). They have made the same argument that MacArthur made in that all believers have been equipped by God to accomplish a task or mission for man's greatest good and God's greatest glory. One of the tasks to be accomplished is biblical counseling.

Paul confirms the Holy Spirit's working in and through believers for this purpose in I Corinthians 12:1-3: "Now concerning spiritual gifts, brethren, I would not have you ignorant. Ye know that ye were Gentiles, carried away unto these dumb idols, even as ye were led. Wherefore I give you to understand, that no man speaking by the Spirit of God calleth Jesus accursed: and that no man can say that Jesus is the Lord, but by the Holy Ghost." The Holy Spirit is responsible for endowing believers with spiritual gifts to be used to counsel other believers.

Preventative Biblical Counseling

The meaning of the phrase "preventative biblical counsel" conveys the idea that major life challenges may be headed off when biblical teaching and mentoring are consistently taught and exemplified before young people. Relationship patterns are

---

[215] Clinton and Ohlschlager, *Competent Christian Counseling*, 421.

formed early in children's lives, and thus, teaching must begin early. Proverbs 22:6 says, "Train up a child in the way he should go: and when he is old, he will not depart from it."

Because biblical counseling is, in a sense, biblical teaching, one could say that parents, teachers, and youth workers are counseling children before they need counseling. Counseling is often thought of as a corrective measure, but teaching biblical relationship principles to children and teens is a directive.

John Piper gave a biblical approach to how men and women should relate to each another as follows: "The tendency today is to stress the equality of men and women by minimizing the unique significance of our maleness or femaleness. But this depreciation of male and female personhood is a great loss. It is taking a tremendous toll on generations of young men and women who do not know what it means to be a man or a woman. Confusion over the meaning of sexual personhood today is epidemic. The consequence of this confusion is not a free and happy harmony among gender-free persons relating on the basis of abstract competencies. The consequence rather is more divorce, more homosexuality, more sexual abuse, more promiscuity, more social awkwardness, and more emotional distress and suicide that come with the loss of God-given identity."[216]

One can see in Piper's list of relationship problems, the direct results of unbiblical thought toward relationships that have been destructive to many lives. So preemptive biblical counseling begins to teach the young person biblical principles regarding relationships. In doing so, the biblical counselor is providing directive counseling that will prevent relational problems when

---

[216] Piper and Grudem, *Recovering Biblical Manhood*, 33.

young people grow up and, thus, prevent the need for corrective biblical counseling.

Preventative relationship counseling must hold to the premise that unless committed Christian parents, teachers, pastors, and every church member take the biblical mandate seriously to teach and mentor children in a Christian worldview, one can expect that children will grow up with an incorrect worldview of marital relationships. The basic truth that deals with one's worldview is found in Luke 6:48: "He is like a man which built an house, and digged deep, and laid the foundation on a rock: and when the flood arose, the stream beat vehemently upon that house, and could not shake it: for it was founded upon a rock."

Young people need to be taught to have a worldview of relationships that is built on the foundation of biblical principles. Simply said, if Christians do not teach children and teenagers what a biblical relationship is, then the world will, and the consequences can be devastating to the couple and to a local church.

John Stormer discussed these foundations that served families so well for over a hundred years. Stormer documented how the foundation of marriage came under assault by the reformers in public education. Stormer wrote, "America was once a society which had its roots in the Bible. The founding fathers were the product of western civilization. That civilization developed over several centuries after Gutenberg invented the printing press and published the Bible. In a Bible-based society, America grew great on the twelve foundational concepts. They were proclaimed in the nation's churches and taught in the nation's homes and schools."[217]

---

[217] John A. Stormer, *None Dare Call it Education: The Documented*

Stormer researched the history of public education and policy from before the founding of the country. He drew a direct connection between the public education that has grown incrementally toward secularism and the growing dysfunction and destruction of the family. The primary principles that apply to relationships and, ultimately, preventative biblical counseling are: "(1) The Sanctity of Marriage and the Family, (2) No Sex Outside of Marriage, (3) The Sanctity of Life, and (6) There are Absolutes of Right and Wrong."[218] Stormer's evidence and arguments for these foundational principles have and will uphold the foundation of the family relationship, but without these foundations, the family is destined for destruction.

For those devoted Christian adults that commit to the preventive biblical counsel of those young people in their homes, Christian schools, and local churches, these foundation principles are the cure for relational problems before the problems can even accrue. If these relationship foundations are installed in little hearts and minds before young people reach their teen years, they will have the principles and, hopefully, the convictions to prevent relationship patterns that might otherwise cause major relationship failures later in life.

Preventative biblical counsel also begins with instilling in believers, preferably when they are young, the principles to develop their worldview around the concept that biblical marriage is for the purpose of glorifying God and the glory of the woman. But for this conviction to take hold in the hearts and minds of young people, they must have a worldview that believes

---

Account of How Education "Reforms" Are Undermining Academics and Traditional Values (Florissant, MO: Liberty Bell Press, 1999), 52.

[218] Ibid.

that the Word of God is truth and that it applies to every aspect of human relationships.

Nancy Pearcey made this plea for the worldview of young people to be challenged in an intellectual way. She wrote, "Not only have we lost the 'culture,' but we continue losing even our own children. It's a familiar but tragic story that devout young people, raised in Christian homes, head off to college and abandon their faith. Why is this pattern so common? Largely because young believers have not been taught how to develop a biblical worldview. Instead, Christianity has been restricted to a specialized area of religious belief and personal devotion."[219]

The argument that Pearcey has built throughout her book is that without a comprehensive biblical worldview, the believer is overcome by the influence of the world. The greatest battleground for competing worldviews is in the marital relationship. What Pearcey is saying is that if the young people are not equipped with a biblical worldview, they will be lost to the world.

Pearcey explained, "We constantly see young people pulled down by the undertow of powerful cultural trends. If all we give them is a 'heart' religion, it will not be strong enough to counter the lure of attractive but dangerous ideas. Young believers also need a 'brain' religion—training in worldview and apologetics—to equip them to analyze and critique the competing worldviews they will encounter when they leave home."[220]

The apostle Paul challenged his hearers to not only think biblically but also to have a biblical worldview. Paul confronted

---

[219] Nancy Pearcey, *Total Truth: Liberating Christianity from Its Cultural Captivity* (Wheaton: Crossway Books, 2005), 19.
[220] Pearcey, *Total Truth*, 19.

the religious of his day. He challenged the philosophers' worldview on life, death, and eternal life. He got right down to the thoughts and heart attitudes when he penned Philippians 4:8, 9: "Finally, brethren, whatsoever things are true, whatsoever things are honest, whatsoever things are just, whatsoever things are pure, whatsoever things are lovely, whatsoever things are of good report; if there be any virtue, and if there be any praise, think on these things. Those things, which ye have both learned, and received, and heard, and seen in me, do: and the God of peace shall be with you."

Paul was drawing a connection between one's thinking and living out the Christian life, and, in the context of this writing, living out relationships in a biblical worldview. The prevention of marriage problems begins long before a couple walks down an aisle and says their marriage vows. Preventive counseling begins with children and teenagers. As young people are mentored into mature Christian adulthood, they adopt the relational skills that will help them live in Christian harmony, holding each other in high moral regard.

Premarital Biblical Counseling

Premarital biblical counseling is a continuation of discipleship. In the continued context of preventative biblical counseling, premarital biblical counseling seeks to instruct young adults in a biblical worldview of the marital relationship. Colossians 3:18–20 summarizes a biblical family clearly and distinctly in just a few brief words. "Wives, submit yourselves unto your own husbands, as it is fit in the Lord. Husbands, love your wives, and be not bitter against them. Children, obey your parents in all things: for this is well pleasing unto the Lord."

If young couples have a worldview that their marriage is to glorify God rather than please one's self, whey will have a vastly different worldview with a vastly different outcome. Colossians 3:23, 24 illustrates this idea: "And whatsoever ye do, do it heartily, as to the Lord, and not unto men; Knowing that of the Lord ye shall receive the reward of the inheritance: for ye serve the Lord Christ."

Chip Ingram has illustrated and communicated the difference between the Hollywood worldview of relationships and a God-centered worldview of relationships in an instructive way. He explained, "The revolutionary method begins by establishing that a spiritual component is the only foundation broad and strong enough to sustain the rest of the relationship. This spiritual component includes a clear understanding of God's entire prescription for love, sex, and lasting relationships."[221] Ingram made the argument that since the Hollywood worldview of relationships begins in the wrong place, it is not possible for those relationships to end up in the right place.

What Ingram has done is reveal the deception and failure of the worldview of dating by contrasting it with the worldview that he pointed to in Ephesians 4:3:, "And be ye kind one to another, tenderhearted, forgiving one another, even as God for Christ's sake hath forgiven you." Ingram explained that this is the biblical principle that will formulate a biblical worldview of relationships. He continued, "Our love for others flows out of our sense of being deeply loved. Instead of constantly looking for the right person, God tells us to become the right person. Instead of looking for love, God tells us to realize that love has already found us! God loves us as no one else ever can."[222]

This contrast is biblical and powerfully influential in the counseling ministry to demonstrate to couples the way most

---
[221] Ingram, *Love, Sex*, 46.
[222] Ingram, *Love, Sex*, 52.

people think, including Christians, and to challenge them to embrace God's worldview for a biblical relationship. As young people are taught and accept this biblical worldview of relationships, many relationship problems can be eliminated before they have the opportunity to develop. As a result of teaching the biblical worldview of marriage relationships, the amount of marriage counseling that might otherwise be necessary may very well be greatly diminished or not needed.

Part of the purpose of premarital counseling is to make sure the couple has the right worldview of marriage. Secondly, that the couple has the convictions and foundational beliefs that will give their relationship the strength to endure for a lifetime. Norman Wright discussed these foundational principles. He called them pillars. Wright asked the question, "What are the factors necessary for a lasting relationship? What would you say? What foundation stones or 'pillars' are essential for strong relationships?"[223] Wright was building the case that a couple must have a biblical worldview in order to have a lasting relationship. He explained, "There are actually many (pillars), but what is needed in any relationship, especially a lifelong marriage, are the following: love, trust, respect and understanding."[224]

The biblical foundation being taught here is derived from I Corinthians 13:13: "And now abideth faith, hope, charity, these three; but the greatest of these is charity." Charity is the Old English word for love. As a young couple prepares for a lifetime relationship, they are building these foundations into their lives and their marriages. These foundations are critical to their worldview in order to have lasting relationships.

[223] H. Norman Wright, *Relationships that Work and Those That Don't: The Singles Guide to Looking for Love in All the Right Places* (Ventura: Regal Books, 1998), 27.
[224] Wright, *Relationships that Work*, 27

Much of premarital counseling is actually educating the couple as they prepare for this important transition to married life. Norman Wright described premarital counseling this way, "Part of this teaching involves helping the couple to understand themselves and what each one brings to marriage, to discover their strengths and weaknesses, and to be realistic about the adjustments they must make to have a successful relationship."[225]

What Wright is talking about is the pulling back the curtain of who each marital partner is so that the couple may either move forward with their plans to marry or decide otherwise. Wright says that "one of the main purposes is to help the couple eliminate as many surprises as possible from the impending marriage. By eliminating those and helping them become more realistic about the future, marital conflict will be lessened."[226] His intent of premarital counseling is instructive, and to a great degree, works to prevent marital problems. Premarital marriage counseling is a significant help for the couple as there are many complexities with two personalities and lives coming together.

BIBLICAL COUNSELING FOR ADDICTIONS

Biblical counseling with regard to addictions requires first an understanding of the human makeup. Neil Anderson was helpful in describing from a biblical standpoint the different parts of man and how addictions can be overcome. Anderson explained it like this, "To understand the gospel and who we are in Christ, we need to look at the creation account and the subsequent fall of mankind."[227] He documented the creation of mankind by

---

[225] H. Norman Wright, *Premarital Counseling: A Guidebook for the Counselor* (Chicago: The Moody Bible Institute, 1981), 39.

[226] Ibid., 39.
[227] Neil Anderson, *Victory Over the Darkness: Realizing the Power of*

referencing Genesis 2:7: "And the LORD God formed man of the dust of the ground, and breathed into his nostrils the breath of life; and man became a living soul."

Anderson then described the different senses of body and soul: "Sufficient to say, we have a physical body that relates to this world through the five senses, and the inner self that relates to God and is created in His image."[228] He referenced Genesis 1:26, 27, to point to the significance man has. "And God said, Let us make man in our image, after our likeness: and let them have dominion over the fish of the sea, and over the fowl of the air, and over the cattle, and over all the earth, and over every creeping thing that creepeth upon the earth. So God created man in his own image, in the image of God created he him; male and female created he them." Anderson further explained the parallel between the Trinity and the human makeup. "Being created in the image of God is what gives us the capacity to fully think, feel and choose."[229] The case that he is building here is that people are made in God's image; that is, people have great significance to God. And people are free moral agents that are able to make decisions on their own and are responsible for the ones they make.

The counselee that is dealing with addiction may or may not yet be a Christian, but certainly, if the counselee is not a Christian, the first order of business is for the counselee to understand his fallen nature. Anderson explained the fallen nature like this: "What happened to Adam and Eve spiritually because of the Fall? They died. Their union with God was severed

---

Your Identity in Christ (Ventura: Regal Books, 2000), 28.

[228] Ibid.
[229] Anderson, *Victory Over the Darkness*, 28.

and they were separated from God."[230] He referenced Genesis 2:17, "But of the tree of the knowledge of good and evil, thou shalt not eat of it: for in the day that thou eatest thereof thou shalt surely die."

Anderson pointed out the tragic change because of original sin. "Innocence was replaced by guilt and shame; therefore the need for a legitimate sense of worth has to be restored."[231] The counselee must be shown that he is spiritually dead and that to be brought into a relationship with Father God, he must be saved. John 3:3: "Jesus answered and said unto him, Verily, verily, I say unto thee, Except a man be born again, he cannot see the kingdom of God."

This is the starting point for the counselee to see his sin the way God sees his sin. Before the counselee comes to this point, he may not think there is any problem in his life; he may just not like the consequences of his actions. Once the counselee comes to this point, he can make a positive change in his life. The theme of Anderson's book, as well as Jim Berg's book that will be referenced, is that only Christ can make permanent, transforming change in one's life. As Philippians 4:13 states, "I can do all things through Christ which strengtheneth me." It is God's strength, not self-determination or man's wisdom, that changes and upholds people.

The counselee that is not saved or has just been saved in counseling sessions has likely never had it occur to him that he was lost or that he was a slave to his flesh. This is where counseling and discipleship cross over each other. Paul stated in

---

[230] Ibid., 32.

[231] Ibid., 37,

Romans 8:13, "For if ye live after the flesh, ye shall die: but if ye through the Spirit do mortify the deeds of the body, ye shall live."

The drug user will eventually kill himself if he continues down this destructive path. Jim Berg uses scripture to explain that the believer is no longer under bondage to this sin of drug addiction. Berg stated, "Romans 6 teaches us, however, that because of Christ's death and Resurrection, we have been ;made free from sin' (6:22). We no longer have to obey its pull to go our own way."[232] What Berg was saying was that the counselee must be taught to be controlled by the Spirit of God rather than give in to these fleshly impulses to use drugs.

The other aspect of the changed life that Berg discussed may also be a new concept to the counselee through the changed life he now wants to live to glorify Christ. Berg referenced II Corinthians 3:18: "But we all, with open face beholding as in a glass the glory of the Lord, are changed into the same image from glory to glory, even as by the Spirit of the Lord." Berg discussed those that saw the Shekinah glory and equates this to the radiant countenance of the victorious believer. He stated, "As God shows them His in His Word, they experience a very specific change. By God's Spirit, they display an ever-increasing reflection of those 'glories' in their own lives."[233] As the counselee begins to be changed into the image of Christ, and more of the bondage of sin falls away, the counselee reflects more and more the image of Christ.

BIBLICAL COUNSEL FOR DIVORCEES

---

[232] Jim Berg, *Changed into His Image: God's Plan For Transforming Your Life* (Greenville, SC: Bob Jones University Press, 1999), 94.
[233] Berg, *Changed into His Image*, 143.

A BIBLICAL WORLDVIEW OF COUNSELING IN THE LOCAL CHURCH

As the local church seeks to minister to those within its membership as well as those outside its membership, divorce is a widespread problem that pastors and others that counsel within the local church must deal with. A study by George Barna demonstrated that the level of divorcees among non-Christians and Christians is similar. Barna found that "in fact, when evangelicals and non-evangelical born again Christians are combined into an aggregate class of born again adults, their divorce figure is statistically identical to that of non-born again adults: 32% versus 33%, respectively."[234]

Pastors and other counselors have a widespread problem with divorce to deal with. Needless to say, in the local church, this issue must be dealt with according to biblical principles and mandates. Divorce is always a challenging problem to deal with, and as children may be involved as well as family members and friends in the church, the need for wisdom from on high and the need for grace is significant. Pastors and other counselors are honor-bound to teach, counsel, and edify those that come to them for help, skillfully using the Word of God to bring about healing and hope.

Jay Adams dealt with whether Christian couples should divorce or remain together. Scripture makes this situation clear. I Corinthians 7:10, 11 states, "And unto the married I command, yet not I, but the Lord, Let not the wife depart from her husband: But and if she depart, let her remain unmarried, or be reconciled to her husband: and let not the husband put away his wife." Adams added to this verse,"The basic, twofold command in these verses

---

[234] George Barna, "New Marriage and Divorce Statistics Released," The Barna Group (March 2008), Available from http://www.barna.org/barna-update/article/15-familykids/42-new-marriage-and-divorce-statistics-released (accessed Nov 4, 2012).

is that neither the Christian wife nor the Christian husband may divorce one another."[235]

Adams then moved on to deal with the clause that states, "Let her remain unmarried." His argument is that if one will contest that they have a biblical marriage and quote Matthew 19:9 ("And I say unto you, Whosoever shall put away his wife, except it be for fornication, and shall marry another, committeth adultery: and whoso marrieth her which is put away doth commit adultery."), one should go back to the command in I Corinthians 7:11 and "remain unmarried, or be reconciled to her husband."

Adams stated, "He is saying, stay unmarried in relationship to all others. Or, he says (better still), repent right away and remarry the man you wrongly left. Indeed, if she does remain unmarried for a space of time, it is in order to allow for the possibility of reconciliation."[236] Adams argued from scripture that the intent is to preserve the marriage if the couple can possibly reconcile together.

Biblical Counseling for Strong Marriages

Strong marriages are a result of the strong foundations and principles that uphold them. As pastors and counselors, these foundations are not learned by themselves but must be taught. As previously mentioned, much of counseling is discipleship. When it comes to marriages, it is the local church that is at the front lines as a defense and proponent for marriage.

The first foundation of marriage understands God's purpose for marriage. Paul Steele and Charles Ryrie explained,

---

[235] Jay Adams, *Marriage, Divorce, and Remarriage in the Bible* (Grand Rapids: Zondervan Publishing House, 1980), 40.

[236] Adams, *Marriage, Divorce, and Remarriage*, 42.

"Our understanding of marriage principles begins with the fact that God created man and woman distinct from all animals and plant life. Imprinted on man's very being is the image of God, so that man is a personal, rational, and moral being possessing intellect, emotion, and volition (Genesis 2:19–20; 3:6–7)."[237] When counseling couples, it may go without saying, but the counselor should strive to get the couple to see their marriage in the big scheme of God's plan for their lives and marriage.

Steele and Ryrie discussed a second foundation. "In discovering the purposes of God in marriage, the bottom line is the covenant of marriage given in Genesis 2:24 and repeated by Christ and the Apostle Paul (Matthew 19:5; Mark 10:7-8; Ephesians 5:31)."[238] The counselor again must impress upon the couple the Third Person in their marriage, the Lord Jesus Christ, and that when they make or made their vows, Christ was present. When the couple makes a vow to each other, they are making that vow to Christ as well.

The third foundation in the bigger picture of marriage is that society is made up of marriages. Steele and Ryrie explained, "When one considers the signs of our times, it calls to mind the desperate question David posed in Psalms 11:3 'If the foundations be destroyed, what can the righteous do?' The very foundation of society is marriage, the home, and the family. If this foundation is destroyed we are set adrift on the sea of human solutions that never work."[239]

---

[237] Paul E. Steele and Charles C. Ryrie, *Meant to Last: A Christian View of Marriage, Divorce and Remarriage* (Wheaton: Victor Books, 1984), 18.

[238] Ibid., 23.
[239] Steele and Ryrie, *Meant to Last*, 62.

The couple must have impressed upon them the gravity and significance of every marriage. Along with the joy and lightheartedness of getting married, the couple should see themselves as, in part, making up the very fabric of human society. Pastors and counselors carry a lot of weight in helping marriages attempting to knit themselves back together and instructing new couples to lay solid foundations for their new and upcoming marriage.

CONCLUSION

This discussion on the counseling ministry in the local church began with a brief ecclesiological argument for counseling's greatest effectiveness to be done in the local church. Both Good and MacArthur provided material for a definition, as well as scripture, describing biblical counseling. This study found that all members of the local church ought to be involved in the ministry of biblical counseling and the edification of other members. A definition of preventative biblical counseling was offered for consideration. Premarital counseling is a staple of every local church ministry and is important to the next crop of families.

An ever-increasing problem in the local church is addictions. A biblical response to this problem was given as pastors stand in the gap trying to save souls and lives. Another epidemic in local churches is couples divorcing and pastors and counselors in the local church seeking to hold these families together with biblical counseling. Lastly, biblical counseling for strong marriages was discussed. The foundations of scripture will encourage couples to have a biblical worldview and God-view of their marriage and how it can last a lifetime.

A BIBLICAL WORLDVIEW OF COUNSELING IN THE LOCAL CHURCH:

QUESTIONS SIX

A Biblical Worldview of Counseling in the Local Church—Questions Six

Questions:

1. Where does counseling's greatest effectiveness take place?

   _____

2. James Beck and Bruce Demarest contrast Evolutionary Psychology with biblical counseling, pointing out the cavern between the two regarding relational worldviews.

   A) What does evolutionary psychology elevate above all else? B) What does biblical counseling elevate above all else?

   A) _____

   B) _____

3. **Matthew 16:24**: "Then said Jesus unto his disciples, If any man will come after me, let him deny himself, and take up his cross, and follow me."

   What standard does Christ give to his followers?

   _____

4. What mandate is seen in I Thessalonians 5:11 ("Wherefore comfort yourselves together, and edify one another, even as also ye do.")?

_____

_____

_____

_____

5. **I Corinthians 12:1-3**: "Now concerning spiritual gifts, brethren, I would not have you ignorant. Ye know that ye were Gentiles, carried away unto these dumb idols, even as ye were led. Wherefore I give you to understand, that no man speaking by the Spirit of God calleth Jesus accursed: and that no man can say that Jesus is the Lord, but by the Holy Ghost."

From where are believers endowed with the spiritual gifts needed to counsel other believers?

_____

6. What is the goal for directive Biblical counseling?

_____

_____

7. Relative to preventative biblical counseling, Stormer gives what primary principles for biblical relationships?

   A) _____

   B) _____

C) _____

D) _____

8. Nancy Pearcey points out the problem with young people today abandoning their faith once they leave home for college. To what does she attribute the commonality of this pattern?

_____

_____

9. **Colossians 3:23-24:** "And whatsoever ye do, do it heartily, as to the Lord, and not unto men; Knowing that of the Lord ye shall receive the reward of the inheritance: for ye serve the Lord Christ."

   How does this passage apply to marriage?

   _____

   _____

10. Wright asserts that marriage counseling lessens marital conflict by 1) "help[ing] the couple eliminate as many surprises as possible," and 2) "helping them become _____."

TRANSFORMATIONAL TRUTH VOLUME II

A BIBLICAL WORLDVIEW OF COUNSELING IN THE LOCAL CHURCH—

ANSWERS SIX

Answers:
1. Where does counseling's greatest effectiveness take place?

    Answer: The local church

2. James Beck and Bruce Demarest contrast Evolutionary Psychology with biblical counseling, pointing out the cavern between the two regarding relational worldviews. A) What does evolutionary psychology elevate above all else? B) What does biblical counseling elevate above all else?

    Answer:
    A. Self first
    B. Christ first

3. **Matthew 16:24**: "Then said Jesus unto his disciples, If any man will come after me, let him deny himself, and take up his cross, and follow me."

    What standard does Christ to his followers?

    Answer: Denial of one's self

4. What mandate is seen in I Thessalonians 5:11 ("Wherefore comfort yourselves together, and edify one another, even as also ye do.")?

Answer: Paul mandates all believers to be involved in counseling others in encouragement and building up one another in the faith.

5. **I Corinthians 12:1-3**: "Now concerning spiritual gifts, brethren, I would not have you ignorant. Ye know that ye were Gentiles, carried away unto these dumb idols, even as ye were led. Wherefore I give you to understand, that no man speaking by the Spirit of God calleth Jesus accursed: and that no man can say that Jesus is the Lord, but by the Holy Ghost."

   From where are believers endowed with the spiritual gifts needed to counsel other believers?

   Answer: The Holy Ghost

6. What is the goal for directive Biblical counseling?

   Answer: Preventing future problems in young people's lives

7. Relative to preventative biblical counseling, Stormer gives what primary principles for biblical relationships?

   Answer:
   A. The Sanctity of Marriage and the Family
   B. No Sex Outside of Marriage
   C. The Sanctity of Life
   D. There are Absolutes of Right and Wrong

8. Nancy Pearcey points out the problem with young people today abandoning their faith once they leave home for

college. To what does she attribute the commonality of this pattern?

Answer: These young people have not been taught how to develop a biblical worldview.

9. **Colossians 3:23-24:** "And whatsoever ye do, do it heartily, as to the Lord, and not unto men; Knowing that of the Lord ye shall receive the reward of the inheritance: for ye serve the Lord Christ."

How does this passage apply to marriage?

Answer: A marriage's goal should be to glorify God.

10. Wright asserts that marriage counseling lessens marital conflict by 1) "help[ing] the couple eliminate as many surprises as possible," and 2) "helping them become ____."

Answer: "more realistic about the future"

CHAPTER SEVEN

CONCLUDING THOUGHTS

CONCLUSION

Knowledge Gained from this Research

The first volume of Transformational Truth discussed developing a biblical worldview, contrasting naturalism and theism, the strengths of presuppositionalism and the weaknesses of classical apologetics, the comparison of Islam with Christianity, prophecy in future events, and the apologetic practices of the first- century Christians.

This second volume begins in chapter one with an explanation of the term *philosophy* in its original understanding relative to the Greek philosophers. Following this explanation were the more generic uses of the word philosophy. These explanations led the conversation to a biblical philosophy. The significance of this explanation of terms was to educate the reader: first, that the origins of Greek philosophy were no friend to the Christian worldview, and second, to help the reader to understand better and apply the terms as they relate to biblical apologetics.

The classic Bible account of Paul confronting the Greek philosophers at Mars Hill was referenced in Acts 17. This account and other references were given as a biblical precedent for presuppositional apologetics. The other important principle noted from the book of Acts was Paul making the argument from the scriptures. In other words, he employed expository preaching and teaching.

In the pursuit of understanding apologetics, the definition and biblical origin of knowledge and truth were given a brief explanation. The importance of understanding the origins of knowledge and truth is for skeptics to arrive at the conclusion of God's existence. The understanding of knowledge and truth leads to a discussion on the philosophy of education. The argument was made to connect education to the Great Commission. Notable preachers and educators from history were discussed. The path from Mars Hill to the Greek philosophers, to the Renaissance, to Western thought was outlined. Furthermore, we saw that while secular humanism was on the rise, several great awakenings occurred. The picture that has been seen throughout human history is the spiritual battle between good and evil. The question of evil in the world is one of the topics of chapter two.

The problem of evil was discussed in order to help both the skeptic and believer alike. This topic was addressed to take away the skeptic's objections of why not to believe in the Lord. One primary objection of skeptics is that there is a misunderstanding of scripture. The clarification and the proper application of hermeneutics will pave the way for skeptics to become believers in Jesus Christ. The explanations for the problem of evil will be a help to the believers to accept hardships as a result of evil in the world. The Fall of man in the Garden of Eden and the free moral agent of each human being will help the believer to understand when evil befalls even those that are living for the Lord.

One major accusation that skeptics and atheists have towards God is that if God allows evil in the world, then maybe He is not a moral God. This accusation was dealt with, and with reasonable people and a sound understanding of the scriptures, the Lord is by every account moral, just, holy, and compassionate. The Lord loves you!

One of the amazing discoveries found while researching the problem of suffering is that if there were no suffering, people would have no reason to demonstrate the godly attribute of compassion toward those that are suffering. One major point that debunks the atheist attack against the existence of God is that if one agreed with the atheist that God was the author of evil, the atheist would be honor-bound to believe in the existence of God. If the atheist trusts Christ as Savior, everyone wins. If the atheist does not trust Christ, the atheist has exposed his objection to belief in God to be a falsehood.

The argument was made that suffering went right along with and was a central part of the Gospel story. Christ suffered to give salvation to the world. Among other factors, Christ's own suffering leads to the morality of God. He is moral and righteous and has no conflict with the facts that God in His sovereignty allows for evil and suffering in the human experience.

In that chapter, we also discussed the problem of miracles. This is a misnomer for Christians because they have no problem with miracles, but communicating with the unbelievers about miracles is where help was offered. The clarification is that the "laws of nature" are not really laws but rather perceptions. This understanding gives clarity to the believer and the unbeliever.

Chapter three dealt with the belief systems of Arminianism and Calvinism, relative to how they related—or better stated, how they do not relate—to presuppositionalism. This author argued that Calvinistic teaching has primarily come from Presbyterian theologians. Furthermore, as Cornelius Van Til began to popularize presuppositionalism, he interjected his beliefs on

Calvinism into his theory of presuppositionalism. The argument is that the two theories are mutually exclusive. Calvinism's beliefs can stand alone without any aid from the theory of presuppositionalism.

Presuppositionalism, though popularized by Van Til and Greg Bahnsen, was first practiced by the apostle Paul (Acts 17:2). Presuppositionalism stands alone without need or aid from Calvinism. Presuppositionalism is the clearest biblical approach to apologetic teaching and must be applied to a "whosoever salvation" biblical principle. Presuppositionalism is consistent with scripture as it is the Word of God that convicts the heart of sin, and it is the Word of God that is absolutely necessary for conversion. One could very well argue that the mind is the gatekeeper to the heart, but it is most certainly the heart that must be converted. It is the scriptures that change the human heart. Thus, argumentation from the Bible, with the intent to persuade every listener to place his faith in Jesus Christ, is the task of presuppositional apologetics.

The fourth chapter discussed a biblical worldview of manhood and womanhood. This topic alone demonstrates how broad a body of study that apologetics is. The chapter begins with sourcing the Danvers statement, which was a counsel on manhood and womanhood. Apologetics does not end with salvation, but salvation is where one's entire biblical worldview begins to develop. Making an argument from the Bible for one to place his faith in Christ is presuppositional apologetics. Making an argument from the Bible relative manhood and womanhood might well be called apologetic worldview development. An unbeliever will undoubtedly have a worldview of one's manhood and womanhood. However, only a Christian can hold to a biblical worldview on manhood and womanhood, and only a biblical worldview leads back to the biblical account of Creation.

Concluding Thoughts

Chapter five dealt with the biblical worldview of sex and marriage. The basis of a Christian worldview is a biblical presupposition. As one looks around our world today, there are many different worldviews that people hold. The worldview that has God's blessing, brings that greatest joy to families, and continues to further the human race, is the biblical worldview of marriage and sex within the marital relationship. On the contrary, a secular worldview of sex and marriage leads to God's judgment: lives destroyed, babies aborted, the rise of divorce, the rise of single-parent homes, the rise of one-sex unions, and the rise of disease and mental illness. The call for society to come back to the biblical norms could not be louder. The need for biblical worldview teaching is enormous. The blessings that God has provided for through a biblical worldview of sex and marriage are as real as all the promises recorded in the Bible.

One could argue that all preaching, teaching, debating, witnessing, and counseling are forms of biblical apologetics. What are any of these endeavors for if not to persuade with the Word of God? There are competing worldviews many times within Christian thought. This author's view of the local church is that it is a local body of called-out believers for worship and service. Therefore, in chapter six, biblical counseling in the local church is discussed. The local church is the biblical model for applying the Great Commission, preaching, teaching, fellowship, and counseling. God blesses His Word, and God blesses the institution of the local church. It is God's Word that changes hearts, minds, lives, and worldviews. Biblical counseling is best applied in the local church; it prepares marriages in the premarital counseling process; it changes hearts when dealing with addictions; it may prevent divorce and can help heal those that have been divorced. And finally, biblical counseling can help marriages stay strong and give glory to God.

Transformational Truth Volume II

Remaining Research to be Accomplished

Apologetics is most certainly a broad body of study. Apologetics has many layers included in the subject. This writer would argue that beyond the many primary subjects relative to apologetics, there are even more secondary subjects related to apologetics, as seen in the subject of marriage and family.

The next area of study yet to be discussed is apologetics in the Old Testament. We will be going back to look at the Old Testament patriarchs, prophets, and others that apologetic principles can be attributed to their practice of communicating the things of God in their Old Testament era. We will also look at those recorded in the New Testament to see how the disciples, apostles, and others practiced apologetics in the first century. Special attention will be given to the ministry of the apostle Paul, including his apologetics, his rhetoric format of speaking, and his expositional style of preaching.

Once the biblical history has been looked at, our attention will turn to the history of the modern practice of apologetics. Special attention will be given to Cornelius Van Til and Greg Bahnsen. Within the body of apologetic study is the body of the study of logic. This will be useful in one's witness to the unsaved. The next area that will be covered will be pluralism and world religions. This will give the Christian better awareness of how Christianity fits into world history and events, and how Christians will be victorious. We will also look at the practice of rhetoric and how it can be used in our witness for the Lord. Paul employed rhetoric in I Corinthians 15 when discussing the resurrection of Christ and in Romans 10 when discussing the Great Commission. We will conclude in Transformational Truth Vol. II, by discussing the current trends of biblical apologetics.

APPENDICES

APPENDIX A

REVIEWS OF WRITERS ON EVANGELISM IN A POST-MODERN WORLD

AN EVALUATION OF C.H. SPURGEON'S MESSAGE.

Spurgeon's message began with a brief text from the book of Isaiah, in which he gave an excellent historical background of this passage. Spurgeon's narrative style immediately draws the reader into his message. His description of the passage drew a picture of an unsaved heart that is crying out for a Savior. He described the Jewish people of the day who were looking forward to the promised coming Messiah.

The people's hearts were heavy with grief for their sins and wanted relief. He referenced king Josiah and how the temple was left in shambles. The correlation was made of a spiritual life or lives that were in shambles because of their sin-wrecked lives. Spurgeon also gave an interesting description of Nehemiah and the idiosyncrasies of his personality. He reiterated the anguish the hearts of the people felt in their need for the Lord.

Spurgeon gave interesting details regarding the life and ministry of Martin Luther and the Reformation period. This detail might not be surprising because Spurgeon was closer to the time of the Reformation than modern times, as well as his being closer geographically closer to the events of the Reformation. In his description, he referenced several other European countries. Spurgeon then equated the travail of a woman in labor with the travail of those acquiescently waiting on the appearing of the Lord.

Spurgeon then referenced Elijah to discuss the need for men to have a burden for the lost. He talked about the ravens feeding Elijah. The point being discussed was that men should not be hard-hearted to the things of God and, per this conversation, that they have a burden for lost souls.

Spurgeon also discussed the character of Christ as an example to follow. Jesus prayed over Jerusalem, as we are instructed to do; He prayed so hard that He sweat blood. Christ really did demonstrate how we should have a burden for the lost. Spurgeon made an analogy to a cannon and cannonball, as it relates to being an aggressive soul winner. In other words, the soul winner must be enthusiastic and assertive when presenting the Gospel. There is no room for a lack of confidence or excitement about sharing the Gospel with one's friend and prospect.

Spurgeon told another story of how a couple wept over a soul-stirring sermon, but others could not understand why. Spurgeon then discussed several axioms relating to personal evangelism and made the connection that God has designed Christians to have and demonstrate compassion. Christians, he argued, are divinely designed to demonstrate compassion by sharing the Gospel with the lost around them.

Spurgeon made the argument that the Christian must have a fire in his soul to force him to pray for the lost. Furthermore, Christians must have a fire in their souls to share the Gospel with the lost and to minister to people. The inference is well stated that the Christian life is not normal without this fire for lost people. Spurgeon continued as he argued that a zeal for lost souls provides the purpose of life. He also explained that eloquences were not necessary for the conversion of souls because the heavy burden of an average Christian lady who begs God for souls would be far more productive.

Spurgeon made a great argument that those that do not travail for the lost souls of men would not be the ones that God wants to use to win the lost. The argument turned the typical thought process of unconcerned Christian thinking on its head. In other words, the Christian may think that the preacher is trying to recruit soul winners for his benefit, but the preacher is actually saying that the unconcerned Christian is missing one of the greatest blessings in the Christian life.

Spurgeon further argues that the convert would be in dangerous hands to come into the faith from the witness of an unconcerned Christian and that the baby Christian would be harmed by this poor spiritual attitude.

Spurgeon made another interesting point about time. He referred back to the woman in travail, an application to having a burden and being in the struggle for lost souls. The reference to time that Spurgeon made was likely an explanation that in God's work, more can get done in a small timeframe than with all the ingenuity applied to the world's progress in the same amount of time. He continued with two biblical examples of God's work being accomplished quickly. The first reference was the rebuilding of the state of Israel, and the second was to the earnestness of prayer in the upper room and after three thousand souls were saved in Jerusalem.

Spurgeon discussed the burden for the world, for China, and for the city of London. He made the argument, how will these souls be saved without a burden? He then brought the argument home to the lack of burden within their own ranks. He further argued that the church would either have new children in Christ or the church would die from the inside out. He gave the church these options and asked, "Which one do you want for your church and for your city, London?"

Spurgeon continued his argument that a church member cannot be uncommitted to the work of God through the local church without being a hindrance. He further stated that a church would have an impact on the politics of the town, but the politics should be left outside the church.

He also addressed the issue of offenses within the church, concerning the service of the Lord, that a Christian should be willing to be a doormat for others within the church. And of course, a Christian should avoid any offense to others in the church. He was really saying, "Christians keep your focus on reaching the lost for Christ."

As Spurgeon closed his message, he continued to argue that in each relationship, teaching, or ministry, everyone must prepare his heart to be able to handle the Lord's blessing. He continued to challenge the church to press forward together, and continue to pray, be burdened for, and witness for the Lord to the lost world around them. He encouraged them that they would be blessed as they fervently served the Lord.

An Evaluation of Modern Approaches to Evangelism.

What is the best way a believer can get an unbeliever to become curious about spiritual matters?

A soul winner must be winsome in order to win some. Dwight L. Moody was famous for saying that "he would first win a sinner to himself, and then to his Savior." One cannot get past the fact that personality and being personable are paramount in the endeavor of evangelism. As taught in Proverbs 18:24, "A man that hath friends must shew himself friendly: and there is a friend that sticketh closer than a brother."

The Christian minister and/or church member who is to be a witness does well to be friendly, likable, and hospitable while witnessing and/or discipling people into the faith and helping them grow in the faith. In business, it is said that people do business with those they know, like, and trust. How much more important is it for the one who knows Christ to befriend the lost and foster relationships of trust? In doing so, an environment of trust is cultivated, and the opportunity for one to receive Christ as Savior increases.

One method that is not passive, but is non-confrontational, is to give a testimony of how Christ has changed lives. A soul winner can go one of two ways with this: he can offer his personal testimony, or he can testify to another person's changed life. The latter may be even better as it is hard to challenge the changed life of one that is not present in the current conversation. Billy Graham used this extensively at Harvard University. Graham referenced numerous people from around the world who had their lives changed by having come to Christ.

Felt-needs have a strong appeal to the lost person as they do to anyone. The reason that felt-needs are a useful tool while witnessing to the lost is that they are a basis of common ground between the lost and the saved. Now, it is true that the lost and saved really have very little in common. Paul talked about the lack of agreement that believers and unbelievers have between them in II Corinthians 6:15–16: "And what concord hath Christ with Belial? or what part hath he that believeth with an infidel? And what agreement hath the temple of God with idols? for ye are the temple of the living God; as God hath said, I will dwell in them, and walk in them; and I will be their God, and they shall be my people."

Though this passage deals with the marriage relationship, the principle is clear. However, there are more, what one might call, "surface things" common to the human condition that believers and unbelievers might have in common.

For example, an unbeliever may become friends with a Christian. They both may have wives and children, work in the same field of business, and like to hunt and go to the shooting range. They both may have a child in the baseball league at the same public school. None of these things have anything to do with salvation, but they all may be common ground for the believer to befriend the unbeliever. As the unbeliever learns more about the believer, he may grow more interested in what makes this family so different from others.

It is interesting to note that Mormons when they are trying to convert men into their group, will ask, "How is your marriage? How is your family?" They will use marriage as a point of common ground to reach out to those outside their group.

There is one Christian pastor on TV whose broadcast revolves significantly around the subject of marriage. Many times the pastor and his wife will converse between themselves or with a guest on the program. Other times the pastor will speak to his congregation. The conversation is always about marriage. Yes, there is a felt-need being addressed. And certainly, marriage is both a bridge into conversation and a bridge into people's hearts to address the deeper need of salvation.

Other men put on marriage seminars that address the marriage and family, although those are both evidence of a deeper problem or a confirmation that families are following the Lord or need the Lord.

Many times, churches will use activities as an outreach to the community. This may take the form of a church baseball league, a hunting club, or a pig roast on the church property, and other times churches will put on a play or musical production. If children are involved, family and friends are bound to come out to see their children or grandchildren.

One Bible topic that is of great interest to many people, including those outside the faith, is future things. Some pastors, like the pastor in San Antonio, John Hagee, major in teaching on future things. Everyone is interested in his own future, and sometimes when life is going upside down with an unbeliever, he or she becomes more open to what the Lord says about the future of humanity. When unbelievers come under the sound of the preaching of future things, they then realize that there is accountability for their sin and unbelief. The biggest problem in their lives is not temporal but rather eternal. When the unbelievers begin to observe the believers in the church, the witness of God's remnant speaks to the unsaved and their curiosity.

An Evaluation of Billy Graham's Message: "Evangelism and the Intellectualism."

Billy Graham is an intellectual and a brilliant mind. It is interesting that Graham does not think of himself as an intellectual theologian, but also did not think of himself as an evangelist. He has since changed his mind. He explained that he did not know the difference between a lecture and a sermon but thought he might do a little of both.

Graham addressed the students and faculty at Harvard University. He declared that he was going to make a case for the Gospel, though he did not say "Gospel." Graham's ministry has consistently mentioned the possibility of nuclear holocaust. He used illustrations from around the globe to begin to frame his argument for the need for the Gospel, though he had not yet mentioned the Gospel or even a little scripture.

Graham listed off multiple problems that result from not knowing Christ; still, he did not mentioned the Bible. Graham demonstrated to his hearers that he is widely read and can stand toe to toe with any intellectual from Harvard's student body or faculty. He would most likely stand head and shoulders above the brightest of the bright.

Graham posted three questions that he intended to answer: (1) Is there an exit from the human dilemma, (2) what is the cause of this dilemma, (3) and is there and answer to this dilemma? What is the cause of this dilemma? Sin. Graham explained that within the body is a spirit that will live on somewhere beyond this life.

Graham illustrated with the lives of the Ela Indians. They were savages about to exterminate their entire people group. Then he referenced a modern city like New York. The take-away, he explained, is that economic security or education has not changed what the savage Elka Indians demonstrated. He concluded his illustration by stating that man is its own problem. He then bridged over to the verses in Romans that reveal man's sinful nature.

He continued with a version of the Roman's Road—the plan of salvation. Graham wove into his lecture that one of the strongest drives man has is to seek and find the truth.

Appendices

Graham gave another illustration from the psychologist's department-head at Yale. The department-head made the statement that if the churches do not fix the human problems, then the psychologists would have to fix them.

Graham then gave a couple of illustrations about men who were once vile people and very hateful but eventually were saved. These same men now preach God's love. Graham used this to illustrate the profound, positive impact Christ has on a person who comes to faith in Christ.

One man from Long Island was told to do more to restrain evil than any other force to date. Graham gave the illustration of William Wilberforce;he stood up against slavery, and eventually, England abolished slavery. Graham told accounts of how he has seen intellectual students and professors submit to Christ, and he made the case that he has seen changed lives all over the world.

Graham discussed that man has a destiny, and that destiny was not written by Kennedy or Crustchoff but by Christ. Graham talked about his own life and how he committed it to Christ. He stated he would not change his commitment to Christ for all the money in Fort Knox.

A Harvard student asked whether people need a shoulder to cry on or something more? Graham stated he was not calling people to Christianity, but to the person of Christ.

Professor Okanogay was asked a question that was riddled with criticism of the right-wing ideas of government. Professor Okangay did mention that the Bible talks about personal responsibility. Graham gave a great answer that a Christian should be able to live under any form of government, even the Roman government.

Another professor asked about his conversion. Graham explained the three forms of love and that agape love is only found in the Lord Jesus Christ.

Graham was then asked why one should become a Christian over another religion. Graham explained that Christ did something that no other religious leader has done: Christ died for His followers. This example demonstrated how Christianity is the only belief system that could live up to the ethics taught in the Bible.

Graham explained how people like Wilbur Wilberforce and D.L. Moody could practice ethics because of the commitment that these men and many others had to Christ. The inference was that it would not be possible to hold to an ethic, and Graham referred to the Moral Law and the Laws of the Universe, without a personal relationship with Jesus Christ.

This forum held at Harvard University demonstrates how influential Billy Graham has been. This audience was not made up of those in the seminary at Harvard but was attended widely from those across the campus. In the closing moments of the mp3, there was an indication of the number of students from the Harvard School of Law in attendance.

A fair amount of Graham's presentation included ethics. This body of study has wide appeal and certainly was front and center in this forum. Graham was very skilled at handling himself in front of this type of audience and, in particular, how he handled questions from the students and professors alike.

WHICH GOSPEL RECORD GIVES THE BEST APPROACH TO EVANGELISM?

The book of Matthew is an interesting book, not only because it is a transitional book (from Old to New Testament) but also because of its audience. The audience Jesus was addressing in the book of Matthew was Jewish. There was a clear strategy for getting the Gospel to the known-world as seen in Romans 1:16: "For I am not ashamed of the gospel of Christ: for it is the power of God unto salvation to every one that believeth; to the Jew first, and also to the Greek."

This may seem like a side note, but actually, it is central to understanding the book of Matthew, relative to evangelistic approaches. In Matthew 24:14: "And this gospel of the kingdom shall be preached in all the world for a witness unto all nations; and then shall the end come." Jesus was in the biblical theater during His earthly ministry, and here His preaching pointed His hearers to the return of Christ. Why is prophecy a strong position for evangelism? Because there is a deadline, which is unknown when judgment will happen. Prophecy, therefore, by its nature, is evangelistic. It is like one standing in the streets, yelling, "Prepare to meet thy Maker!"

One must agree, as Benjamin Franklin said, "Nothing makes one more efficient than the last moment." And certainly, no one should put off getting saved. II Corinthians 6:2: "For he saith, I have heard thee in a time accepted, and in the day of salvation have I succoured thee: behold, now is the accepted time; behold, now is the day of salvation." Jesus communicated the Gospel in an excellent way to His audience in the book of Matthew. Now we will consider how the Gospel was presented in the book of Mark.

The book of Mark's primary audience was the Romans. Mark used the word "preach" four times in his Gospel, and Matthew used this word four times as well. Mark records the early ministry of John the Baptist, the forerunner of Jesus Christ, in Mark 1:3-4: "The voice of one crying in the wilderness, Prepare ye the way of the Lord, make his paths straight. John did baptize in the wilderness, and preach the baptism of repentance for the remission of sins." One might argue that John had an evangelistic ministry and a ministry of heralding the fulfillment of the promised Messiah.

John the Baptist's evangelistic ministry was strongly and simply for sinners to repent. In doing so, sinners would obtain remission of their sins. The more pastoral aspect and response to John the Baptist's preaching are seen in verse 5: "And there went out unto him all the land of Judaea, and they of Jerusalem, and were all baptized of him in the river of Jordan, confessing their sins." As people repented of their sins, they made their public professions of faith as they responded to the evangelistic preaching of John the Baptist.

John the Baptist was an itinerant preacher because he moved from town to town throughout Galilee. Notice John the Baptist's evangelistic strategy seen in Mark 1:38–39a: "And he said unto them, Let us go into the next towns, that I may preach there also: for therefore came I forth. And he preached in their synagogues throughout all Galilee." In Romans 1:16, it came to be understood that the Jews would not receive the Gospel from the Gentiles. The Jews were the "religious" people, while the Gentiles were referred to as "dogs" because they were considered pagan, or non-religious. Thus, the evangelistic strategy was to get the Gospel to the Jews first, and then the Jews would give the Gospel to the Gentiles.

The best-known passage in the book of Mark, relative to evangelism, is found in Mark 16:15: "And he said unto them, Go ye into all the world, and preach the gospel to every creature." This passage may very well be the best strategy of evangelism as our Lord directs the Gospel to be preached to every living person.

Appendices

The book of Luke used the word "preach" five times in its pages. The human writer was Dr. Luke, who was a Greek like his audience. As a physician, he viewed his audience as he would a patient, which is to say using empirical evidence. Like a physician inspects his patient, so did Dr. Luke spiritually inspect his audience as he preached the Gospel. This was seen in Luke 4:18: "The Spirit of the Lord is upon me, because he hath anointed me to preach the gospel to the poor; he hath sent me to heal the brokenhearted, to preach deliverance to the captives, and recovering of sight to the blind, to set at liberty them that are bruised."

This is to say that Luke, though addressing the spiritual needs of his audience, was well aware of the human condition. He thus framed his Gospel presentation in terms of being poor, brokenhearted, losing freedom, blind, and bruised. In so doing, Luke illustrated the Gospel in a very tangible way. Now, notice how John framed evangelism in quite a different manner.

There are the synoptic Gospels, and then there is John's Gospel. This is to say the synoptic Gospels very much parallel the narratives of the other Gospel writers. Matthew's Gospel addressed the Jews (a transitional book from Old to New Testaments). Mark's Gospel addressed the Romans. And while Luke's Gospel addressed the Greeks, John's Gospel addressed everyone. John's Gospel is also thought to be a much simpler sentence structure than the other Gospels. Let's consider a couple of thoughts regarding the narrative seen in John's Gospel.

First, one should conclude that John's narrative is that of a personal soul winner as described in John 1:12: "But as many as received him, to them gave he power to become the sons of God, even to them that believe on his name." The reason the Gospel of John is so useful in personal soul winning is that it is easy to understand and gives logical steps to how one comes to faith in Jesus Christ.

Secondly, John's appeal is to the whole world, as seen in John 3:16: "For God so loved the world, that he gave his only begotten Son, that whosoever believeth in him should not perish, but have everlasting life." The third aspect that must be mentioned about John's Gospel is that it describes clear doctrine as in John 14:6, "Jesus saith unto him, I am the way, the truth, and the life: no man cometh unto the Father, but by me." The book of John is written in such a usable and teachable manner and is so practical in its application to personal evangelism.

The Gospel of Matthew demonstrates that it was written in a very strategical manner and is a narrative of preaching to groups of people. The preaching style is both prophetic and evangelistic. Mark's Gospel seems to be a heralding style of preaching that announces the fulfillment of the Old Testament prophecy of the coming Messiah. Luke's Gospel and style of preaching seem to be very pastoral as he framed the Gospel in terms of human needs. John's Gospel is both doctrinal and a personal soul-winning approach to presenting the Gospel.

Though every approach to evangelism in the four Gospels is Divinely written and vital to accomplishing our Lord's Great Commission to His churches, the Gospel of John would seem to be the most used and needed in its application of God's people doing their part to accomplish this Divine task.

An Evaluation of Adrian Roger's Message "Apostasy of a Dead Faith."

Adrian Roger preached for several years at First Baptist Church in Merritt Island, FL. At that time, he preached evangelistically across Florida daily. It has always been this writer's belief that the reason any preacher gets on the radio is because he is highly motivated for as many as possible to hear the Gospel of Jesus Christ. Later, Rogers became pastor at Bellevue Baptist Church in suburbia Memphis, TN. While he was pastor of the church, it grew over twenty thousand in membership. Needless to say, Rogers brought his evangelistic fever with him.

In Adrian Rogers' sermon, "Autopsy of a Dead Faith," he used the passage of James 2:17. Rogers preached on this topic often and demonstrated his heart for alive, soul-winning Christians. After reading the passage, he began his homily by stating emphatically that salvation is by grace alone. It is very practical and necessary when dealing with any type of service to the Lord and the local church that church members are instructed and reminded that any work in the service of the Lord, whether it be as a volunteer or paid, can in no way be misconstrued to be payment for one's sins.

The motivation for Christian service must always come with the idea that one is using his time, talent, and resources for God's highest glory and man's highest good. This is based on Ephesians 2:8–9: "For by grace are ye saved through faith; and that not of yourselves: it is the gift of God: Not of works, lest any man should boast."

Rogers continued his clarification between grace and works as he referenced Acts 16:31: "And they said, Believe on the Lord Jesus Christ, and thou shalt be saved." Rogers then referenced Romans 4:2, 5–6: "For if Abraham were justified by works, he hath whereof to glory; but not before God. But to him that worketh not, but believeth on him that justifieth the ungodly, his faith is counted for righteousness. Even as David also describeth the blessedness of the man, unto whom God imputeth righteousness without works."

Rogers argued from this passage that one is not saved from works. He pointed out that righteousness came without works. Next, Rogers referenced what sometimes is called a hard passage. This is to say, though it might appear on the surface to be a contradiction, what has to happen is to study deeper in a given passage to more clearly understand what God is revealing to humanity. Rogers referenced James 2:21 ("Was not Abraham our father justified by works, when he had offered Isaac his son upon the altar?") and 24 ("Ye see then how that by works a man is justified, and not by faith only."). Rogers explained this apparent contradiction and made the two passages very clear.

He stated that James and Paul were not contradicting each other but were instead stating the same point relative to justification. The way Rogers explained these two passages, Paul was discussing justification before God, while James was talking about justification before man. He further explained that God sees your faith in your heart. According to Paul, God can judge or, in this case, may justify the believer. On the other hand, James dealt with what man can see, as stated in James 2:14, "What doth it profit, my brethren, though a man say he hath faith, and have not works? can faith save him?" This points out the error of when a person says they are a Christian, but in effect, they have no evidence of the Spirit of God.

What James was saying is that one's works reveal to others the faith one possesses. Rogers summed it up as Paul discussing the root of salvation while James was talking about the fruit of salvation.

Adrian Rogers offers his expository message in a very understandable way. To clarify, this may very well be a topical message, but, to be sure, Rogers expounded on these two different passages. First, he showed a contrast, and then he gave the explanation of the two passages. Paul and James were saying the same thing about justification. Rogers said the difference was Paul discussed a knowing faith, while James talked about a showing faith. Rogers has a good way of stating biblical principles in a way that is memorable.

Next, Rogers gave the autopsy of a dead religion. His first point about a dead religion was that it demonstrates no compassion. Rogers made a powerful argument when he referenced James 2:15-18: "If a brother or sister be naked, and destitute of daily food, And one of you say unto them, Depart in peace, be ye warmed and filled; notwithstanding ye give them not those things which are needful to the body; what doth it profit?

Even so faith, if it hath not works, is dead, being alone. Yea, a man may say, Thou hast faith, and I have works: shew me thy faith without thy works, and I will shew thee my faith by my works." In other words, how can one claim to have a love for God and not have a love for God's people? A Christian must have a changed life.

Rogers secondly made the argument that one without works does not have any communion. Rogers challenged the listeners whether they really loved Jesus Christ. The third argument Rogers made was that there was no real conversion. Rogers then made a great point from Ephesians 2:8-10 that people are saved by faith, through grace, and unto good works.

Rogers does an excellent job of helping people to understand the scriptures. In this message, Rogers first contrasted an apparent contradiction. Then he explained and developed the two contrasting passages and biblical writers. He not only cleared up the apparent contradiction but also explained why Paul and James were actually in sync with each other's writings.

Rogers closed the message by continuing to make the point that for the church, there must be evidence of conversion. Throughout the passage in the book of James, Rogers demonstrated excellent expository development while holding the listeners' attention. Rogers pushed for two significant points in this message: first, that religious people would get saved, and second, that saved people would serve the Lord through the local church.

Is the Terminology "Receive Christ" Proper to Use in Presenting the Gospel?

In order for one to best understand repentance relative to receiving Christ as Savior in response to the Gospel presentation, one must understand how repentance fits into soteriology. Lewis Sperry Chafer explained, "Since repentance—conceived of as a separate act—is almost universally added to believing as a requirement on the human side for salvation, a consideration of Biblical meaning of repentance is essential."

An old saying is "no conviction, no conversion." *Repentance* is clearly a biblical word and one that is a requirement for conversion to happen and salvation to be received. Chafer offered this definition for the word repentance. He stated, "The transliterated Greek word, metanoia {met-an'-oy-ah} is in every instance translated repentance. The word means a change of mind."

This is a must for one to receive salvation. One must repent and receive Christ as his personal Savior. There is no other way, as Christ does not force His way on anyone. Christ comes into one's heart by personal invitation. God made human beings to be free moral agents. God can only get glory from human beings who decide to repent of their sins and receive Christ as their personal Savior.

The Gospel of John records the terminology *receive* many times, as seen in John 3:27: "John answered and said, A man can receive nothing, except it be given him from heaven." It is reasonable from the language John used that if one gets the eternal gift from heaven, one must receive it into his heart.

As a soul winner, it has always been this writer's practice to use in his Gospel presentation John 1:12: "But as many as received him, to them gave he power to become the sons of God, even to them that believe on his name:" Frankly this writer does not know and could not imagine not using the terminology receive while giving out the Gospel. Furthermore, this writer would always make the point to the sinner that receiving is equal to believing.

The previous verse gave an example of those who had not "received" Christ as their Messiah. John 1:11: "He came unto his own, and his own received him not." The negative here proves positive, which is to say those that did not receive Christ made the argument that they should have received Christ.

The Galileans responded by faith when they received Christ as their Messiah. John 4:45: "Then when he was come into Galilee, the Galileans received him, having seen all the things that he did at Jerusalem at the feast: for they also went unto the feast." This was an example of a spiritual response to the miracle of Jesus turning water into wine. In other words, the Galileans were persuaded by the miracles, and they received Jesus as their Savior.

John recorded for us how the apostles were persuaded by the words that Jesus used when speaking to them. In other words, no ordinary man could say the things that Jesus said. John 17:8: "For I have given unto them the words which thou gavest me; and they have received them, and have known surely that I came out from thee, and they have believed that thou didst send me." Even the apostles, who saw and touched Jesus, who were part of His earthly ministry, and followed Him for three and one-half years had received Him as their Messiah.

One of the greatest evangelistic events recorded in scripture is found Acts 2:41: "Then they that gladly received his word were baptized: and the same day there were added unto them about three thousand souls." A theologian may look at this passage as a theological one. As we are studying the doctrine of soteriology and its implications, it goes without saying that salvation comes before baptism. Here in this passage, those that "received His Word" clearly trusted Jesus Christ as their personal Savior. Following this event, immediately in this example, the new believers were all baptized into the local church in Jerusalem.

So is it acceptable to use the term "receive the Lord" in the soul-winner's Gospel presentation? It is not only acceptable; it is absolutely necessary. The word, receive, is imperative.

An Evaluation of Ron Comfort's Message

Ron Comfort began by asking those in attendance to open their Bibles to Romans 7:4, which he then quoted. He stated that the church has as much enthusiasm for evangelism as it does for righteousness.

He then shared two stories of how he went to a large church in California to hold a training meeting on evangelism. Many cars were in the parking lot, but it was because there was a woman's meeting being held at the church at the same time. He told another story about a large crowd in the church parking lot, but he came to find out it was only because traffic from an accident was being funneled through the parking lot, not because of the service.

Ron Comfort told how he was saved out of the hippy culture, and that a ninety-one-year-old Presbyterian pastor was his mentor. When the man died two years later, he sang a hymn as he passed. Comfort gave his testimony of how he lived terribly. He then suggested that he had made a false profession before actually getting saved. Comfort gave an illustration about a young man speeding through town whose father had to spring him out of jail. The fruit of the son was repentance and fruitfulness. The fruit of repentance was good works, which was a result of gratefulness for the dad's graciousness to him.

Comfort continued to frame the argument of his message of false conversions. He quoted several passages to make his case. He continued to argue for the one that was likely lost in a false profession. He talked about running off those that have made false professions and stated that those that have genuinely been saved would desire the Word, fellowship, and want all the things that they should they want. Comfort then argued that true converts would not lust, steal, lie, and so forth. However, this seems to be a high bar for most Christians.

Comfort gave several examples of evangelists from antiquity that quoted false converts. He then told a story of an angry church member who cut his pastor with a knife; he concluded that the man could not have been a Christian because he did not possess love, joy, peace, and restraint. He then gave examples of mass murderers that were once in Christian churches and told a similar story of those in rock bands who had previously been in a church.

Then, he shared the story of a loud, bombastic Christian and another of a Christian who was quiet but took copious notes from the sermons. The bombastic Christian fell away, but the quiet Christian stayed plugged into the church. Comfort continued by sharing Bible examples from the time of Jesus' earthly ministry, such as Judas and other false believers. Comfort also mentioned Demas, who loved the world rather than the things of God.

Comfort continued with the story of a church that moved into an old jewelry factory. The church people found thousands of dollars of dust in the building, which they were able to sell. Comfort made the spiritual connection that the Lord has to refine Christians through heat. He continued that we are tried by challenges to purify us for Christ.

Comfort then argued that a Christian's fruitfulness would be based upon whether he used the Bible lawfully. Comfort told about a time when he witnessed to a Muslim, and he convinced the Muslim that he was a lying, cheating, lusting, thief that was an enemy of God. He left him with no hope.

Next, he demonstrated how to witness to a Catholic. Ron gave the same presentation over and over again with a gay man and then an intellectual. Then, after Comfort had made an hour-long argument on how to talk Christians out of their faith in Christ, he argued (after witnessing to the intellectual) that we overcomplicate the Gospel. We are now making the soul-winning too difficult for people to believe.

Comfort focused his whole argument on the law from the book of Romans. He gave numerous arguments that were somewhat apologetic and, to some extent, philosophical when dealing with witnessing. He talked about reasons not to have a fear of men to be a witness for the Lord. He closed his talk by admonishing the lost people in his audience to trust Christ as their Savior.

The narrative of Ron Comfort's message was nearly ninety percent about false professions. The reason this message does not register with this writer is that I have started two churches in heavily Catholic New England. Part of the equation is winning people to Christ. It is essential to do a good job presenting the Gospel and continue discipling the new convert.

Once they are saved, I would talk with them about baptism and church membership. I would also have them read the church by-laws and doctrinal statements. We might go over the doctrinal statement together, and then would set a date to baptize by immersion. Once I gave the Gospel, and they understood it and trusted Christ, I would never hunt them down to suggest that they were not truly saved. I must trust God's Word, and I trust someone that gives testimony that they are indeed saved, as to do otherwise is above my pay grade. I must trust God to help me present the Word of God accurately and to do all that He has commanded me to do. Everything else I have to leave with Christ.

DO YOU BELIEVE IN LORDSHIP SALVATION, EASY-BELIEVEISM, OR SOMETHING ELSE?

Lordship salvation began to be popular in or around the 1970s and was very likely popularized by John MacArthur. Another one that comes to mind that emphasized Lordship salvation was Billy Graham.

Graham would end his evangelistic meetings with an altar call. In that call, he would appeal to the people's need to be saved. Within that appeal, he would give the charge that people must make Christ Lord and Savior of their lives. But they had to commit their whole lives to the Lordship of Christ right then and there in that stadium.

Billy Graham is a brilliant man, but he may have overthought the doctrine, which is supposed to God's free gift to the world—not a transaction event. On the other hand, because John MacArthur is not only an intellectual but also a biblical scholar, he has poured over this doctrine of salvation and written and taught on it for years. Why some want to take a free gift (the Gospel) and turn it into a payment plan is beyond this writer.

MacArthur has pushed this idea of Lordship salvation, in some ways, to the greater extent. Through MacArthur's books, seminary, and daily speaking on the radio, he has pushed Lordship salvation continually. This writer knows of several pastors in the Chicago area that have to deal with the fallout of MacArthur's false teaching regularly. One church in the western suburbs of Chicago has a national TV broadcast. They ask viewers to call in to get saved, from which they have over one hundred professions per week. As a result of their broadcast, many people call in who have been sitting under the teaching of John MacArthur, and so many are confused and just lost. The simplicity of the Gospel message and offer has been mottled.

Although Lordship salvation is a contemporary issue in the local church today, this issue has been around since the first-century church. Paul had to address this problem with the church at Galatia. Paul wrote under the inspiration of the Holy Spirit in Galatians 1:6–9, "I marvel that ye are so soon removed from him that called you into the grace of Christ unto another gospel: Which is not another; but there be some that trouble you, and would pervert the gospel of Christ. But though we, or an angel from heaven, preach any other gospel unto you than that which we have preached unto you, let him be accursed.

As we said before, so say I now again, If any man preach any other gospel unto you than that ye have received, let him be accursed." Thus, after this church had filled up with those that had converted to Christianity, Paul had to go in and reteach them what was biblical salvation and what was a works-salvation. Works-salvation is what the Galatians had come out of. This is why Paul was so surprised when the Galatians fell away or, rather likely, were not saved before now and had to revisit the salvation doctrine and trust Christ as their personal Savior.

Easy-Believism became popular in the 1960s and 1970s with the methodology employed by Jack Hyles and those that fell under his spell. To be sure, Fundamentalism was doing well in the 1970s. The Christian school movement had grown out of the events of the Supreme Court's removing Bible reading and prayer out of the public schools in 1962 and 1963. During the 1970s, Lee Robertson, Jerry Falwell, and others had soul-winning churches that were growing fast. This writer only puts Hyles in the Easy-Believism camp, although other Baptist groups were certainly winning people aggressively to the Lord.

There are likely several causes of this movement. One obvious one was populating Baptist churches with men who were not seminary trained. Although some men have a propensity for more in-depth learning in the ministry and away from the classroom, most pastors teach on a level of skim milk. Most preaching revolves around the operation of the local church, soul-winning, tithing, and faithful attendance. A primary Sunday morning preaching theme is a salvation message for most weeks.

Though no Bible believer could disagree with the content, the church member needs expository preaching that feeds his soul. Disciples make disciples.

A clear Gospel message begins with sound hermeneutics and solid Bible doctrine. As was mentioned previously in this class on evangelism in a post-modern world, the witnessing Christian must begin the Gospel presentation with the Creation account in Genesis. The unbeliever must learn about the Fall in the Garden of Eden and the Law that was handed down to Moses. This writer has had his worldview of evangelism move from a door-to-door model to a discipleship model. In other words, the elevator conversions may or may not be true.

This writer knows this much: growing in grace with the Savior takes time. One must be in a hurry to see the lost come to Christ, but one must also be patient like a farmer to watch and see the seed grow into the harvest. As a parent must be patient so that his child understands instruction, so must the Christian while working in the Lord's harvest.

An Evaluation of Ken Ham's Video.

After reading Ken Ham's book, *Why Won't People Listen*, and listening to his audio, this author felt that it was generally good material covered. One thing which occurred to this writer is that much of the material on the audio, if not all of it, was covered in his book. From an analysis perspective, it is clear that Ken Ham is not a Classical apologist, an Evidential apologist, or a Presuppositional apologist. One might make the argument that he is a Creationist apologist, but this does not even seem to fit any of the apologetic models which have previously taught in this program.

Ham's principal argument throughout the book and video was that the spiritual foundation has been removed from the culture of the Western Hemisphere. As previously mentioned, this writer's pastor told him about having to go back to Creation in Genesis when witnessing thirty years ago. When witnessing to someone nowadays, it is almost as if there was a Creation blackout.

Ham did, however, bring an interesting perspective, being from Australia and having traveled to many places around the world. Ham discussed how the culture in England has gone from a reasonably high percentage of evangelicals to somewhere less than five percent. He made the argument that what has happened to England is going to happen to America.

He further argued the point that America is not listening. He pointed out all the Bible colleges, seminaries, Christian radio and TV stations; yet, the country is still mostly unsaved. All these were valid points to be made, but Ham never referenced I Timothy 4:1: "Now the Spirit speaketh expressly, that in the latter times some shall depart from the faith, giving heed to seducing spirits, and doctrines of devils." These are all things that have been prophesied by the apostles since the first century.

On one side of Ham's argument, it appeared as though he was saying that the CCM and the entertainment culture of contemporary churches have lessened the impact of the Gospel on these church attendees. This writer would have to agree. Ham, at the same time he was arguing that the "seeker-sensitive churches" are not influencing the culture like the traditional churches have, also argued that American churches are not speaking the same language (so to speak) as the unsaved culture around us that they are trying to reach with the Gospel. Now, Ham did not state his own position on the most biblical eschatology, but if this writer understands what Ham was saying, 1) churches are too much like the world, and 2) churches are not communicating in a way that unsaved people understand.

This is part of what Ham was saying, of which the only logical way to respond it that one cannot have it both ways. This is to say, the church cannot change its message. On the other point, the church cannot compromise its message in music if it wants to impact the culture for eternity. The local church is not a bar or a dance hall, and it certainly is not an entertainment center. The more the church tries to be like the world in order to win the world, the less it impacts the culture for Christ.

The main area of miscommunication by Christians trying to be a witness is that the culture is such in the current climate that some cannot be won to Christ until the foundations of Christianity have first been established in the minds of the non-churched person. This writer whole-heartily agrees with the cultural shift and that churches and soul winners must be willing to take the time to lay the foundation of explaining the Creation, the Fall, and the Law, before moving on to the death, burial, and resurrection of Jesus Christ.

Ham made some good points for those in ministry and/or soul winners to be cognizant of the culture and time in which we minister to people. It is always good to have a spokesman for Creationists evangelism. The time in which we live in is certainly the last of the last days before Christ's return. Every believer must sharpen and put all his tools in his toolbox as he engages in the winning of the lost culture.

Explain and Defend the Doctrine of Eternal Security.

The topic of eternal security has been a hotly debated and controversial biblical, doctrinal issue for the best part of the thirty years this writer has been involved in fundamentalism. There are good men on either side of the debate. The local church has been called the first American institution of politics. It has been this writer's observation that many times, men's positions are derived by the doctrine which is held by their pastor.

Many times, pastors hold the position that is also held by the college and or seminary which they attended. Other times, pastors hold to a doctrine based on a favorite theologian and/or author. As a Biblicist, one errs if pastors, Bible colleges, seminaries, theologians, and authors are his final authority on matters of faith and practice.

A Biblicist does do well to consult many and broad theological teachings from the most biblically sound and reliable sources one can find. Because the Biblicist is also a free moral agent who will give the final account for his stewardship, he must be transparent and nakedly honest with his biases and presuppositions. After all, one cannot throw the theologian and seminaries out with the bathwater.

Every disciple needs a discipler. As this writer likes to say, every creature needs a preacher. Thus, the Biblicist must have as his final authority—after all his seeking wisdom—the Word of God. Said simply, the Biblicist must exegete the doctrines that he holds to out of the Bible. The broader method of developing one's doctrines is by cultivating one's systematic theology of eternal security.

The Biblical Basis for Eternal Security.

This Biblicist argues for eternal security with the verses from John 1:12, "But as received him, to them gave he power to become the sons of God, even to them that believes on his name," and John 10:27–29, "My sheep hear my voice, and I know them, and they follow me: And I give unto them eternal life; and they shall never perish, neither shall any man pluck them out of my hand. My Father, which gave them me, is greater than all; and no man is able to pluck them out of my Father's hand."

One of the strongest arguments comes from Paul's writings in Romans 8:35 ("Who shall separate us from the love of Christ? Shall tribulation, or distress, or persecution, or famine, or nakedness, or peril, or sword?") and verses 38-39 ("For I am persuaded, that neither death, nor life, nor angels, nor principalities, nor powers, nor things present, nor things to come, Nor height, nor depth, nor any other creature, shall be able to separate us from the love of God, which is in Christ Jesus our Lord."). Paul used what one might call Aristotle's form of argumentation when he spoke. Certainly, this was the style Paul used here in the book of Romans.

The scripture passage this writer refers to as his salvation and eternal security verses is found in I John 5:11-13: "And this is the record, that God hath given to us eternal life, and this life is in his Son. He that hath the Son hath life; and he that hath not the Son of God hath not life. These things have I written unto you that believe on the name of the Son of God; that ye may know that ye have eternal life, and that ye may believe on the name of the Son of God." This writer sees this passage as a mathematical equation—meaning, if one has Jesus, he has eternal life. There is no ambiguity in this passage. These passages strongly suggest eternal security.

Theological Reasons for Eternal Security.

Charles Ryrie dealt with the doctrine of eternal security. He stated, "Eternal security is the work of God which guarantees that the gift of salvation, once received, is forever and cannot be lost. The concept of eternal security emphasizes God's activity in guaranteeing the eternal possession of the gift of eternal life. It relates to those the Holy Spirit regenerates, and its veracity does not rest on feelings or experiences."[240] Ryrie not only defined eternal security but also gave biblical reasoning for eternal security.

He explained, "Basically security is based on the grace of God and the fact that eternal life is a gift and is eternal. When a person believes in Christ, he is brought into relationship with the Godhead that assures his salvation is secure.... But the regenerated person's salvation is secure because of that relationship of God which he has through faith."[241] Ryrie not only discussed general reasons that one trusts Christ as Savior but also gave reasons relative to the Spirit of God.

He taught, of course, that scripture gives no hint that a Christian can lose the new birth, that he can be disindwelt, or that he can be unsealed. "Salvation is eternal and completely secured to all who believe."[242] The doctrine of eternal security is part of the doctrine of salvation.

What Instruction Does the Book of Acts Give for Witnessing in Today's Culture?

The first thing this writer sees as an instruction to local churches and individual Christians is that they must be witnesses near and far, in their home town, and to the far reaches of the globe. A well-known Creationist, missionary, and conference speaker, Dr. Carl Baugh, and his wife went to the Fiji Islands some

---

[240] Charles C. Ryrie, *Basic Theology*, 328.

[241] Ibid., 330.
[242] Ryrie, *Basic Theology*, 332.

forty-five or so years ago. The Fiji Islands are the furthest point on Earth from Jerusalem.

Dr. Baugh's leading came from the Lord and the Lord's word right here in Acts 1:8: "But ye shall receive power, after that the Holy Ghost is come upon you: and ye shall be witnesses unto me both in Jerusalem, and in all Judea, and in Samaria, and unto the uttermost part of the earth."

Thus, Dr. Baugh and his wife went and were witnesses to the Fiji people, and now, over forty years later, virtually the entire island is Christian. The president of the island is saved, and he gives the pastors carte blanche to go into all of the public schools throughout the whole island. When they go and present the Gospel, almost all the students and the teachers get saved. The first church that was started years ago now has over 3,500 souls in her.

The antecedent of the charge to be "witnesses" is found in the tiny word within this verse, "ye." Now one could point to the whole verse and see genesis, but if one looks to the Greek behind the word "ye," this tiny word takes on greater meaning. "Ye" answers the question of who should be a witness. But if the Greek indicated that the English were the word "you," no one would know if our Lord meant singular or plural. Since "ye" is translated in the plural vowel, the Lord's people know that He gave a command to everyone to be a witness for our Lord. No one is excluded; everyone has the happy task of being a witness and sharing his faith with the world.

We can back up for just a moment to notice that our Lord gives a promise at the beginning of the verse: "Ye shall receive power." This is a great promise from our Lord to give us wisdom, strength, confidence, and the words to say, that we may testify of the love and power of God to those in darkness.

APPENDICES

Before the believers were sent out to be witnesses for our Lord, they were to identify with the Lord and the local church in Jerusalem. They were instructed to be baptized by believer's baptism as seen in Acts 1:5: "For John truly baptized with water: but ye shall be baptized with the Holy Ghost not many days hence." This writer still remembers the day he was baptized by emersion and identified with the Lord and Calvary Baptist Church in Windsor Locks, CT. B was this writer's second step of obedience to the Lord. Baptism is only the beginning, but for everyone that is to be a witness for the Lord, it is the first step of obedience after one is saved.

Another church organizational principle is leadership and church growth as seen in Acts 1:14: "In those days Peter stood up in the midst of the disciples, and said, (the number of the names together were about an hundred and twenty)." Here we see a man of faith and courage, Peter, and God using him as he was motivated to be a witness for his Lord. We see Peter again being a witness for the Lord in Acts 2:14: "But Peter, standing up with the eleven, lifted up his voice, and said unto them, Ye men of Juda, and all ye that dwell at Jerusalem, be this known unto you, and hearken to my words."

Peter again demonstrated great leadership as he preached to many who were still lost there on the day of Pentecost. The biblical instruction here is that when one sees a need and opportunity to serve the Lord and be a witness, he should take it as he might just change the world.

Especially in American cities, a local church should reflect the demographics of the community around the church as seen in Acts 2:8–10: "And how hear we every man in our own tongue, wherein we were born? Parthians, and Medes, and Elamites, and the dwellers in Mesopotamia, and in Judaea, and Cappadocia, in

Pontus, and Asia, Phrygia, and Pamphylia, in Egypt, and in the parts of Libya about Cyrene, and strangers of Rome, Jews and proselytes."

Thus, the local church must endeavor to reach all the people groups that she can reach within a short distance to the local church. This writer has seen this in Baptist churches in Windsor, CT, Jacksonville, FL, and Atlanta, GA, where black people, Asian people, and white people all work together, worship together, and serve each other together. This writer does not know any other institution where the walls of race are broken down other than the institution of the local Baptist churches.

One of the greatest strengths of the first-century local church was its complete commitment to faith in Christ (Acts 2:44-47). Here, the new church met daily in the temple or in house churches. The lost saw an incredible commitment to the Lord, the commitment the Christians had to one another, and the Christians' commitment to being a witness for the Lord. The changed lives were unmistakable. No one could see these Christians worship and witness day after day and not be influenced by God's people.

MESSAGE ONE AND TWO FROM EWIN LUTZER: "HOW YOU CAN BE SURE."

Lutzer is one of the most polished speakers of our day. He reminds this writer of D. James Kennedy. Every word which Lutzer speaks is meticulously crafted and put in place.

Lutzer is known as a classical apologist. All of his messages are clearly framed in a classical apologetic fashion. Lutzer speaks at an even pace and is as methodical as most any other preacher alive today. He begins his sermons with an illustration and then he gives an explanation of that story and bridges it into what he plans to discuss in the remainder of that thought or principle.

APPENDICES

Ewin Lutzer began his homily in message one with a poem from Michaelangelo and gave an explanation of people's fear of meeting God. Lutzer posed the question to his church: how might they react to meeting God in an hour? He asked if they would be fearful as the artwork of Michaelangelo's paintings revealed.

Lutzer's message revolved around the concept of eternal salvation and how one might be sure he will go to heaven when he dies. Lutzer offered a list of reasons why people may have doubts. The first reason was that one might have doubt if he forgets the date on which he was saved. Lutzer also suggested a reason for doubts might be poor teaching. In other words, one might have been exposed to Reformed theology or Lordship salvation or just poorly communicated theology that confused the hearts and minds of believers. The third cause of doubt that Lutzer suggested was that believers might have a disposition of lack of confidence, and as a result, may have a habit of doubting their own salvation.

Lutzer then made a much stronger point by describing a false faith that may be true in the mind but not in the heart. This is not hard to prove. Romans 10:10a: "For with the heart man believeth unto righteousness." Lutzer made the argument that one could consent to the idea of getting saved but not repent or actually trust Christ as Savior. Lutzer also made the argument of misdirected faith and even called out any Catholics who might have been in the congregation.

This writer would state that a works-salvation is no salvation; thus, false faith is no faith. In a cultural climate where people like to say they are "spiritual" but not "religious," the religious but unsaved are everywhere. Northern Illinois, especially Chicago, is very Catholic, and thus, the religious unsaved are very prevalent in that area. Lutzer did an excellent job of both communicating and explaining the difference between being religious and having what he referred to as "decisional faith." A Christian must have the experience of being born again in order to actually be a Christian.

Lutzer also dealt with the issue of children doubting their salvation. Lutzer did well to warn the parents not to hinder their children from getting saved if the child was expressing concern about their salvation. Lutzer referenced Hebrews 11:1 ("Now faith is the substance of things hoped for, the evidence of things not seen.") and I John 5:10–11 ("He that believeth on the Son of God hath the witness in himself: he that believeth not God hath made him a liar: because he believeth not the record that God gave of His Son. And this is the record, that God hath given to us eternal life, and this life is in His Son."). Lutzer gave testimony to counseling that he had done and that counselees had declared remorse for sins committed because of their love for God.

Though this writer entirely agrees with the previous paragraph, the next segment makes this writer a little confused about Lutzer's remarks. Lutzer's final segment discussed the assurance of salvation, especially with children. Lutzer listed off several reasons one should doubt his conversion. This writer believes in salvation by grace alone, through faith alone. Furthermore, this writer believes that once saved, always saved.

Lutzer made a public appeal for what is sometimes called "shock conversions." This has a much bigger appeal than if one or two people announce that after years of being a member and serving in a local church, they have come under conviction and declare their need to be saved. If shock conversions result from regular altar calls, making a public appeal has the potential to make shock conversions to generate decisions into a hard appeal because he referenced altar calls as a source of false professions.

Appendices

Lutzer continued with the second part of his series on "How to Be Sure." He began with a reference or two to the philosophy of the day, which suggested that everyone could do as he pleased. Israel lived like this as referenced in Judges 21:25: "In those days there was no king in Israel: every man did that which was right in his own eyes."

Lutzer further discussed signs of false professions of faith. He stated that praying the sinner's prayer does not save a person's soul. Lutzer certainly meant well, but one should never make this type of declaration. Furthermore, Lutzer suggested that asking Jesus into one's heart is not biblical. Romans 10:13 states, "For whosoever shall call upon the name of the Lord shall be saved." John 1:14 says, "But as many as received him, to them gave he power to become the sons of God, even to them that believe on his name."

Lutzer referred to this point as the root. The next point Lutzer made was the fruit of the Spirit. He referenced Romans 8:14, "For as many as are led by the Spirit of God, they are the sons of God." Certainly, evidence that the Spirit is working in people's lives is a good assurance of one's salvation. This lead to Lutzer's final point, which was that spiritual growth would help eliminate doubts that a believer may have about his salvation. Lutzer demonstrated through his messages that he is one of the most gifted Bible teachers of our day.

APPENDIX B

AN APOLOGETIC PRACTITIONER'S STRATEGY

INTRODUCTION

How does one define an apologist? This, of course, is not a name, word, or profession that is discussed daily by the general public. Though an apologist may very well describe who argues in favor of any number of areas or pursuits, in this writing, an apologist's objective is to teach, preach, witness, and persuade unbelievers and skeptics. The apologist continually employs a significant amount of apologetics tools and skills while in the process of discipling believers. Thus, the apologetic tools must be employed inside the local church as well as outside the walls of the church.

This apologist will outline numerous platforms, venues, and initiatives as a practitioner of Apologetics. The biblical basis for apologetic witnessing, teaching, preaching, and writing is based on I Peter 3:15: "But sanctify the Lord God in your hearts: and be ready always to give an answer to every man that asketh you a reason of the hope that is in you with meekness and fear." This is to say that all platforms, venues, and writings will contain elements of apologetics in them.

The objective is to lead skeptics and unbelievers to a saving knowledge of salvation through faith in Christ and to an ever-increasing maturity in one's stewardship for the Lord. This apologist will begin by describing his apologetic outreach to

Christians and skeptics on social media. This will include the platforms, the content, and the objectives of this apologetic ministry.

A description of apologetic books that have been published and manuscripts that are in progress will be detailed. The next step in advancing the apologetic outreach that will be explained is the launch of the national broadcast on Christian TV beginning in March. As a balanced approach to apologetics, this author will discuss how to organize and execute a worldview forum on secular university campuses.

The next progression in the apologetic teaching ministry will be to explain the establishment of seminary module classes at local Baptist churches. This writer will offer his explanation and an apologetic basis for founding a seminary dedicated to teaching apologetics and leadership. The final and ultimate apologetic endeavor to be outlined are the plans to launch two-hundred-fifty new church plants in America and send four hundred well-trained apologetic missionaries across the world.

Apologetics on Social Media.

An apologetics ministry began about nine years ago while church planting in Connecticut. It occurred to this apologist that one can witness, teach, and invite people to church on social media, even if it is six degrees and dark outside.

Two criteria came to mind when beginning this outreach: first, one needs people to be an apologist to, and second, one must consider whom they want to reach out to. It goes without saying that everyone is a sinner in need of a Savior, but it occurred to this apologist that no one can reach everyone. The term *demographics* came to mind. This is generally considered business terminology, but all it really means is types of people, groups, and ages. So this apologist thought that he could most likely and effectively reach people ten years younger and ten years older than himself.

This apologist began adding to the Facebook account the contacts of young adults up to their 40's or so, who were from the same town as the new church and surrounding towns. The list grew to 5,000 on Facebook and over 15,000 on LinkedIn. These people could see scripture and testimonies and engage in apologetic conversations. The best result was a woman who ended up coming to the church for relationship counseling and eventually trusted Christ as her Messiah.

The social media ministry today has become much larger and influential. That list of friends and contacts on Facebook has grown to 5,000 and to over 15,205 on LinkedIn. These platforms are now connected to this apologist's missions website, www.ExcellentWay.tv. A ministry channel has been created on YouTube, and new apologetics sermons are taped weekly and posted across all platforms. Social media contacts have been made throughout the country on Facebook and with many national pastors, Christian individuals, and skeptics across the Philippines, Pakistan, India, South America, Nepal, East, West, and South Africa.

On LinkedIn, contacts tend to track those of one's professional area. As a result, LinkedIn has led this apologist to hundreds of alumni and students from Pensacola Christian College, Bob Jones University, Crown College, West Coast Baptist College, Liberty University, Maranatha Baptist University, and Piedmont International University, as well as many professionals from other backgrounds.

Social Media has been extremely instrumental in the past few years of apologetic outreach, not only to many by way of

Appendices

postings, but also through personal communications, teaching videos, and apologetic and theological papers posted on the missions' website. This may seem like a hobby rather than an apologetics ministry, but it is making a difference.

This writer recently called one of the 5,000 friends on Facebook because he had liked a scripture posting. This man was an immigrant from Pakistan. The first time this apologist talked with him, the man said that he had been following the posts for a couple of years. The fact is that with any media ministry, one will not know until he gets to glory how many lives have been touched by his apologetics media ministry. The national pastors in the countries this apologist has reached out to have received books, electronic theological libraries, teaching videos, theological articles, and apologetics sermons. This apologist has lectured in a seminary in India to twenty-three students by way of Skype, and also preached in Indian and Pakistan Baptist churches through Skype.

Research and Published Apologetics Books.

The command of our Lord is to "teach all nations." Matthew 28:19: "Go ye therefore, and teach all nations, baptizing them in the name of the Father, and of the Son, and of the Holy Ghost." As this apologist would argue, backed by recent reading, all doctrinal teaching is apologetic in nature. One could break the Great Commission down to teaching the Bible, which is an apologetic endeavor. One can further argue that writing is discipleship. Writing is discipleship beyond one's reach.

Thus, this apologist has made the practice of not only putting books in print but also making teaching and training tools to include in each chapter. These first two books, *Children's Leadership Ministry* and *Leadership the Lord's Way*, have been sent by email to national pastors to many places around the world.

These national pastors have begun translating these books, and those that know some English have been trained by the national pastors with these books to do the work of the ministry better.

This apologist's next manuscript will be two volumes, which will be called *Transforming Truth*. The first of these two volumes will go to the publishers by December. Each chapter will have an apologetics lesson in the back of each chapter. In addition, the new books will have all seven lessons that are in *Children's Ministry Leadership* (which focus on the Great Commission and training parents on how to lead their children to the Lord) put in the appendix of the new books. There will be a total of nineteen lessons in the first volume of *Transforming Truth*. This book will also be distributed free of charge to the national pastors around the world for them to distribute to other national pastors and church members.

These pastors will use these books in their churches and Bible institutes. These books are all written in order to teach doctrine, improve the practice of the local church ministry, help families raise their children for the Lord, and to persuade in the things of God.

Teach Doctrines and Apologetics on a National Broadcast

This apologist and his cameraman tape apologetics messages every week and post videos and the pdf versions on the missions foundation website. These apologetic sermons are receiving reactions and views from social media contacts all over the world. Through the LinkedIn page, the videos are getting upwards of 600 views per video per week. This is not for naught, but it is somewhat a dry-run as the plan is to put a Bible teaching, apologetics broadcast on a national Christian TV channel.

Appendices

This broadcast will seek to fulfill several objectives from a teaching perspective. First, the broadcast will teach eleven major doctrines of the Bible. This teaching will attempt to communicate deep scriptural truths in as understandable a way as possible. This will be a lengthy series that we plan to call "Doctrines for Dummies." Notes and outlines will be provided for the viewer on the website.

This apologist will develop more substantial notes to teach from and to edit for a manuscript for publication and distribution. The second objective to fulfill though this broadcast outreach will be to make apologetics arguments throughout this endeavor to teach the eleven major Bible doctrines on national Christian TV.

The two major forms of apologetics to be employed in this broadcast outreach will be presuppositionalism and evidentialism. The reasons for emphasizing presuppositional apologetics are that first, the supremacy of scripture demands that arguments begin and end with scripture. Truth must be employed to advance the truth. John 1:17: "For the law was given by Moses, but grace and truth came by Jesus Christ." And John 17:17: "Sanctify them through thy truth: thy word is truth."

One cannot prove truth without truth, and one cannot teach truth without truth. Thus, all presuppositional apologetics must begin with Genesis 1:1: "In the beginning God." All other writings, such as linguistics, history, geography, archeology, scientific discovery, and the biographies of those that were human authors and the translators of the King James Bible, have been immensely helpful to the advancement and defense of biblical Christianity.

In addition, the profiles of those that have defended, preached, taught, or commentated on the scriptures, and those that have faithfully lived their lives according to God's Word are all useful in advancing and defending the Word of God. All extra-biblical sources are incredibly useful but are limited by their lack of divine origin and canonization. Scripture as the primary source of truth, and thus the scriptures stand tall with supremacy as the ultimate apologetic tool.

The second reason for employing presuppositional apologetics is that because its foundations are built on the doctrines of the Bible, this teaching will lay the groundwork of truth in people's hearts and minds. When one teaches the doctrines of the Bible, they are teaching presuppositional apologetics. Truth upon truth and reason upon reason is why one puts his faith in the Lord Jesus Christ.

The primary reason evidential apologetics will be employed is that Peter used this specific language in I Peter 3:15b: "A reason for the hope that is in you." The secondary reason for this is that people are rational thinkers. One could argue that the mind is the gatekeeper to the heart. As the apologist appeals to the mind, he will then be granted access to the heart. The apologist formulates his arguments for the purpose of inching his hearers further to maturity in Christ.

Hold Worldview Forums at Secular Universities Campuses

An apologist is a warrior by nature and function—not physical but rather spiritual warfare. Ephesians 6:11–12: "Put on the whole armour of God, that ye may be able to stand against the wiles of the devil. For we wrestle not against flesh and blood, but against principalities, against powers, against the rulers of the darkness of this world, against spiritual wickedness in high places." As such, the apologist must be in what the military calls the "forward operating base." This is to say, the apologist is not the support staff, but rather is on the spiritual and cultural frontlines, defending and advancing the Word of God. He must be in the thick of it.

This apologist will use the TV broadcast to promote worldview forums on college campuses. Other marketing tools would be employed, including Eventbrite and social media, press release services, and direct mail. These events will be designed to be evangelistic, not just informative, or a debate. These forums would take place in a college or university auditorium. This apologist likes the idea of using a team member to ask planned questions from the apologist.

This tactic gives the impression that there is a conversation happening, and like a tennis match, the audience will be watching back and forth as the questions and answers are asked and answered. This technique accomplishes two things: first, it controls the conversation, and second, it provides visual motion for people to follow. The next step, which is less controlled but more engaged, will be taking questions from the audience.

The key to this is not losing control of the microphone. We will qualify the questions to the subject matter of the worldview topic being discussed. All the time, the apologist will be giving answers that will lead his audience to the most important question, "Where will you spend eternity?" The team will speak with people after the question and answer time and answer all their questions. We will also give out literature at all the doors and make sure that everyone goes home with good information and the Gospel in their hands.

TEACH ONE-WEEK MODULE CLASSES AT LOCAL CHURCHES.

This apologist will continue to expand his teaching and apologetic influence by extending his teaching ministry to hold one-week module classes at local churches across the country. These seminary classes will be set up under the auspices of Constitution Baptist Church and Constitution Baptist Theological seminary. The classes will focus on Apologetics, Leadership, Systematic Theology, Old and New Testament Biblical Theology, and Christian Education.

All of these classes will have a strong emphasis on applying the bodies of the study of Apologetics to the local church outreach. Every subject has an application for apologetics. This would include both sharpening the teaching tools within the local church and the apologetic ministry to the unbelievers and skeptics outside the local church.

Local Church Seminary Focus on Apologetics and Leadership.

Many seminaries have as their basis for existence a mission verse, sometimes called their mission statement. II Timothy 2:2 says, "And the things that thou hast heard of me among many witnesses, the same commit thou to faithful men, who shall be able to teach others also." As apologists, we are not called to reinvent the wheel, but rather to be faithful to defend and advance God's Word and His Gospel throughout the world and to train faithful men to do the same.

The credits and transcripts of the module classes from Baptist churches throughout the country will be matriculated through the local church's Baptist seminary. The weekly TV broadcast will continue to teach doctrines and apologetics, and in doing so, will continue to attract seminary students to the modules remotely and through the local church location. The only real way for any seminary to have a particular emphasis is to talk about it continually.

Appendices

Apologetics, world missions, and church planting will be kept at the top of mind in word, print, and as the major focal point of the institutional existence. One of the major objectives of Centurion Education Foundation is to fund the training and full support missionaries for life and church plants to maturity. The national broadcasts will do a lot of this fundraising for the seminary and missions.

Launch Church Planting and world Missions Initiatives.

The initiatives for an apologetic training seminary, church planting, and world missions are posted on the website for Centurion Education Foundation at www.CEF.gives. The first objective besides teaching doctrine and apologetics on national Christian TV would be to raise an endowment of $440,000,000, which will fund the missionaries for life and fully support the church planters in America. These new American churches, once established and fully self-supporting, would contribute to the support of the missionaries that went through the local church seminary and are sent out by Constitution Baptist Church.

One of the major reasons for supporting the apologetic missionaries 100% is that these 400 missionaries, which are sent in groups of two families to each of 200 countries, would have the full support of a local church. Support would include, but not be limited to, quarterly visits from the short-term missions teams which would lend support and fellowship while far from home. Another objective would be to train them through the local church seminary so that when missionaries are sent to the four corners of the globe, they will have a strong group of church family members who stay in constant contact with the missionary families.

The apologetic missionaries, who are fully supported, will also save precious time—which is to say, they will spend more time on the field and be able to more frequently return to spend time at their home church. Under the current schedule of many missionaries, they spend five years on deputation, four years on the mission field, and then come home to raise more support and report to upwards of 100 churches over the course of another year.

Over the course of ten years, the missionary will have only spent four years on the field being the apologist. Under the model where the church and foundation support the missionary apologist 100%, the missionary family completes their apologetic training and then prepares to leave for their respective missions field. Every year between Thanksgiving and Christmas, the missionary family would return home to their home church. At the end of ten years, the missionary family will have spent just over nine years on the mission field and ten months in their home church.

The new church planters will graduate from the apologetic training seminary each year, and when they do, they will have a short-term church planting team or teams that will work with them for the first three months of the new local church. This will resemble a barn-raising that the Amish farmers practice. These churches and church planters will be closely watched for any problems in the fragile work of birthing a new local church. Like a training hospital many times provides the best medical care, this "training church and seminary" will go to great lengths to ensure sound apologetic training in the classroom and strong apologetic practitioners in the field.

CONCLUSION

This apologetic ministry started with humble beginnings on social media. The steps of progress thus far and into the future, if the Lord tarries, have been outlined. The motives for writing books for the purpose of advancing apologetics and leadership were discussed. The steps that have been taken, and will be taken to launch a national broadcast, in order to teach apologetics and doctrines, and to raise missions endowments have been detailed. A detailed plan to organize and conduct worldview forums on secular campuses has been offered for consideration.

The plans and objectives to promote and teach apologetics and leadership in local Baptist churches across America have been detailed, along with the plan to matriculate apologetic students through the local church seminary. The next major step in the progression of this apologetic ministry to develop the seminary around the study of apologetics and leadership and the detailed plan to implement sending Apologists around the world were elaborated upon. Finally, the rationale and steps to fund and support apologists across America and across the globe were highlighted.

APPENDIX C

A REVIEW OF JOHN FRAME'S BOOK *APOLOGETICS: A JUSTIFICATION OF CHRISTIAN BELIEF*

INTRODUCTION

The first part of this review will offer an analysis of the purpose of John Frame's book, *Apologetics: A Justification of Christian Belief*. The second part of this review will focus attention on the less agreed upon aspects as this writer offers an analysis of Frame's volume. The third aspect of this paper will highlight the favorable aspects of Frame's volume as this writer offers his analysis. Finally, the conclusion will summarize the analytical review for consideration.

The first purpose which the author mentioned was the need for a biblical approach to apologetics. John Frame's first purposes were stated, "A biblical apologetic targets unbelief wherever it may be found, strengthening the faith of Christians and calling unbelievers to repentance and faith in Christ."[243]

Frame began with a brief biblical definition and outline for Presuppositional Apologetics. First, he referenced the biblical basis of apologetics, I Peter 3:15–16, and outlined "1. Apologetics as proof,"[244] followed by "2. Apologetics as defense,"[245] and then

---
[243] Frame, *Apologetics*, 36.
[244] Frame, *Apologetics*, 1.

"3. Apologetics as offense."[246] Frame demonstrated a clear way of understanding as he outlined and taught the basics of Presuppositional Apologetics.

Frame touched on both of his themes when he stated, "But Christianity is not just an alternative to the secular philosophies or a set of moral standards better than those of current society. It is gospel, good news." Frame seems to have pointed out to the Christians that apologetics is a source of encouragement to one's faith, and to the unbeliever that apologetics is a source of reasons to except God's gift of salvation.

Frame made an argument that benefitted Christians and unbelievers alike when he argued for the Transcendental Argument for God's existence. Frame stated, "For God is the Creator of all, and therefore the source of all meaning, order, and intelligibility."[247] Whether the unbeliever knows it or not, both the believer and the unbeliever benefit from the existence of God. The believer is encouraged by a reasonable argument for his faith in God, and the unbeliever has a reasonable argument to put his faith in Christ.

Frame went on to make numerous other arguments that edified believers and appealed to unbelievers, such as the Theistic Argument. The apologetic defense, which this writer believes most helps unbelievers and believers alike, is one of the subjects Frame dealt with: the problem of evil. Frame explained, "In his view, all the wimpish theologians who have agonized over the problem down through the centuries (such as Augustine), who

---

[245] Ibid., 2.

[246] Ibid., 50.

[247] Ibid, 69.

have mumbled 'mystery' and tiptoed around the issue, have simply failed to see the answer that has been right there in black and white in front of their noses! That answer is Romans 9:17."[248] Here Frame did a service to both believers and unbelievers because he put the believer at ease with the problem of evil, and he gave the unbeliever a reason to discard this issue as a reason for unbelief.

John Frame has done a great service for his students and readers relative to the body of the study of Presuppositional Apologetics. In particular, Frame has done a masterful job of laying out the framework (pun intended) of the apologetic apparatus and explaining the many parts and pieces to this way of looking at scripture and arguing for the faith.

Frame did insert into his explanations of apologetics one aspect of this body of study which, to this writer, seemed to be unessential. This topic was predestination.

Frame stated, "The doctrine that God foreordains and directs all events is generally regarded as Calvinistic, and I am not embarrassed to be called a Calvinist."[249] Frame goes on to discuss Arminianism. The question to ask is, "Can the study of apologetics stand on its own without inserting Calvinism into it?" This writer believes so. Good men, of course, can disagree and should be able to remain amicable with one another, especially in higher Christian education.

Furthermore, the whole problem with the argument for being foreordained in Ephesians 1:11 is that it misuses the antecedent of whom and when those were predestinated to eternal life. Paul

---

[248] Frame, *Apologetics*, 158.

[249] Ibid., 43.

was speaking to the saved, baptized members of the church at Ephesus; thus, these believers were indeed predestined from the point of their conversion. By far, every other aspect of Frame's work had excellent thought and content. Frame did a great job of explaining even the more technical aspects of Presuppositional Apologetics.

A vast majority of this work that John Frame wrote was both informative (as it is a new body of study to this author) and edifying to this writer's spirit. As this writer read, the wheels were turning on the many ways this Presuppositional Apologetics study could aid through soul-winning outreach and through the pulpit ministry.

Frame's explanation of the Transcendental Argument for God was the first of many new aspects of this body of study that was spiritually enriching. For example, Frame offered numerous arguments such as, "My point here is not merely that if God doesn't exist, for example, the law of non-contradiction will fail. Rather: it does not even make any sense to talk about a world in which God doesn't exist. If God does not exist, we cannot argue either the presence or absence of logic in the world."[250] This kind of apologetic argumentation exemplified is helpful to put into practice apologetic conversations and apologetic preaching.

The two chapters on the problem of evil were a welcome sight to this writer as it appears that this topic is dealt with in numerous apologetic programs and in many apologetic seminars. Frame wrote about this topic in such a way as to convey the need for believers and unbelievers to find answers to this dilemma. Frame gave the best answer one could give when he cited Romans 9:17, "For the scripture saith unto Pharaoh, Even for this same purpose have I raised thee up, that I might shew my power in

---

[250] Frame, *Apologetics*, 71.

thee, and that my name might be declared throughout all the earth."

Frame made other significant points relative to the unbeliever's strawman arguments. Frame argued, "Marxism claims scientific status, but preaches ethical relativism. If ethics are relative, why should we value science? Modern public schools claim religious neutrality. What this means in practice is that they are relativistic in their values, but dogmatic in excluding Christianity from all substantive discussions."[251] What Frame offered in this work was a layout of the foundational principles in this body of study. He outlined it in such a way that it could be understood and processed. Frame also was practical in his presentation so that his readers could see how to put Presuppositional Apologetics into practice in real-life ministry.

CONCLUSION

This critical book review of John M. Frame's book, *Apologetics: A Justification of Christian Belief,* is a brief analytical overview of the book. This writer first reviewed Frame's stated purpose for his book. Frame was very accurate in addressing each of his stated purposes to be accomplished. This work that Frame wrote had very little for anyone to be critical of but one differing viewpoint was offered. Several passages of Frame's book were sited with much favorable analysis, which was offered. Frame's book was seen overall as an excellent teaching and practical application to Presuppositional Apologetics.

---

[251] Frame, *Apologetics*, 204.

APPENDICES

APPENDIX D

A CRITICAL BOOK REVIEW OF *IS YOUR CHURCH READY?: MOTIVATING LEADERS TO LIVE AN APOLOGETIC LIFE*

INTRODUCTION

This writer will first review the stated purposes of the authors Ravi Zacharias and Norman Geisler for their book, *Is Your Church Ready?: Motivating Leaders to Live an Apologetic Life*. Secondly, a positive analysis of this book will be offered in order to point out its highlights. Thirdly, a negative critique and analysis of the book will be offered for consideration. Fourthly, a final analysis of this book will be presented for consideration of the book's apologetic training and motivation of the local church.

ZACHARIAS AND GEISLER'S STATED PURPOSES

Ravi Zacharias and Norman Geisler's gave several stated objectives for this book. First, Zacharias stated that the purpose of training church members for an apologetics ministry was to "Frame the Gospel."[252] This is to say that the pastor is an apologist by his preaching and his message of the Gospel is, in effect, an argument for the Gospel. Zacharias stated, "With such a challenge, one can safely say that the pastoral call may in fact be the most

---

[252] Ravi Zacharias and Norman Geisler, *Is Your Church Ready?: Motivating Leaders to Live an Apologetic Life* (Grand Rapids: Zondervan, 2003), 16.

difficult call to fulfill today. It is at once an unenviable task and an easy target for anyone to hit, but I know of no more important role for the shepherding of the soul in a vagabond culture that ours has become. Properly understood and pursued, the calling and gifts are of pristine value in a society accustomed to counterfeit. Recognizing this challenge let us look at the pastor as apologist."[253] The pastor is the apologist, the one in society standing for truth.

Zacharias also made the argument for the pastor's presence as an apologist when he stated, "This is the best thing pastors can do. Nothing I say from here on will diminish that role. Pastors as apologists have the best apologetic in their very presence, and that is a unique privilege."[254] The pastor speaks for God just by being present with God's people.

Zacharias made the argument that the implantation of apologetics is action and is seen in its practice in the local church. He said, "In other words, apologetics is often first seen before it is heard. For that very reason the scriptures give us a clear picture of the pastor as an apologist."[255]

A Positive Analysis of Ravi Zacharias and Norman Geisler's Book

This writer appreciated that the author, Ravi Zacharias, put an outline into his text. He began, "The first assignment for the church leaders is to clarify truth-claims."[256] He continued by stating, "Second, leaders have a responsibility to remove obstacles

---

[253] Zacharias and Geisler, *Is Your Church Ready*, 17–18.

[254] Ibid., 19.

[255] Ibid., 22.

[256] Ibid., 26

APPENDICES

in the path of the listeners."[257] Zacharias made the teaching understandable, practical, and logical to follow. The discussion questions at the end of each chapter were also a practical way to review what had been taught in the chapter.

John Guest also had an excellent teaching acumen, as seen in chapter three. His section on the use of apologetics within worship was a teaching moment for the use of apologetics. Guest stated, "By worship I mean a vital expression of people loving God through songs and hymns, prayers, preaching that inspires, and fellowship that is enjoyed. Skeptics can thereby witness existential as well as intellectual persuasion when people gather. They can sense the power of God."[258] The experience of worship can push people to seek God's Word and conversion.

A NEGATIVE ANALYSIS OF RAVI ZACHARIAS AND NORMAN GEISLER'S

BOOK

The negative aspects of this book are the apparent and intentional appeal to the evangelical feminists in churches who desire to be pastors. This is an egregious mistake that should be avoided. Many hard passages in the Bible take much careful study and hermeneutic skill to understand and apply correctly, but it is not the case with this subject matter. It only takes courage, as the seminary at Clarks Summit does not allow women to pursue what are typically pastoral degrees.

Zacharias stated, "One who has set apart Christ in his or her heart as Lord and who then responds with answers to the questioner and does so with gentleness and respect."[259] He also

---

[257] Zacharias and Geisler, *Is Your Church Ready*, 28.

[258] Ibid., John Guest, 43.

[259] Zacharias and Geisler, *Is Your Church Ready*, 22.

discussed the issue this way: "A pastor should also address throughout his or her messages the tough questions raised by unbelievers or make them the focus of a complete series."[260] Though Christianity elevates women, the Bible makes it clear that men and women are equal but different. Thus, the Lord makes no provision for women to be pastors. Zacharias and Geisler know this and should employ sound hermeneutics in this matter.

CONCLUSION

The Final Analysis of Ravi Zacharias and Norman Geisler's Book:

This writer enjoyed reading Ravi Zacharias and Norman Geisler's book on apologetics training for the local church. Many of the numerous areas covered were encouraging and helpful for future apologetic endeavors. Ravi Zacharias' use of the metaphor of the arrows and the swords was an excellent teaching tool. His use of poetry is a good teaching tool, too. Judy Salisbury made a significant and rare contribution when she discussed the home as the most effective environment to apply apologetics to the children.

Chapter seven, which J. Budziszewski offered, was important, regarding young people keeping their faith when they go off to college. The problem with his approach is that one cannot Christianize secular education. Christian education is central to the Great Commission, and the parents are required to raise their children in the nurture and admonition of the Lord. On the contrary, Dean Halverson made a strong case to reach some 650,000 foreign students that study in American universities. His

---

[260] Ibid., 57.

instruction to learn one set of worldviews in order to answer them with the appropriate apologetic answers was practical and sound advice. This apologetic strategy would make one more effective at apologetics in his outreach to international students.

APPENDIX E

A REVIEW OF THE BOOK *CHRISTIAN THEOLOGY*

Biographical Sketch

Millard J. Erickson is a professor of theology at Truett and Western Seminaries in Portland, Oregon. Erickson has been noted as a nationally known spokesman for evangelicalism. He has authored numerous books, including *God the Father Almighty, God in Three Persons, The Word Became Flesh,* and *Post-Modernizing the Faith.* [261]

Summary Review of Verbal Plenary Inspiration

Definition of Inspiration

Millard Erickson explains the inspiration of scripture as a supernatural influence by the Holy Spirit. As the writers of scripture wrote, he stated, the Holy Spirit influenced the writers to transcribe the revelation of the Word God accurately. Erickson stated that the revelation of God is the primary source of communication between Himself and humans.

The truth communicated from God to man is so that man can properly relate to God. Erickson believed that the Word of God was preserved as, he stated, oral communication and tradition might lose meaning in the transmission. The significances of preservation, he stated, was never more

---

[261] Erickson, *Christian Theology*, 177–285.

imperative than from the time the revelation was penned until the time of the canonization of the scriptures. Erickson argued that preservation was needed as relying on the oral passing on of revelation would not be reliably accurate.

Erickson stated that the difference between revelation and reservation was that revelation is vertical, and inspiration is horizontal. He stated that revelation and inspiration were not contingent upon each other. For example, Erickson said that there are times the Bible records the words of unsaved people. He then referenced John 21:25 to argue that there were many times that there was revelation but no inspiration to pen words and events that were said or took place during Christ's earthly ministry.

The Fact of Inspiration

Erickson began his argument for the inspiration of the Bible as a defense attorney would for his client. He then talked about circular reasoning and its limitations. He stated that one could begin with the Bible as a historical document and then build his evidence out from that starting point to other evidence. Erickson then referenced the main verses that speak to the inspiration of scripture, such as II Peter 1:20, 21; II Timothy 3:16, 17; and Matthew 5:18.

He pointed out that the two things that were considered sacred in Jesus' day were the Temple and the scriptures. He concluded, along with the Old Testament prophets and New Testament preachers, that the Bible is the Holy Word of God. The Bible is the inspired Word from the Holy God to the human race. He claimed that the next issue to arise is the interpretation of scripture.

Issues in Formulating a Theory of Inspiration

Erickson first asked his readers if there could be any theory of inspiration in the Bible. Then he asked his readers whether there was a theory of inspiration taught in the Bible. If there were, were the readers obligated to accept this view of inspiration? Erickson then mentioned the analysis of scripture both inductively and deductively. He then asked his readers whether inspiration guaranteed the accuracy of the writers, whether inspiration was broadly or narrowly related to the scripture writers, and whether inspiration was related to the scriptures themselves or the writer?

Theories of Inspiration

Erickson began this section discussing the first five theories of inspiration. The more liberal part of Christendom believed in an institutional form of inspiration. Erickson stated that the human writers of scripture were brilliant religious thinkers. The Illumination Theory states that the Holy Spirit influenced the writers of scripture. The Holy Spirit heightened the writers' consciousness. The Holy Spirit has a higher degree of influence but of the same type.

Erickson next discussed the dynamic theory whereby the human and divine inspiration of the writing of the Bible came together. The Holy Spirit directed ideas and concepts to be included while the personality of the biblical writer came through in the Bible. Next, Erickson stated that the verbal theory of inspiration meant that every word that was penned by the writers was precisely as God intended it to be recorded. Then Erickson talked about the dictation theory which says that God dictated to the biblical writers the entire Bible. This school of thought is smaller than the verbal plenary school of thought.

APPENDICES

The Method of Formulating a Theory of Inspiration

The first method Erickson referenced was focused on what the biblical writers wrote and how those words were used. The second method focused on how the Bible was analyzed and how the biblical writers recorded biblical events.

The Extent of Inspiration

When Timothy stated that "all scripture is given by inspiration of God," he was talking about the entirety of scripture. That is to say, the Law and the Prophets in the Old Testament and the Gospels and the Epistles in the New Testament.

The Intensiveness of Inspiration

The New Testament writers looked at the Old Testament writers as having recorded the very Words that God had spoken. These Words were seen as authoritative. Jesus many times used the phrase, "It is written," referring to an Old Testament passage.

Model of Inspiration

The writer here is arguing that the Bible is inspired not because of the nature of God but rather because of the didactic material. The writer discussed the word-versus-thoughts issue. He stated that the words had to match the thoughts precisely, or they could not be used. Erickson ultimately argued that it was the leading of the Holy Spirit upon the human authors of scripture that led them to use the exact right words. He stated that though the Holy Spirit had directed the scriptural writers to specific words, the words could have been more general or more specific.

Erickson stated that the way to determine the specificity was by studying the original biblical languages. He concluded that inspiration was verbal, including the choice of words. Furthermore, Erickson stated that the biblical writers were not novices. They had walked with the Lord for some time, and they and were grounded in the faith. He referenced Paul as stating that he was chosen before the world began.

Erickson then discussed that the words recorded in the Bible were not just human words penned in the Bible. He stated that these words were derived from a long-standing relationship and influence from God to man. The other influences that affected the biblical writers were their education and many other earthly experiences. God also had a pool of words that He intended the biblical writers to use. Then God also influenced the thoughts of the minds of the biblical writers. The writer equated this to mental telepathy.

Erickson continued to suggest the connection between God and the biblical writers was not divinely dictated from the mind of God to the writers penning the words. He argued that these biblical writers were already devoted followers of Christ and had been immersed in the truth.

Next, Erickson gave a comparison between himself and his secretary: she knew his thoughts and was able to write a letter on his behalf because she knew her boss so well. He then stated that there was a vast difference between literature and inspired writing. Erickson then addressed the fact that there is a distinct difference between devotional materials and the Sermon on the Mount. His point was that inspired writing has a distinction all its own.

Erickson then stated that he did not believe in a literal interpretation of the Bible, but at the same time, he said, one must

Appendices

take the interpretation very seriously. He then stated that inspiration takes into account both the writing and the writer. He compared it to revelation, including both the revealed and the revealing.

Erickson, in this chapter, gave attention to inspiration as well as the phenomenon of scripture. He concluded this chapter stating that he was motivated to study God's Word and have confidence that it is a sure Word from God.

The Constitutional Nature of the Human

Summary Review of the Nature of Man

Erickson began this chapter discussing the three different views that make up the human constitution. First, he stated, there is the trichotomism, then dichotomism, and finally there is monism. Erickson wanted his readers to pay particular attention to A.T. Robinson's view on monism. Erickson believes these three views should be rejected and replaced with a conditional unity model. He suggested this model has five implications that he intended to bring to the readers' attention.

The three questions to be asked regarding humanity are about its origin, its purpose, and the ultimate human's destiny. The next basic question is, "What are human beings?" The author gives one caution to his readers to be careful in their study of anthropology and not to superimpose into the scriptures Greek dualism or modern behavioristic monism.

Basic Views of Human Constitution

Trichotomism

Erickson stated the position of many conservative Christians that trichotomism can be traced back to ancient Greek metaphysics. But right after stating that, he went into a list of scripture that indicated three distinct parts of a human. Erickson continued his discussion by stating that the Greek philosophers taught that there were a body and soul, and the spirit brought the two together. He stated that trichotomism lost the regard of the early church fathers who referred to it as heretical until revived by English and German theologians.

Dichotomism

Erickson began discussing dichotomism as a view that was popularized at the time of the Council of Constantinople in 381. This belief began to become universal in the church. Dichotomism is attributed to the Old Testament, while dualism is attributed to the New Testament. It claims that the body was what died at death, and the soul was what survived beyond the body.

Erickson stated that dichotomism made arguments against trichotomism in order to try and prove itself over the latter. Erickson argued that soul and spirit were used interchangeably, thereby demonstrating there are only two parts to humans, not three. He then continued his argument that the body and the spirit are the only two parts of a human being. He stated that at death, the spirit lives on while the body dies. Erickson also brought out examples of other theologians that had different ideas about the makeup of a human being.

Erickson discussed the liberal view that in immortality, they do not believe the body is resurrected. Harry Emerson Fosdick said that resurrection was just an event of its current time in the New Testament. Fosdick stated that the resurrection was more like a perseverance of the personality. The conservatives, though, believe in a resurrected body and the survival of the soul.

Monism

Erickson began this section stating that the dichotomist and trichotomist are similar in that they both believe the human is made up of two or three parts. Monism believes a human is made up of one part, or a self. They do not believe in immortality apart from the bodily resurrection, nor do they believe in an in-between state. Erickson stated that monism was popularized by neo-orthodoxy. He referenced A.T. Robinson as saying that there is no Old Testament word for body, that is equivalent to the Greek word.

Robinson stated that the Old Testament word for body is flesh. What he was saying is that these words both refer to the whole person. He stated there is, therefore, no difference in the meanings of the words. Robinson argued that the Old Testament word for body and soul was a synonymous term. His understanding then was that there was no difference in the body and the soul. The body, he stated, was all one unit.

Biblical Considerations

Erickson then contrasted other views with the full view of scripture. Erickson referred to both Luke 23 (the thief of the cross) and Luke 16 (the rich man and Lazarus) and suggested that these men were both in intermediate locations apart from their bodies. He did well then to reference II Corinthians 5:8, which teaches separation from the body and soul. He then referenced Jesus' words in Matthew 10:28, where Jesus taught that there was a difference between body and soul.

In the next passage, Erickson showed a challenge between two theologians, John A.T. Robinson and James Barr. Barr believed that Robinson ignored a lot of biblical data to have stated that there is no distinction between the words, body and flesh. Part of the argument has to do with whether the Greeks had any knowledge of the contrast or distinction between form and matter or not. Barr did not believe that the Greeks had this knowledge at that time. He also pointed out that Robinson lacked documentation of the Greeks in this matter.

The final argument that Erickson used was that of languages and context. He first argued that someone with a different language would have a correct understanding in their own tongue. Mainly, he stated, understanding would happen because of the words in their context. The words would give meaning based on the context in which they were placed in their sentencing.

Philosophical Considerations

The first philosophical argument that Erickson put forth was the differentiation between the soul and the body. The point here is that the Bible refers to two different deaths. The first reference was the physical body. The Bible, he stated, refers to the physical death of the body. The second reference to death was a second death. He then referenced the second death, which was separate and distinct from physical death. The second death had to do with the soul.

Next, Erickson referenced Penelhum, who stated that personal identity was dependent upon the body. Paul Helm remarked that memory was adequate to be considered personal identity. Helm then divided the person into two categories: E1 and E2. Penelhum responded by stating that if two different parts did not have different properties and essences, they would be meaningless.

Erickson then referenced Wittgenstein, who did not believe in a disembodied existence or separation of the body from the soul. Erickson offered some examples of religious models of disembodied existence. The religious models were not conducive to a scientific analysis of the body and soul.

Erickson stated that the concept of the behavior of humanity is flawed because it is not an authentic replica of human behavior. He explained that without recognition of the introspective element of human beings and a clear representation of people's observable behavior, this is not a good representation of humans and human life.

Unless human behavior is seen and assessed properly, human beings will be viewed as equal to a highly developed animal. Erickson then chided a behaviorist that has just given birth to her own child. He asked the behaviorist if she would consider her newborn child just the birth of a mammal? It seemed to be a rhetorical question and one that would have shamed the behaviorist. The central-state materialist does, he stated, believe in the subjective experiences.

An Alternative Model: Conditional Unity

Erickson concluded this section on the nature of man with an alternative model he referred to as conditional unity. This approach was his alternative to both dualism and monism. Erickson also referenced Henri Bergson's view of creative evolution. Erickson reiterated that the Old Testament referred to the body in unity, while the New Testament introduced the terminology of body-soul.

The New Testament idea, he continued, does not clearly state whether the soul-body is depicted as an embodied or disembodied being. Erickson moved on to discuss that the New Testament does teach a point between immaterial and material existence. This intermediate state is the place between the death of a person and the universal resurrection of all the dead and the living to a new and perfect body made for eternity (II Corinthians 5:2–4).

Erickson then moved to his closing arguments, which was how the question was answered, "How does this differ from the usual views of trichotomy, dichotomy, and monism?" Erickson termed this biblical approach to the essence of man from the point of death until the resurrection "conditional unity."

Erickson argued that the Bible never encouraged the believer to escape from the body. Although the soul is separated from the body at death, at the resurrection, the two will be reunited together again. He then warned about a neo-orthodoxist's idea of humans not persisting past death. He also warned against the liberal idea of an immortal soul that needs no resurrection. He encouraged the orthodoxy thought in both of these areas.

Implications of Conditional Unity

Erickson ended with important advice for a Christian counsel to treat a person holistically. This, he stated, would include addressing people's spiritual issues along with their physical, mental, and emotional state. He wanted people to understand that humans are complex. He also stated that "the gospel is an appeal to the whole person."

Summary Review of the Fall of Man

Appendices

Evil in General

The question that Erickson asked and needed to be answered is, "Could Adam have died prior to the Fall?" This writer will seek to answer this question. Erickson began by discussing racial sin. The human race, Erickson stated, had violated the human state of innocence. Death fell on humanity as a result of the original sin. He also stated that the whole creation was affected by human sin and is awaiting redemption from the bondage that it is in. Another important aspect that Erickson brought out was the connection that natural evil has had with human sin.

The first challenge that Erickson tried to solve was whether there was sin from Satan's fall until Adam and Eve's temptation. Erickson gave some speculation about a theory he called the "germ theory." However, he then stated that sin was more than a result of someone's will to do the wrong thing. Sin is a result of a wrong relationship with God. Erickson's conclusion on this matter was that God did not create sin. True freedom, he stated, was the ability to do wrong, but choose the right thing. The conclusion Erickson came to was that Adam could not have died before the Fall.

Specific Evil

Erickson then addressed the very practical issue of how sin's results affect people directly or indirectly. Erickson first referenced Job chapter 22, where Job suffered by evil, but there was no sin connected to Job that might have been punishable. Erickson's take away was that there did not have to be any personal sin for there to be suffering from evil.

Erickson then addressed an interesting problem found in John 9, where it was assumed that someone in a family must have sinned for a man to be born blind. Jesus' response, of course, was that no one sinned. Something evil happened to someone that did not sin so that God would be glorified and that His work might be accomplished.

Erickson then brought out the more obvious and predictable result from personal sin. He referenced the account of the sin of King David and Bathsheba found in Psalm 51. David's sin with Bathsheba led to him murder her husband, followed by the death of their child. Erickson moved on to mention Paul, who charged his readers not to be deceived into believing that one's sin would not be judged.

Animal Nature

One of the theories that Erickson described as a reason for the source of sin was that man had evolved from its original species as an animal. The timeline when this theory became popular was in the late nineteenth and early twentieth centuries. Erickson, recording this theological and cultural shift, paralleled the advent and expansion of the theory of biological evolution. Erickson further explained that when the Genesis account of creation and sin became untenable, another explanation for original sin was sought.

Anxiety of Finiteness

Erickson next explained another philosophy that was popularized by Reinhold Niebuhr. In this belief, Erickson stated, the problem of sin arose from human finitude and the freedom to aspire. Niebuhr believed that humans tried to overcome the insecurities of having intellectual limitations. This intellectual pride and the lust for power, Erickson stated, caused a disturbance in the creation's harmony. He explained that these two matters were the fundamental forms of sin.

He further explained that these issues have both a moral and a religious component of sin. He stated that pride was a rebellion against God and that a lust for power was a human injustice. Erickson showed Lucifer's sin of pride in Isaiah 14 when Lucifer gave his intent to be supreme above God. Erickson stated this was Adam and Eve's sin as well, wanting to know good and evil.

Existential Estrangement

The next concept Erickson dealt with was existential estrangement. First, he stated that this estrangement was likened unto sin. Then he backed off from that position, stating that estrangement was backing off from what one ought to be. Sin, he said, was becoming estranged. Erickson was referencing Paul Tillich, who argued that to have existence was to be estranged; thus, the two concepts could coexist.

Erickson further discussed Tillich's position on the Fall of man. Tillich stated that he did not go along with the Genesis account of man's nature changing in an instant from good to evil. What Tillich believed in was called "actualized creation and estranged existence." Erickson stated that this view was similar to that of Origen.

Economic Struggle

Erickson then turned to identify a number out of mainstream theology. First, he discussed liberation theology. This belief system, he stated, skipped over the original sins in the garden in Genesis 3. Liberation theology looks to the sin in Exodus 3. Liberation theology begins, he stated, by rejecting the personalization of sins.

He referenced James Cone, who stated that sin was not religious but rather political and economic. He then referenced Gustavo Gutierrez and explained his view that if one does not love his neighbor, he cannot love God. Erickson then referenced James Fowler as stating his view of God as either oppressed or an oppressor. Cone believed that black theology meant that God must represent blacks and thus be against whites.

Erickson then made a startling statement as he compared liberation theology to Marxism. He did not force his readers to say that they were the same, but rather that they did have similar stated problems and outcomes that created an observable parallel. He stated that the problem was one of power and wealth inequalities.

Individualism and Competitiveness

Erickson continued as he highlighted other unbiblical views of sin. He referenced Elliott, a liberal professor of Christian education. Elliott's idea of sin was not using one's full potential of his ability. Elliott had rejected the thought that sin could be reduced to one act or to egoism. She defined sin as any demonstrated striving or any individualism that might be misconstrued as egotistical. On the contrary, she argued that for the underachiever, it was not sinning for them to strive to better their economic standing.

Elliott further stated that she thought it harmful for humans to be thought of as sinners. She also thought it harmful for one to be thought of as having sin and guilt. Elliott saw sin as something that was a learned practice, not an innate character. Egoism and aggressiveness only become sinful when it is in excess. She referred to this as ruthless and a competitive struggle against each other. Elliott said this struggle went far beyond the wild kingdom.

APPENDICES

The Biblical Teaching

Erickson recapped the previous study stating the review of five flawed views of the source of sin. He first reviewed the fact that God does not tempt anyone to cause them to sin. Erickson squarely placed the blame for sin on one's own sinful desires. Erickson then clarified the sin of strong desires. He stated that everyone has a desire for food and intimacy. Misplaced desires will lead to sin, but without fulfilling these desires, the human race ends. Erickson then contrasted the difference between the command in God's economy to "subdue it."

Thus the Christian, he argued, should be industrious and acquire material goods. "When does this command have a limitation?" he asked. When this quest becomes so compelling that one would do or say anything to acquire goods. When one, he stated, goes beyond this point, it becomes "the lust of the eyes" and thus, becomes sin for the Christian.

The next aspect that Erickson pointed out regarding material goods and the heart was the attitude toward those material things. The attitude, he suggested, was the spiritual barometer that gauged the temperature of one's Christianity. He referenced I John 2:16, "the pride of life," to support his statement. Erickson further argued that when Satan tempted Jesus, he used legitimate desires to try and entice Him (Christ could not have sinned).

He then concluded his point by stating that Adam and Eve chose to sin when, in fact, they were induced externally by Satan. Jesus, on the other hand, Erickson stated, was also externally induced by Satan with an appeal to legitimate desires, yet He refused. His final point was the contrast between the flesh and the spirit. He claimed that the body in and of itself is not evil. He explained it was the natural bias man has toward sin and the propensity to reject God.

Physical Death

Erickson explained the obvious result of sin, which is death, and that the mortality of every human being was fixed. Erickson asked the question of whether people were made to be mortal or immortal. He also dealt with the squeamish topic, whether the original sins in the garden brought spiritual or physical death. His answer was that people were made in God's image, which is eternal. Erickson answered both of these issues when he explained that sin separated man from God; thus, spiritual death is the issue, not physical death.

Spiritual Death

Erickson explained the difference here between physical death and spiritual death. Concerning Adam and Eve eating of the knowledge of the fruit of good and evil, the death they experienced, Erickson stated, was not physical right away but rather spiritual. He explained that the spiritual death took place immediately upon the original sinning in the garden. Physical death would take place in the future.

SUMMARY REVIEW OF ERICKSON'S FOUR ASPECTS OF ATONEMENT

Effectual Calling

Erickson began this chapter (45) by referencing back to the previous chapter and his conversation about leading to one's effectual calling, conversion, regeneration, justification, and adoption. Erickson began discussing the general calling to salvation. He gave Matthew 11:28 to show that the invitation is given to all people. He then referenced Isaiah 45:22 to demonstrate the universal dimension of salvation. Erickson next stated that this seemed to be a universal offer, but then seemed to walk that statement back.

Erickson gave several references to support his point of view. Next, he explained his extra-biblical terminology, "God's effectual special calling." He explained that this "special calling" is the only real way anyone can get saved. He referred to the chosen ones as the elect. In Erickson's elect intellect, he stated that these elect are the only ones that can respond in repentance and faith. Erickson then moved on to make a strange comparison between Jesus choosing disciples and a dinner guest, and the elect that get saved. He listed a number of those in the New Testament that were saved, but then argued from the Bible's silence that God chose others not to be saved. This approach does not seem to have any exegetical basis.

Erickson further discussed his thoughts regarding the special or effectual calling. He gave his continuing reasoning that this extra-biblical concept allows people to understand the gospel that might not understand it otherwise. He then explained that this effectual calling is in a logical order that leads one to conversion. Erickson then parsed out the salvation experience into two parts, conversion and regeneration, or, special and effectual calling. He concluded with a special calling, conversion, and regeneration.

Conversion

Erickson began this part by stating that conversion is the starting point in the Christian experience. Erickson then gave references from the Old and New Testaments that conversion has two different parts, repentance and faith. He broke conversion down this way: repentance was the unbeliever turning away from his unbelief, and faith was turning to Christ.

He termed these two aspects as the negative and the positive of the same event. He stated that each of the two aspects is incomplete without the other. Erickson stated that scripture indicates that conversion generally takes place in a moment of time. He gave the examples of Nicodemus, the day of Pentecost, Saul, and Lydia.

Erickson then discussed some history of evangelistic campaigns whereby the evangelist had all aspects of the Gospel but was pressuring the hearers for a decision. He summed this up as being a crisis decision. His thinking was that everyone is different, so all will not have an identical response to the Gospel presentation.

Repentance

Erickson described repentance as the negative part of the conversion. He called it a feeling of godly sorrow. Erickson stated that it is only logical to deal with repentance before dealing with where one is going. He then referenced the well quoted Old Testament scripture, II Chronicles 7:14, with particular reference to God's people being humble and repenting of their sins. He also stated the repercussions of sins that were generational. Erickson then moved to New Testament references such as Matthew 21:39: "He answered and said, I will not: but afterward he repented, and went." He also referred to John the Baptist in Matthew 3:2: "And saying, Repent ye: for the kingdom of heaven is at hand." Erickson explained the word repentance has the idea of changing one's mind, and that repentance was a prerequisite for salvation. He went on to talk about the connection between repentance and discipleship as one matures.

Faith

Erickson then began the faith aspect of conversion, the part he referred to as the positive aspect. He referred to faith as the heart of the Gospel, even calling it the vehicle in which people receive the grace of God. Erickson first referenced the well-know Old Testament verse, Habakkuk 2:4: "Behold, his soul which is lifted up is not upright in him: but the just shall live by his faith." The Hebrew in the Old Testament does not have a noun form of the word faith. The Hebrew concept rather is not that they possess faith, but rather it is a verb, something that they do.

In the New Testament, Erickson explained that the word faith had one meaning. The idea is that a statement that was made was believed upon. So he defined faith as believing that something was true. He stated that faith was more than a statement of faith, but a significant personal trust. Erickson concluded his point regarding faith by stating that for salvation, one must believe in a statement and believe in the One he is trusting in. His concluding thought was that those that believe in the revelation of God's Word see the twofold nature of faith: affirming a statement of faith and then trusting in the Lord. Lastly, he described faith as a form of knowledge; thus, faith and reason are intertwined.

Regeneration

Erickson broke down salvation into two parts. He stated that conversion was the individual's response to God's offer of salvation. Regeneration, Erickson explained, was all God's working. He stated that this was God doing the transformation. He further explained that the unregenerate person was completely unaware and unable to respond to spiritual matters. To support this position, Erickson referenced Romans 3:9–20.

Erickson then declared that there is a biblical description of the new birth. He discussed the Old Testament example of

God's renewing work. He referenced Ezekiel 11:19, 20. Erickson then made New Testament references such as Matthew 19:28.

Erickson continued his discussion about regeneration and stated the clearest passage was John 3 when Jesus was talking with Nicodemus. This matter of being born again is a supernatural work that only God can do, and it is the only way one comes into the kingdom of God. This is the new birth, he stated, that gives one new life as a regenerated person.

Erickson moved on to explain that because this was a supernatural event, it took some explaining. It was not like any natural thing in the world that one could see, he explained. Erickson continued his discussion on regeneration by stating that this supernatural event affected the individual. It crucified the flesh. He explained this meant to be dead to the flesh (natural desires) and alive to Christ.

Erickson brought out an interesting point that this new nature in Christ is not foreign to human nature but rather a restoration of the way human nature was originally intended to be before the Fall. This event of regeneration is complete in a moment but is just the beginning of the process of an individual maturing in Christ, he specified.

This process, he stated, is called sanctification. Erickson then discussed what he called the manifestation of the spiritual ripening. This, he said, is the fruit of the Spirit. Erickson concluded this matter of regeneration with and oxymoron in the Christian experience. He stated that although from the Christian perspective, the human experience without Christ is hopeless, with Christ, it and the future could not be brighter.

Sanctification

At this point, Erickson said, the work of God has just begun in the life of the new believer. He stated that this is the beginning of making one holy. Sanctification, he said, was the process of making one's moral condition in alignment with his legal status before God. The first of two aspects that Erickson discussed was the idea of holiness. The believer, he explained, was set apart, or separated from the world and/or the unholy.

Erickson continued with his discussion on sanctification, referencing Exodus 13:2: "Sanctify unto me all the firstborn, whatsoever openeth the womb among the children of Israel, both of man and of beast: it is mine." The second aspect of sanctification that Erickson mentioned was the moral goodness and spiritual worth of a Christian. He explained that the new birth has a direct connection to the conduct of the believer.

Erickson further explained that the purpose of the divine work of God in the believer's life is progressive. The objective of the divine work, he explained, is Christ-likeness. He then said the fruits that come from sanctification are things like love, joy, peace, patience, kindness, goodness, and so forth. Erickson concluded with discussing sinlessness; although it is the aim of sanctification, it is not likely in this life.

Glorification

Erickson referred to this aspect as the final stage of the doctrine of salvation. He referenced Paul looking forward to this future state with Christ. He also stated that this glorification would bring about the perfecting of the bodies of all believers. Erickson explained the Old Testament meaning of the term *glorification*. He stated that the word refers to an individual's display of splendor, also one's wealth and pomp. He referenced Psalms 24:10: "Who is this King of glory? The LORD of hosts, he is the King of glory. Selah."

Erickson then gave the New Testament definition that he stated gave the idea of brightness, splendor, magnificence, and fame. He reminded his readers that Christ's second coming is an event that will demonstrate His glory. He referenced several scriptures next, including Matthew 24:30: "And then shall appear the sign of the Son of man in heaven: and then shall all the tribes of the earth morn, and they shall see the Son of Man coming in the clouds of heaven with power and great glory."

APPENDIX F

A REVIEW OF THE BOOK *THE DEATH CHRIST DIED: A BIBLICAL CASE FOR UNLIMITED ATONEMENT*

INTRODUCTION

BIOGRAPHICAL SKETCH

"Robert Lightner has had a very focused history of study and as a professional educator in the area of Theology. Lightner began his study in Theology at Baptist Bible Seminary, where he did his undergraduate work in theology. Then he moved on to receive his Masters and Doctoral degrees in Theology at Dallas Theological Seminary. Lightner also earned a Masters in Liberal Arts from Southern Methodist University." [262]

APPENDICES

Robert Lightner is the Professor Emeritus of Systematic Theology at Dallas Theological Seminary. He has also distinguished himself as a member of the Evangelical Society. He serves on a board of directors on the Bible Memory Association International and is a prolific author of several books and articles such as "The God of the Bible and Other gods," the "Handbook of Evangelical Theology," and "A Biblical Case for Total Inerrancy."

Purpose

"Why did the author write this book?" Robert Lightner wrote this work with the intent of explaining the atonement that was provided for all mankind by the death that Christ died on the cross of Calvary for all that would place their faith in Christ alone. The problem that Lightner attempted to solve for his readers was the detraction of two unbiblical philosophies that he addressed in this book. He addressed both Calvinism and sufficient grace.

Lightner referred to the different systems as both limited atonement and unlimited atonement. What he wanted to do after defining these different positions was to show the strengths and weaknesses of each and then show the biblical approach, intending to demonstrate the unlimited atonement position and why it is a position of strength.

Summary of Contents

Introduction

Robert Lightner began his introduction with the main focal point of this theological debate: who did Christ die for? Lightner indicated that this debate began during the Reformation, as he

---

[262] Robert P. Lightner, *The Death Christ Died: A Biblical Case for Unlimited Atonement,* Revised Edition (Grand Rapids: Kregel Publications, 1967, 1998), 171.

mentioned that the first-century Christians all believed that Christ had died for everyone. He mentioned that some of the early church fathers did believe in an unlimited atonement. The first area of concern that Lightner addressed was regarding the essence of Christ and His finished work on Calvary's cross.

Lightner drove his position home right in his introduction as he referred to John 3:16 with his focus on the word, "whosoever." He then stated that this offer of salvation was open to all and that no unbeliever has any excuse for not being saved. Lightner then discussed how the different creeds and confessions, as well as John Calvin, were not in favor of the unlimited atonement position. He also mentioned that the unlimited atonement did not begin with Arminianism.

The limited atonement, he indicated, was not widely held until the Westminster Confession in 1647. Lightner made one clarification of his terminology when he stated that he would be using the words *atonement* and *redemption* as synonymous terms. Lightner went on to explain that as a Christian ambassador, one must believe that Christ died for all or else his heralding of the Gospel would be insincere—that is if the Gospel were for some but not all. In other words, if one believed in limited atonement, they would not be at liberty to preach a universal Gospel.

Robert Lightner's Introduction

This writer thought the introduction was good as it gave the reader a sense of where the author was going on his theological positions. It was good that Lightner was transparent with his readers in that he wanted to show all sides of the theological issues; but even from the introduction, the reader relatively knows that the author will end up with a biblical approach to the person of Christ and the purpose of the cross as it relates to atonement of mankind. This writer did not find any real fault or area of deference with the author's introduction.

Chapter One

Lightner began chapter one with a discussion of the nature of the Lord Jesus Christ. He affirmed that Christ was and is sinless, as God the Father is sinless. Lightner referred to Jesus as "the most unique Person that ever lived." Lightner further stated that not only did Jesus not sin, but because of His nature, He could not have sinned. He said that theologians insist on the impeccability of the nature of Christ.

He further stated that both scripture and reason confer that Christ could not have sinned. Lightner continued his argument by logic that if Christ sinned, then He could have sinned now. This, of course, is impossible, illogical, and unbiblical. Lightner did an excellent job of documenting from scripture and arguing for the impeccability of Christ's nature.

Lightner continued as he described the suffering of Christ: He was righteous and pure, and yet He condescended Himself to live among sinners, even those that outright rejected Him. Lightner gave accounts of how Christ was burdened and thus suffered for the individual and the multitude that were lost. He gave scripture that documented Christ's grief that He felt for mankind and their infirmities.

Lightner continued discussing Christ's suffering physically when He suffered on the tree for the sins of mankind. He referenced the Isaiah 53 passage that foretold Christ's suffering. Lightner described the suffering of Christ as the substitutionary death for the transgressions of man. He then stated that Christ's suffering was because of Christ's divine compassion. Lightner identified the one act of Adam that was the root of all suffering in

Romans 5:18. And then he identified the one act of obedience that Christ did on Calvary's cross to take away the sin of man. To conclude this point, Lightner stated that Christ's suffering during His earthly ministry was non-atoning, yet His sinless life qualified Him to be the sacrifice for man's sins.

Lightner stated that one of Christ's accomplishments of His death was that He ended the Mosaic Law as a pattern for life. The obvious benefit that Lightner stated is the redemption of mankind. He then detailed the Savior's death, further referring to His death as vicarious, and saying that He was the sinless Vicar that took the sinner's place as the sacrifice for sins. Lightner qualified the death as satisfactory to God the Father, whether anyone ever applies faith to Christ's offer of salvation or not.

Lightner moved on to discuss the magnitude of God's love for mankind that He would give His own Son as the sacrifice for man. This also showed, Lightner stated, the enormous sin debt that needed to be paid for the sins of the world. He then stated the two sides of the cross. There was the side of gloom and the side of glory. Man's side was gloom, and God's side was the glory. Lightner explained that the cross was God's provision for sin, and its necessity was not a plan B in the whole scheme of things. In fact, Lightner showed from scripture that the Cross and the determinate counsel were from the foundations of the world.

He also explained that the gloom of Golgotha was countered by the glory of Christ's divine accomplishments. Lightner finished the chapter by talking about the atonement, and that Christ was a propitiation for man through faith in Him. He also stated that God could not have been the justifier outside of Christ's death on the cross. He finished by stating that it was man's sin for which there must be accountability and which was the cause of Christ needing to die on the cross.

APPENDICES

Lightner did an excellent job of making clear not only the doctrinal part of Christ atoning work on the cross but also the position he has taken to let scripture answer the question of "Why Christ had to go to the cross." He also put together a good argument for his position.

Chapter Two

Lightner began this chapter with the purpose of answering the question, "whom did Jesus die for?" Lightner framed the question very well and then qualified it further by stating that the answer is found in no other place than the scriptures. He further stated that the entire argument of limited atonement versus unlimited atonement centers on the redemptive work of Christ. He made the argument that the believer must not succumb to man-made construct for the sake of not making people uncomfortable with their unscriptural traditions. Lightner's argument for one to be a Biblicist was convincing but straightforward. Any other position would quickly compromise the authoritativeness of scripture.

Lightner moved on to state that two views within orthodoxy deal with the purpose of atonement. It may be arguable that the answers of Arminians and Calvinists are orthodox at all, though he was about to stress again that the focal point should be that the final answer is scripture. Lightner began to give some historical background of Arminianism. He stated how numerous variations of it today are nowhere similar to its roots in the early 1600s. Lightner gave the quick historical progression to show where and when Arminianism splintered off into a group that became known as Calvinism. He then recorded the five points of Arminianism before referencing John 3:16, which single-handedly clarifies the biblical position of who can be saved, or who did Christ die for? The answer is everyone.

Lightner then began to talk about the Arminian concept that has made the death of Christ for man's forgiveness go from being a work of God to becoming a shared work of man and God. He stated that this, in effect, makes God a bystander. Lightner then discussed a man, Watson, who was an Arminian theologian, saying that though they might believe in the sufficiency of Christ, they seem more likely to discuss the degenerate nature of man. Watson seems to have said two different things. On the one hand, he said that all men have lost any ability to turn to spiritual matters in the Fall. Then he stated that the grace to do these things had been made available to all. The outcome of this belief is that all the work and the decision to have God work in a life rests solely upon the individual.

Lightner then laid out the five points of Calvinism for the reader. He explained one difference between Calvinism and Arminianism when he stated that Calvinism teaches that men in their natural state are completely depraved. Their Calvinist view is that the depraved person cannot cooperate with God. Lightner then referred to John Murray who asked some penetrating questions of the Calvinist, with regard to whom Christ came to save. This line of questioning shot holes in the construct of the Calvinist. Murray's questions were rhetorical as his premise of questioning suggests that indeed Christ did die for all men and that all have the opportunity to receive Him as Savior.

Lightner next brought up a different view of the theologian, Charles Hodge, who seemed to have put salvation a one-sided process. Hodge suggested that the righteousness of Christ secured the salvation for those that He wrought. Then

Appendices

Lightner introduced R.B. Kuiper as having stated that the atonement intended to save the elect but made no provision for the non-elect. He believed that the cross had and applied its own benefit to the elect. Lightner went on to detail that some Calvinists have no real reason why they believe in a limited atonement.

He stated some that are more moderate Calvinists believe that the atonement was there to provide salvation to the elect, while for those who rejected Christ's offer, it was the basis for condemnation. He then referenced another Calvinist that believed that God could have secured salvation for everyone if that had been God's intent. He then referenced the Arminian view that God provided salvation for all men by supplying sufficient grace for all to believe. However, the Arminian would say that Christ died only for the elect.

Lightner then referenced Isaac Watts, who drew a contrast between the Arminian and the Calvinist. He discussed the difference between those that would take a conditional salvation approach versus the strict Calvinist who says that Christ only died for the elect. The observation from a scriptural approach is that the atonement would be open to all mankind. The benefit of the cross was only realized by those that believe in Christ.

Next, Lightner discussed the Godhead and how that view affects the design of the atonement. The Arminians believe that the design of God's atonement for mankind has been purchased and that His grace is sufficient for redemption. The Calvinist view of the design of atonement is sufficient for redemption but only for the elect.

Lightner presented these two sides but then turned back to the authenticity of the Bible. He discussed the twofold testimony of the Bible and referenced John 3:18. He explained that Christ's message is that He died to provide salvation to everyone that will believe in Him. He again referenced A.A. Hodge as he stated that the two previous views must be rejected as neither one is entirely biblical.

Lightner explained Arminianism this way: God gives each person sufficient grace that allows one to be saved. The Calvinist view, he explained, is that God limits the atonement to only the elect to be saved. He stated that neither one is entirely biblical. Lightner explained that Calvinists minimize the aspect of faith; instead, they believe that salvation was secured on the cross for the elect. Lightner's response to this was to reference Ephesians 2:8, 9, concluding from this passage that the "gift of God" was the whole package of salvation. It is freely given to all that will act by faith and receive it.

Lightner continued by referencing Dr. Aldrich, who stated that there are numerous passages in the New Testament as well as whole books that confirm that faith is a gift from God. Then he further referenced Berkhof, who argued that faith did not begin in the heart of man, but that God has placed the seed of faith in the heart of man at the point of regeneration. On the other side of the argument, Lightner referenced Pink with his strange understanding that the nonelect are not able to be saved but then tells them what they must do to be saved.

Lightner's response to this was to point out that the sole condition of salvation is personal faith in Christ. Furthermore, Lightner argued that God has given us revelation of Himself through nature and the conscience that leads one to the revelation that each one must place personal faith in Christ for salvation. He then stated that the biblical view is faith-followed regeneration rather than the other way around as the Calvinist believes.

Appendices

Calvinist Beliefs

Lightner then referenced Murray, who believes in limited atonement and that regeneration comes before faith. Murray stated that a person could not be saved before they believe in Christ, later saying it is impossible for a saved person not to believe. Lightner began to conclude this section stating that the Spirit's work makes the person receptive to the Gospel that comes by faith. He stated that the Spirit and the faith are always working together and never by themselves. He further stated that salvation is unmerited and unearned favor with God. He finally argued that the idea of man having sufficient grace in order to be saved must be rejected in light of scripture.

Chapter Three

Lightner litigated his case in this chapter as the major flaws of a limited atonement position. He began here by referring to the Isaiah 53 passage and showed from the passage that it, in the strictest sense, is referring to the Jews. This view would, of course, eliminate any Gentiles from being saved, as the personal pronoun "our" is used to refer to the Jewish people. Lightner then referenced Matthew 1:21 that uses the phrase "his people," which also, in its strictest approach, would eliminate Gentiles as well.

Lightner showed these passages to prove his point that God is not in the business of keeping people out of His plan for redemption but rather is all-inclusive in His redemptive work. One other clarification Lightner made was that God's love does not end with those that are believers. God loves unbelievers, as well. His capacity to love is far beyond the comprehension of mankind. Lightner also discussed passages that deal with the redemption of individuals and groups. He stated that these passages in no way contradict what an unlimited redemptionist believes, and there is no scriptural contradiction and that the Bible never says anything about Christ not dying for all men.

Lightner moved on to a new part of his argument for unlimited atonement. He began talking about the cosmos and how God loves the whole world. He argued that the verses that deal with the world (cosmos) are unrestricted in God's love. Lightner then dealt with the New Testament word, "whosoever," to demonstrate that this word also is unrestricted. He also referenced the use of "all" and showed the intent of God was unrestricted in His redemption of man. The word "all," he said, shows the universality of the atonement and that Christ died for all.

The next person that Lightner referenced was John Owen. He stated that Owen changed the meaning of "all" to mean "elsewhere." Then he showed how the Calvinist plays fast and loose with whom Christ died for. The Calvinists believe that Christ died only for the ones that were in Christ when they died, rather than for all men.

Lightner then protested the incorrect view of the limited redemptionists and their treatment of John 1:29 and John 3:16. The Calvinist argued that there was a Jew-Gentile distinction, while Lightner stated that there was nothing in the context that would suggest that there was any distinction. Lightner then referenced Chafer, who mocked the limited redemptionists in how they have imposed their elect views into passages of scripture that plainly teach unlimited atonement. Lightner concluded that the limited atonement view rejects scripture while limiting redemption to the few.

Lightner gave a very descriptive illustration of Jesus' finished work on Calvary's Cross. He referenced Michaelangelo's work to contrast his unfinished work with Christ's finished work of redemption. The meaning was simply that no one could add to what Christ has done to make provision for man's redemption. The freedom received by this redemption is free to the recipient, paid in full by Christ's death on the cross.

Lightner continued his argument to let scripture speak for itself and not super-impose something into scripture. He referenced John Gill again as suggesting that Christ died in vain for those that have rejected Him. Lightner stated that Christ would have died for the redemption of man, whether anyone got saved or not.

Lightner then began to discuss propitiation. He explained that it assumes God's wrath because of man's sin and then explained that through the cross, the redeemed have received God's propitiation. The redeemed, he said, now experiences God's love. He continued his discussion on propitiation and how it relates to atonement, mentioning I John 2:1, 2. Lightner's point was that no one is out of reach of God's redemption. He further mentioned that God's wrath and His vicarious, substitutionary death reach the entire world. This, he said, was an argument for unlimited atonement.

In Lightner's next argument, he again referenced I John 2:2 to discuss the "mercy seat." He argued that this mercy seat is the propitiation of Christ, but it is in reference to the Jews. This is a problem, he stated, for the limited atonement folks. Their problem is that all the Jews would be the elect, and the Gentiles would all be the non-elect. He also said there is a problem to say Christ died for the whole world that is elect, but not for the non-elect in the world. Lightner also referred to Romans 3:19 regarding the "Kosmos." This too is a problem for the Calvinist because the Kosmos makes clear the intent of the passage is the universality of the atonement.

Lightner moved on to discuss the meaning of the word *reconciliation* to clear up God's meaning and intent of atonement. The idea, he stated, was "to change from enmity to friendship." Chafer discussed this meaning as well. He stated the purpose was to remove the cause of the enmity. Lightner finished the clarification by stating that it is man that must reconcile to God, not God to man. He made clear that the scripture teaches that it was the death of Christ on the cross that brought about the reconciliation.

Lightner stated that the reconciliation that God did through His Son to reconcile the world to Himself brings the responsibility of man to be an ambassador for Christ and to encourage men to reconcile themselves to God. Lightner further stated that the main reason we can preach salvation to a lost world is because of Christ's finished work on the cross. He also stated that the main objective of reconciliation is to reconcile the whole world to God. Finally, Lightner stated that the act of reconciliation does not affect the individual, but instead, it makes provision for the individual to be reconciled back to God.

He finished by reiterating that reconciliation is an act of love, freely given to man. It becomes effective upon receiving the gift, and all in the world that have been estranged from God in Adam can now be reconciled in Christ. Robert Lightner did an excellent job of communicating this complicated philosophy. This writer has no qualms with Lightner's position as he stated the other philosophies well and then prosecuted his biblical position very convincingly.

Chapter Four

Lightner stated in this chapter that there are problems with limited and unlimited atonement positions if the Bible is viewed at face value. For the unlimited atonement view, he said that Christ's death does not save if faith is not applied. He also stated that the cross is a basis for judgment. The stated purpose, he said, was that God would be glorified whether they were elect or non-elect, and whether they were saved or not.

Lightner then moved on to discuss universalism and how the Arminianist deals with Christ's death on the cross. The Arminianist looks for sufficient grace to be applied so that one may be saved. Lightner made clear from scripture that Christ's finished work on the cross was all that was needed for man's redemption. He further stated that the only reason anyone was lost because he had rejected Christ's finished work on the cross.

Lightner then discussed that Arminians could not believe in a sovereign God and that His work was finished on the cross. He also stated that Calvinists have trouble believing in unconditional election and unlimited atonement. He referenced Hodge, who taught that challenging the sovereignty of God's saving power of the cross was like believing in double predestination. He did point out an error of Hodge's that the Bible does not teach, which was that God predestinated some to heaven and others to hell. God, he said, is not going to take responsibility for anyone going to hell. Lightner then highlighted the biblical viewpoint, which states the sovereignty of God and the responsibility of man.

Next, Lightner tackled the issue of the "sin of unbelief." His argument is quite compelling. He argued that either Christ died for the sins of unbelief and those that have trusted Him are saved, or Christ did not die for the sin of unbelief, and none of us are saved. His next argument came from John 17, which talks about Christ interceding for believers and those generations to follow that will believe. The takeaway is that Christ was praying for the believers and the unbelievers, thus showing there was no intent on God's part for anyone not to be saved.

Chapter Five

Lightner continued his argument with the problems of a limited atonement view. He pointed to several New Testament words that demand an unlimited atonement view, such as "all," "whosoever," and "world." These words are a problem for the limited view.

Next, Lightner turned his attention to not only the universal use of the words "all" and "world" but also to the fact that the word "love" has universal application without restrictions. He stated that the moderate Calvinist believes that God has a special love for the believer; the inference is that there is not the same love for the unsaved person. Lightner argued that God loves all mankind. When the limited atonement person says that God only loves the elect, that person, Lightner says, is not quoting scripture.

The argument continued with Pink saying that God's truth is just for the elect and not for the enemies of God. He argued that it was basically a waste to give truth to sinners. Lightner argued that God could not have shown more love than to send His Son Jesus to die for a whole world of sinners. He further argued that it was not rational to say God is righteous, just, and holy, but only for the elect. He continued that it is not rational either that God has to wait for one to be saved before He could love them.

Next, Lightner referenced William Cunningham. Lightner responded by asking if Christ died for only the elect, then why are men commanded to give the gospel to the non-elect? James Richards is referenced next, stating that if salvation were offered, it would be reasonable that salvation was provided. Lightner referenced Crawford, who stated that this conflict was too big for a man to solve. Hodge stated that the unlimited view has the same problems as the limited view of atonement.

The next theological challenge that Lightner presented was from Berkof, who was a Covenant Theologian. This is a type of works-salvation because he tied salvation to obedience, instead of eternal life being a free gift. Lightner then stated that the Covenant Theologian tends to put God in a soteriological straightjacket. He stated the Covenant Theology was not in the creeds of the early church, nor is it found in the scriptures. This system of theology was not preached until after the Reformation.

Murray discussed his view of Christ's suffering, breaking it into two parts, both active and passive. Christ's life obedience was active, and Christ's suffering on the cross was passive. Hodge said that all this obedience was suffering. Lightner brought out that Christ's earthly ministry ministered to more than the elect. Berkof is then referenced as saying that all the suffering of Christ should be assessed as the same. Lightner then referenced Owen as saying he acknowledged the need for faith for salvation but then backed off of that necessity for salvation. Lightner concluded that the elect are just as lost as the nonelect until they believe.

He then referenced Crawford's belief that stated that the Holy Spirit gave the grace necessary to put one in a position to be saved. Lightner refers again to Owen, who argued that faith was not necessary for the elect to be saved. Lightner further made his argument in favor of an unlimited atonement when he discussed the work of the Holy Spirit. He argued that if the Holy Spirit did not have a universal scope, then Christ's death on the cross could only reach the elect.

Lightner argued for a worldwide ministry of the Holy Spirit. He further argued that the work of the Holy Spirit and

Christ's work go together. So he stated that it would not be possible for the Holy Spirit to bring conviction that was outside the reach of Christ. He then added that the Savior promised the presence of the Holy Spirit. He also stated that the Holy Spirit was an answer to Christ's petition to the Father.

Lightner began a different line of argument when he discussed Paul saying the god of this world blinded the minds of unbelievers. He stated that if Christ did not die for the non-elect, what are they blinded from? His argument moved on to state that Adam was the federal and natural head of the human race, thus arguing that all sinned in Adam, including the elect and non-elect. Lightner continued his argument that every man from, but including Adam, have sinned and therefore, all men are part of that sin and part of that punishment that is required.

He then contrasted the punishment for all with the free gift for all. He went back to Paul's use of the word "all," arguing how it was contrary to the limited atonement view. He concluded that the limited view was wrong, and the scripture was right in its universal appeal and reach. Lightner then argued that "the many" Paul discussed had grace about many but not all have been saved. So he said that if not all have been saved, one must ask in faith for salvation individually. He stated that man had to receive grace by faith in order to be justified.

Lightner began a different argument demonstrating the resurrection as a basis for both saved and lost to be resurrected in the future. The resurrection showed the universal appeal of the Gospel so that all could be saved if each one would respond in faith to God's plan of salvation. Lightner concludes that the two parts to redemption are the cross and faith. Without faith, redemption is impossible.

Appendices

   This writer had not studied these man-made philosophies before writing this, although he has been aware of them. Lightner was quite skilled in his approach to teaching his readers from a biblical perspective the conflicts that Calvinism and Arminianism have created. Lightner was very helpful in explaining the two different philosophies, as well as how they conflicted with each other. The result and the fruit of this book have been that it has helped this writer to understand better and be better equipped to communicate a biblical view of unlimited atonement.

APPENDIX G

ESCHATOLOGY, THE LAW, AND THE CHRISTIAN

"Individual Eschatology, the Law and the Christian"

I. The Millennial Views

A. Amillennialism

How is amillennialism defined? An Amillennialist is one whose view of Eschatology is that there will be no thousand-year reign of Christ as the Pretribulationalist view of Eschatology. Amillennialists believe that Satan was bound since the time of Christ on earth and that the Millennial reign of Christ does not exist. The other issue that is happening with the Amillennialists in their view of scripture is that much of the Eschatological passages are a metaphoric, and not a literal interpretation of scripture.

B. Postmillennialism

How is postmillennialism defined? Its definition is found in its name. The postmillennialists believe that the Rapture will take place at the end of the thousand-year reign of Christ. In this view, the millennial reign of Christ is suggested to have begun at the beginning of the New Testament era. The view seems to have some uncertainty as to when this millennial reign should have ended. Most Reformed and Covenant theologians believe in postmillennialism.

APPENDICES

C. Premillennialism

How is premillennialism defined? This view holds to the literal second coming of Christ to begin His thousand-year reign on Earth. His return will happen after the seven-year tribulation. The rapture will take place before the seven-year tribulation. The premillennial view holds to a literal interpretation of the events in Eschatology.

More specifically, how is *dispensationalism* defined compared to premillennialism? Dispensationalism is a word to describe different periods throughout history and into the future of how God deals with mankind. Sometimes dispensations are referred to as stewardships of time. There are seven distinct periods: Innocence, Conscience, Government, Law, Church, Tribulation, and Millennial reign, followed by the eternal state. Premillennialism is the view that says when Christ's return will take place, which will be just before the millennial reign of Christ.

What is the difference between historic premillennialism and dispensational premillennialism? Historic premillennialism teaches that Christ's return will happen before the millennial reign of Christ. Dispensational premillennialism teaches that the return of Christ will not only happen prior to the millennial reign but also prior to seven-year tribulation.

Which of the millennial views do you hold, and why? This writer believes in a pretribulation, premillennial return of Christ. There are four primary reasons for this: Hermeneutics are considered to be literal, grammatical, and historical. Thus, Revelation 4:1 and Revelation 11:3 are to be interpreted literally. The second reason for the belief in a pretribulation, premillennial return of Christ is that Christ's return is imminent (Matthew 24:36). The third reason is the significant number of Gentiles saved in the first part of the tribulation (Revelation 7:9). The fourth reason for a pretribulation, premillennial view is the national conversion of Jews (Revelation 7:4).

II. The Basis for Premillennialism

A. The Concept of the Kingdom of God

What does the kingdom of God mean? The kingdom of God in our current dispensation, the church age, has to do with God's sovereign rule in the hearts of Christians as they have trusted Christ as Savior and submit to the leadership of the Lord in their lives (Mark 1:15; Luke 17:20).

What does the Old Testament teach about the kingdom? The kingdom of God in the Old Testament teaches that the kingdom is both eternal and temporal, much like a Christian has eternal life but does not enter eternal life until he leaves this temporal life (Jeremiah 10:10; Psalm 16:10). The Lord established a theocratic kingdom and relationship in Genesis 1:26 and began the kingdom program in Genesis 3:15. The theocratic kingdom also worked through government (Genesis 9:2) and under the patriarchs (Genesis 49:10).

What does the New Testament teach about the kingdom? The offer of a spiritual kingdom was first offered to Israel in the Old Testament, and then again by Jesus in the New Testament. The prophets previously foretold this theocratic kingdom. The disciples misunderstood Jesus' preaching on the kingdom to be an earthly kingdom, but Jesus was speaking of a heavenly kingdom (Matthew 25:1; Luke 1:33; Matthew 10:5–7; Luke 17:21).

How does the church today relate to the kingdom of God? The kingdom of God and His kingdom program continue to be taught in the church age. Jesus instructed the church age in Matthew 13 and laid out the remainder of His theocratic kingdom plan (Luke 19:11-29). God has not forgotten His people Israel and left a remnant that has demonstrated the Lord's faithfulness (Romans 11:1-5) to the church today. Of course, the church trusts in God's Abrahamic covenant (Genesis 12:1-3).

How does the biblical concept of kingdom lead one to be premillennial? First, is the imminent return of Christ (Mark 13:32; John 14:3; Acts 1:11; I Corinthians 15:52; I Thessalonians 4:16, 17). Then after the rapture happens, the seven-year tribulation begins (Revelation 4:1), and the church is called up to heaven. The two olive-skinned tribulation preachers appear in the first half of the tribulation (Revelation 11:1-3). A great multitude of Gentiles will be saved in the first part of the tribulation (Revelation 7:9). And 144,000 Jews are prophesied to be saved in the first half of the tribulation (Revelation 7:4, 5). The thousand-year reign of Christ begins in Revelation 20:1-6. If Christ's kingdom on earth begins in Revelation 20, all these other events must occur before the millennial reign (Christ's kingdom), and prior to the tribulation.

B. The Biblical Covenants

How many covenants are found in scripture? Four.

What is the Abrahamic covenant? This was a conditional covenant offered to Abraham (Genesis 12:1-3). The divine agreement was based upon Abraham following the Lord's directions. If Abraham would follow, then God would bless him there; furthermore, God promised to bless those that blessed Abraham and curse those who would curse God's people.

What is the Palestinian covenant? The Lord has promised that Israel would forever remain in the passion of the Jewish people, and the return of the Jewish people to Israel (Deuteronomy 30:1-10). This covenant is unconditional.

What is the Davidic Covenant? This covenant refers to the lineage of David. The implication is the authority of Christ and His eternal rule. The covenant is to be fulfilled at the second advent of Christ (II Samuel 7:12-16).

What is the new covenant? This covenant is to the house of Israel and the house of Judah. The Lord unconditionally offers to forgive Israel for all of their sins (Jeremiah 31:31-34).

What is the purpose of the covenants in the Bible? The covenants show God's faithfulness to His people and His steadfastness. The covenants show God's desire to have a personal relationship with mankind, and His promises to His people.

Are any of the covenants conditional in nature? The Abrahamic covenant is conditional. If Abraham went, the Lord would bless him.

How do the biblical covenants lead one to be premillennial? The biblical covenants all point to the millennial reign of Christ. Each of the covenants moves the human race closer to Christ's return, and each of the covenants is fulfilled in the millennial reign of Christ (Isaiah 10:21, 22; Isaiah 11:1, 2; Ezekiel 16:60-63; Jeremiah 31:31-34).

III. The Dispensations

A. A Definition of Dispensation

What is a dispensation? A dispensation is a stewardship of whether man will be obedient to the Lord. One could say that it is a test of obedience to the Lord.

B. An Outline of the Biblical Dispensations

How many dispensations are stated in scripture? Seven.

What are the dispensations? Innocence, Conscience, Human Government, Law, Church, Tribulation, and Kingdom.

IV. Dispensationalism

A. The Definition of Dispensationalism

What are the three essential tenets of dispensationalism? A dispensation is a changed government form, changed stewardship of man, and a divine change that allows for these revelational changes.

B. The Biblical and Theological Support for Dispensationalism

What does it mean for the Bible to be interpreted by a grammatical, historical hermeneutic? The grammatical aspect of hermeneutics is a rule of interpretation, which says that unless otherwise indicated, the text of the Bible is a common understanding of the words that are applied to the text of any one given passage of scripture. The historical contextual application of a scriptural text is that the documented events recorded in the Bible took place as they are dated. Each biblical event fits into the time period in each of its historical contexts.

What are some of the hermeneutical views that are in contrast to literalism? The thought of interpreting scripture all as a metaphor diminishes the interpretation of scripture to the individual rather than the Divine. Liturgical or Catholic interpretations of scripture put the authority of scripture on the same level of below Catholic dogma.

What does covenant theology see as the unifying principle to biblical interpretation? Because the covenants are literal interpretations, covenant theology would have a unifying effect from all of the covenants.

What problems exist for those who hold to individual salvation as being the unifying theme for the Bible? God's only plan of salvation is the unifying theme throughout the Bible.

V. The Rapture of the Church

What does the rapture of the church refer to? The rapture of the church refers to the removal of believers that are living from earth to heaven (I Thessalonians 4:17).

What is the origin of the word rapture? The origin of the word rapture comes from Latin, and has the idea of being "caught up" (Revelation 4:1) and "come up hither."

A. Various Views

1. Pretribulation Rapture

What does the pretribulation rapture view of the church teach? The rapture of the church is imminent (Matthew 24:36; I Corinthians 15:52). The Lord calls believers to heaven (Revelation 4:1), with no mention of the church after Revelation chapter three.

What reasons are given to support this viewpoint? The primary reason that forces the rapture to be before the tribulation is the fact that Christ's appearance in the clouds is imminent. Secondly, that the great multitude of Gentiles is saved in the first part of the seven-year tribulation, not before the tribulation, nor in the millennium. The national conversion of Israel takes place right after the Gentiles but before the second half of the tribulation. The rapture cannot possibly happen during the thousand-year reign of Christ. This leaves only the time just prior to the beginning of the seven-year tribulation for the rapture of the church to take place.

Appendices

2. Mid-Tribulation Rapture

What does the mid-tribulation rapture viewpoint teach? The mid-tribulation view teaches that the rapture will happen three and one-half years into the tribulation, or forty-two months into the seven-year tribulation. The church will go through the first half of the tribulation. The thousand-year reign of Christ will happen immediately following the tribulation period.

(Matthew 24:15) What reasons are given to support this viewpoint? The first reason offered was that the Bible suggests there is a focal point halfway through the tribulation period (Daniel 9:27; 12:11). The second argument was based on the Olivet Discourse. The argument suggests that discussions about the spread of the Gospel, the Antichrist, and the persecution of the Christians all point to the first half of the tribulation (Matthew 24:27; I Thessalonians 4:15). The third argument suggested that since the seventh trumpet took place in the first half of the tribulation, then the church must not be raptured until the mid-point of the tribulation (Revelation 10:7; I Corinthians 15:52).

3. Pre-wrath Rapture

What does the pre-wrath rapture viewpoint teach? The pre-wrath rapture is somewhat of a hybrid of the rapture theories. This position is right between the mid-tribulation theory and the post-tribulation theory. The pre-wrath rapture is said to take place three-quarters of the way through the seven-year tribulation. The pre-wrath rapture theory teaches that the church will go through the wrath of man but will not go through the wrath of God (Revelation 6).

What reasons are given to support this viewpoint? This view divided the seven-year tribulation into three distinct parts per their analysis of for Daniel's seventieth week (Daniel 9:27). They also referenced Matthew 24:21 to make the argument that Jesus denoted to the second half of the tribulation as the "great tribulation." The next argument is that the wrath does not take place in the first half of the seven-year tribulation (Revelation 6:17). Next, a reference from Jesus in Matthew 24:22 mentioned that the tribulation days would be shortened. The next argument suggested that the Trumpet Judgments occupied less than the second half of the tribulation period (Matthew 24:21). The second to last argument suggested that the rapture has to take place prior to the Day of the Lord. The final argument is that the pre-wrath rapture theory does not fit into the pre-tribulation rapture position (Joel 2:30–31).

4. Post-Tribulation Rapture

What does the post-tribulation rapture viewpoint teach? This view suggests that the rapture is the second to next eschatological event on God's timeline. This view puts the church through the entire tribulation period. In this view, there is no national conversion of Israel. The post-tribulation model seems to suggest a parallel with classical premillennialism.

What support is given for the post-tribulation viewpoint? The first argument for the post-tribulation rapture is the similarities in vocabulary relative to the rapture and the second coming of Christ (I Thessalonians 4:15; I Peter 1:7). The second argument is the suggestion that John did not really get called up to heaven, and the church was actually left on earth. The twenty-four elders are representing the church that is still on earth (Revelation 4–18; 4:4). The third argument made reference to II Thessalonians 1:5–10, which argues that the end of the church's persecution is at the end of the tribulation period (John 14:1–3; I Thessalonians 4:13–14).

5. Partial Rapture

What does the partial rapture viewpoint teach? This view of the rapture is different from all others as it deals with the individual worthiness to be raptured rather than the timing of the rapture. Each believer that is subsequently raptured based on their being committed to "watching" for Christ appearing.

What support is given for the partial rapture viewpoint? The partial rapture view argues their position relative to the "watching" verses and is mainly dealing with the imminence of Christ's appearing (Matthew 24:41–42; Luke 21:36; I Thessalonians 1:10; II Timothy 4:8; I John 2:28).

B. The Biblical Position

Which of these various viewpoints do you hold to, and why? This author holds to a pretribulation, premillennial rapture of the church. The reason for being pretribulation is that the seventieth week does not allow for the church to overlap any part of the tribulation (Daniel 9:24–27), and the church is kept from the tribulation (I John 2:3). The element of Christ's return, being that it is imminent, forbids the church from having any part of the tribulation. The millennial reign of Christ cannot be before the tribulation, and the millennial reign has certainly not transpired anytime previously. The millennial reign begins immediately following the seven-year tribulation (Revelation 20–21).

VI. The Tribulation

What does the tribulation refer to? The tribulation refers to the dispensation of time from the end of the church age (Revelation 4:1 to Revelation 19). When is the tribulation? The tribulation goes from the end of the church age to the beginning of the thousand-year reign of Christ (Revelation 4–19). Whom does the tribulation involve? The dead in Christ (I Thessalonians 4:16), those alive at Christ's appearing (v. 17), the Gentiles, tribulation saints (Revelation 7:9), one hundred forty-four thousand Jews, and tribulation saints (Revelation 7:4). How does the church relate to the tribulation period? It would seem as though because the church is now in heaven (Revelation 4:1), the saved are preoccupied with worship to the Lord in heaven and at the marriage supper of the Lamb (Revelation 19:7–10). What are the major events of the tribulation? The salvation of a great multitude of Gentiles (Revelation 7:9), the salvation of 144,000 Jews (Revelation 7:4), the abomination of desolation (Matthew 24: 15–16), the Antichrist incarnated (Revelation 13:4–10), the false prophet (Revelation 13:11–18,) and the appearing of Christ (Revelation 19:11–21.)

What are the purposes of the tribulation? The tribulation period sets up Israel for Christ's return (Jerimiah 30:7). Furthermore, the second purpose of the tribulation is the judgment of the unsaved (Revelation 3:10). What is meant by "the Day of the Lord"? The time of tribulation (Acts 2:20; I Thessalonians 5:2; II Thessalonians 2:2; II Peter 3:10).

VII. The Millennium

A. How will it begin

To what does the millennium refer? The thousand years following the seven-year tribulation (Revelation 20–21). Christ will ascend bodily to earth and reign on earth. What is the relationship of the millennium to the eternal state? Satan is cast into the bottomless pit, the earth is on fire, and the white throne judgment occurs (Revelation 20:2, 3; 7,9). How long is the coming kingdom? For eternity. When will the millennial kingdom be established? It will be instituted at the second advent (Revelation 11:15–17).

What events will occur just prior to the establishment of the millennial kingdom? Satan will be thrown into the bottomless pit (Revelation 20), the earth will be purged (II Peter 3:10–13), the unsaved will be judged (Revelation 20:12; 20:3–3, 14).

B. General Description

What is the role of Christ during the millennium? Christ will rule as a theocracy during the millennium (Isaiah 9:3–7; Zephaniah 3:9, 10). What is the role of the believer during the millennium? To worship the Lord (Isaiah 66:23). What will characterize the millennium? It will be governed by divine rule, with no outward temptations, there will be worship, and it will be the final test of Christian character. There will be peace, joy, and justice. What will be the focal point for the world during the millennium? The bodily presence of the Lord Jesus Christ.

C. Coming Events

What will be the role of Satan during the millennium and at the close of the millennium? Satan was in the bottomless pit during the millennium. Satan will be loosed at the end of the millennium and then cast into the lake of fire (Revelation 20:7–10). What events will bring the millennium to a close? The lost from all of human history will be judged at the great white throne out of the Book of Life (Revelation 20:11–15).

VIII. General Eschatology

A. Death and the Intermediate State

Who are the exceptions to physical death and the intermediate state? The believers who are alive at the time of Christ's appearing (I Thessalonians 4:17). When believers die, where do they go immediately? The believers will be in the presence of Christ (II Corinthians 5:8).

What form do believers' bodies take following their death prior to their resurrection? The believers become a disembodied spirit when they leave this world and await Christ's return (I Corinthians 15:20, 23). Where do unbelievers go upon their death? Unbelievers will go to a place of torment (Luke 16:28).

B. The Various Resurrections

When will believers who have died be resurrected? The dead in Christ will be raised to life again at Christ's resurrection (I Corinthians 15:21). What is the significance of this resurrection for those believers? First, those believers who are dead will not only be resurrected with Christ and be in His presence, but they will also be with all other resurrected believers, including Adam (I Corinthians 15:22).

When will the people who died during the tribulation period be resurrected? These saints will be resurrected from the dead at Christ's Second Advent (Mark 12:25; Luke 20:35–36; Acts 4:1, 2). When will the Old Testament saints be resurrected? The Old Testament saints will be resurrected with the church at the rapture (I Chronicles 24:1–4, 19; Revelation 4:1–11). Who will be included in the resurrection following the millennium? Satan, who will be loosed (Revelation 20:2, 3), the tribulation saints (Revelation 20:4), and the dead in Christ (Revelation 20:5).

C. The Various Judgements

APPENDICES

When is the judgment of church-age believers for rewards to occur? The Bema Seat judgment will be at Christ's second coming (II Corinthians 5:10). What occurs at this judgment? The believer's works will be tried by fire to see their worth and what rewards may be received (I Corinthians 3:10–15). Who will be judged at the conclusion of the tribulation? The unsaved, (Revelation 20:12), the saved, those saved that were dead (verse 12), and the unsaved that were dead (verse 13). What is the significance of the White Throne Judgement? This will be the final judgment (verse 12), the book of life will be opened (verse 12), and the dead will be judged and thrown in the lake of fire (verse 14).

D. The Eternal State

Where will believers and unbelievers spend eternity? The believer will be in the presence of the Lord (I Corinthians 15:42), the location will be in the New Jerusalem (Revelation 21:1, 2), and will forever be with the Lord (I Thessalonians 4:17). The unbelievers will be sent to their second death (Revelation 20:14) in the lake of fire (Revelation 20:14). What is heaven like? There is no night there (Revelation 21:25), the throne of God is there, no curses are there (Revelation 22:3), God and the Lamb shall be there, (Revelation 22:1) and the tree of life will be there (Revelation 22:2).

What will hell be like? The lake which burneth with fire and brimstone (Revelation 21:8), wailing and gnashing of teeth (Matthew 13:50), everlasting fire (Matthew 25:41), everlasting punishment (Matthew 24:46), the worm dieth not, and the fire is not quenched (Mark 9:44), everlasting destruction from the presence of the Lord (II Thessalonians 1:9).

What is the significance of the new heaven and the new earth? God will be there (Revelation 21:3), all tears wiped away

(Revelation 21:4), all things made new (verse 5), the water of life freely given (verse 6), a city of pure gold like glass (verse 18), and the Lord and the Lamb are thee (verse 22). Maranatha!

APPENDIX H

ADDITIONAL TRAINING: LESSON ONE

THE BIG PICTURE ACCORDING TO MATTHEW

Community Group Bible Study Class: Lesson 1

Great Commission and Children's Ministry

Matthew 28:18-20: "And Jesus came and spake unto them, saying, All power is given unto me in heaven and in earth. Go ye therefore, and teach all nations, baptizing them in the name of the Father, and of the Son, and of the Holy Ghost: Teaching them to observe all things whatsoever I have commanded you: and, lo, I am with you alway, even unto the end of the world. Amen."

Group Discussion Questions:

1. Based on these verses, what are the three objectives of the believer on earth?

   A._____

APPENDICES

    B. _____

    C. _____

2. Name four ways this teaching can be applied.

    A. _____

    B. _____

    C. _____

    D. _____

Deuteronomy 6:4–8: "Hear, O Israel: The LORD our God is one LORD: And thou shalt love the LORD thy God with all thine heart, and with all thy soul, and with all thy might. And these words, which I command thee this day, shall be in thine heart: And thou shalt teach them diligently unto thy children, and shalt talk of them when thou sittest in thine house, and when thou walkest by the way, and when thou liest down, and when thou risest up. And thou shalt bind them for a sign upon thine hand, and they shall be as frontlets between thine eyes."

Group Discussion Questions:

3. Based on these verses, what is the motivation for our relationship with the Lord?

    A. _____

    B. _____

    C. _____

4. What is the scope of the teaching setting?

    A. _____

B._____

C._____

D. _____

5. Whom does this teaching apply to?

   A._____

   B._____

   C._____

Appendices

Applications for the Group:

1. Participate in personal soul-winning; work a bus route.

2. Discuss baptism with a child that is newly converted, along with the parents.

3. Witness to parents of the children on the bus route.

4. Ask children and parents for F.R.A.N. (Friends, Relatives, Associates, & Neighbors): contacts that may be visited and encouraged to come to Sunday school and church.

5. Commit to learning the Word of God.

6. Commit to teaching others the Word of God.

7. Commit to mentor new believers.

8. Seek to counsel others with biblical principles.

APPENDIX I

ADDITIONAL TRAINING: LESSON TWO

THE BIG PICTURE ACCORDING TO MARK

Community Group Bible Study Class: Lesson 2

Great Commission & Children's Ministry

Mark 16:15: "And he said unto them, Go ye into all the world, and preach the gospel to every creature."

Group Discussion Questions:

1. Based on this verse of scripture, whom does this apply to? Is the "ye" singular or plural in this passage?

   A. _____

   B. _____

Mark 16:9–14: "Now when Jesus was risen early the first day of the week, he appeared first to Mary Magdalene, out of whom he had cast seven devils. And she went and told them that had been with him, as they mourned and wept. And they, when they had heard that he was alive, and had been seen of her, believed not. After that he appeared in another form unto two of them, as they walked, and went into the country. And they went and told it unto the residue: neither believed they them. Afterward he appeared unto the eleven as they sat at meat, and upbraided them with their unbelief and hardness of heart, because they believed not them which had seen him after he was risen."

Appendices

2. What was the spiritual state of Jesus's disciples when He gave this charge?

   A. _____

   B. _____

   C. _____

3. Was this text describing people that are not even saved?

   _____

4. Were the disciples saying that they didn't believe in the Resurrection? And yet they believed on Christ as the Messiah during His 3½ year earthly ministry. What are the possible causes for the carnal reaction that Christ is alive?

   A. _____

   B. _____

   C. _____

5. What excuses do people give for not actively being involved in winning the lost?

   A. _____

   B. _____

   C. _____

6. What are some reasons every Christian can and should be engaged in winning the lost?

   A. _____

   B. _____

   C. _____

APPENDICES

Applications for the Group:

1. Believers must recognize their individual and corporate responsibility to do what they can to help carry out the mission of the Great Commission.

2. Every believer must understand that Great Commission work should be committed to in spite of difficult circumstances or even emotional distress.

3. The believer must guard his heart against unbelief and hardness.

4. Faithfulness to witness for the Lord requires one to overcome the fear of rejection.

5. Christians must train their hearts to overcome the fear of failure.

APPENDIX J

ADDITIONAL TRAINING: LESSON THREE

THE BIG PRIORITY

Community Group Bible Study Class: Lesson 3

Great Commission & Children's Ministry

Matthew **19:14**: "But Jesus said, Suffer little children, and forbid them not, to come unto me: for of such is the kingdom of heaven."

Group Discussion Questions:

1. What does this verse teach us about God's priority to reach children?

   _____

   _____

   _____

2. Why do you think God equates children with the kingdom of heaven?

   _____

   _____

   _____

3. Why do you think the culture's values are different than the kingdom's values?

Proverbs 22:6: "Train up a child in the way he should go: and when he is old, he will not depart from it."

Group Discussion Questions:

1. Why do you think children are apt to continue in their faith for the remainder of their lives?

2. For what reason might God view children as a higher priority in relationship to the Great Commission?

3. How do you think children view the gospel differently than adults?

_____

_____

_____

_____

Psalm 34:11: "Come, ye children, hearken unto me: I will teach you the fear of the LORD."

4. Why do you think King David took the time to teach children about the Lord?

_____

_____

_____

5. What do you think it means to be taught the fear of the Lord?

_____

_____

_____

6. What qualities do you think King David exhibited while teaching the children the fear of the Lord?

_____

_____

_____

7. What do you think the spiritual benefits are in teaching children (in contrast to teaching adults)?

_____

_____

_____

Potential Applications for the Group:

1. As Christians, we must think in terms of kingdom values as relates to children.

2. As adults, we should practice child-like faith in our daily lives.

3. As maturing followers and servants of Christ, we must train our minds and our thinking to resist what the unsaved subculture values and embrace kingdom values instead.

4. As Christians who realize that children have longer to live and serve the Lord, we must refocus our attention on reaching children for the Lord.

5. We must keep in mind while dealing with children that they see the world and the gospel differently than adults.

6. Adult Christians must be humble enough to invest time ministering to children.

7. As Christians, we need to practice the presence of God in order to practice the fear of the Lord in our personal lives.

8. As a Christian, one must remember the spiritual benefits and blessings of working with children.

APPENDIX K

ADDITIONAL TRAINING: LESSON FOUR

THE MASTER'S PLAN

Community Group Bible Study Class: Lesson 4

Great Commission & Children's Ministry

Matthew 19:14: "But Jesus said, Suffer little children, and forbid them not, to come unto me: for of such is the kingdom of heaven."

Plan of Salvation: Children's ministry is a process, and an ongoing process always begins with evangelism. When presenting the gospel to children, it is essential to keep the gospel presentation as simple as possible. It is also important to make illustrations in terms that children understand.

Step One: Children need to be made to understand that they are sinners who have sinned against God. If they want to know for sure that they will go to heaven one day, they need to respond to God's offer of forgiveness and salvation. The best way to illustrate this concept when working with children is to make a connection with parent-child relationships. Children get this!

- **Romans 3:23**: "For all have sinned, and come short of the glory of God."

- **Romans 6:23**: "For the wages of sin is death; but the gift of God is eternal life through Jesus Christ our Lord."

Appendices

- **Romans 5:8**: "But God commendeth his love toward us, in that, while we were yet sinners, Christ died for us."

- **Romans 5:12**: "Wherefore, as by one man sin entered into the world, and death by sin; and so death passed upon all men, for that all have sinned:"

Group Discussion Questions:

1. What are two things that can be done to help understanding while teaching children?

   A. _____

   B. _____

Step Two: After giving scripture to show the child the plan of Salvation from the Bible, one will then want to illustrate the point. This will draw the child into the conversation even more.

- Ask the child, "Have you ever disobeyed your mother or father?"
- Then ask the child, "Don't you want to go to be with Jesus someday?"
- You can also ask, "Wouldn't you like to be in heaven one day with your other family?"

Step Three: Children need to know that Jesus loves them. The point that a child has sinned is a far different point than that God is a good, loving, and forgiving God. One must impress upon the child that God loves him in a profound way.

- Ask the child, "Your mom and dad love you, don't they?"
- Ask the child, "Do you understand that God loves you even more than anyone else could?"

2. What do illustrations do for the child's learning?

   A. _____

   B. _____

3. What other techniques can the teacher employ to draw the child into the conversation?

   A. _____

   B. _____

4. What are two possible outcomes from asking pre-planned questions?

   A. _____

   B. _____

Step Four: Show the child from the Bible how much God loves him.

- **John 3:16**: "For God so loved the world, that he gave his only begotten Son, that whosoever believeth in him should not perish, but have everlasting life."

- **Romans 5:5**: "And hope maketh not ashamed; because the love of God is shed abroad in our hearts by the Holy Ghost which is given unto us."

Step Five: The child needs to be led in prayer to ask Jesus into his heart.

- **Romans 10:10**: "For with the heart man believeth unto righteousness; and with the mouth confession is made unto salvation."

- **Romans 10:13**: "For whosoever shall call upon the name of the Lord shall be saved."

Step Six: Pray "heaven's prayer" with the child and ask the child to pray out loud with you.

Prayer: "Dear Lord, I know that I am a sinner. And I know that You sent Jesus to die on the cross for my sins. I know that You raised Jesus from the grave. Now, I ask Jesus to forgive all my sins and to come into my heart. I trust You alone to take me to heaven one day. I thank You for saving me. In Jesus's name, Amen!"

Step Seven: Give the child a reason from scripture how he can know that once saved, God keeps him saved and will take those saved to heaven one day.

- **John 10:27-29**: "My sheep hear my voice, and I know them, and they follow me: And I give unto them eternal life; and they shall never perish, neither shall any man pluck them out of my hand. My Father, which gave them me, is greater than all; and no man is able to pluck them out of my Father's hand."

- **I John 5:11-13**: "And this is the record, that God hath given to us eternal life, and this Life is in his Son. He that hath the Son hath life; and he that hath not the Son of God hath not life. These things have I written unto you that believe on the name of the Son of God; that ye may know that ye have eternal life, and that ye may believe on the name of the Son of God."

- Ask the child, "Based upon these two passages, do you understand that God will never leave you now that you are His child?"

5. What is the main characteristic of God that one wants to impress upon a child?

   _____

6. What is the name of the prayer that one needs to lead the child in?

   _____

7. What is the Scriptural reason that one would need to give a child after the child prays to ask Jesus into his heart?

   _____

APPENDICES

Applications for the Group:

1. Make the commitment to learn the plan of salvation outline so that one may be confident to present the gospel anytime and anywhere.

2. Commit to memory the verses of scripture included in this lesson so that they can be communicated whenever an opportunity presents itself for sharing the gospel.

3. Commit these questions to memory so that one's conversation with a child flows smoothly and logically.

4. Make a commitment to reaching children and sharing the gospel with children.

APPENDIX L

ADDITIONAL TRAINING: LESSON FIVE

IDENTIFYING WITH CHRIST

Community Group Bible Study Class: Lesson 5

Great Commission & Children's Ministry

Acts 2:41: "Then they that gladly received his word were baptized: and the same day there were added unto them about three thousand souls."

Baptism: The Second Step of Obedience to the Lord

The conflict you may have right away when dealing with children and baptism after conversion is to clearly communicate the different motivation to be saved versus the motivation to be baptized. The connection between baptism and salvation is that one must be saved before they can be baptized. The disconnect between salvation and baptism is that the former is to receive God's gift of eternal life; the latter has nothing to do with gaining eternal life. Baptism is the beginning of stewardship to the Lord.

Step One: Talk to the child about the difference between a gift and obedience. Say to the child, "Do you pay your parents for a birthday or Christmas gift?" Then ask the child, "Do your parents expect you to obey them?" The contrast between Salvation and being baptized will then be made.

- **Ephesians 2:8-9**: "For by grace are ye saved through faith; and that not of yourselves: it is the gift of God: Not of works, lest any man should boast."

- **Titus 3:5**: "Not by works of righteousness which we have done, but according to his mercy he saved us, by the washing of regeneration, and renewing of the Holy Ghost."

Step Two: You will want to give the child a couple of examples from the Bible of those that have followed the Lord in believer's baptism. This will give the child a good example to follow when taking this second step of obedience to the Lord.

- **Acts 8:12**: "But when they believed Philip preaching the things concerning the kingdom of God, and the name of Jesus Christ, they were baptized, both men and women."
- **Acts 18:8**: "And Crispus, the chief ruler of the synagogue, believed on the Lord with all his house; and many of the Corinthians hearing believed, and were baptized."

Step Three: The broader reason for baptism should be explained to the child in the context of the believer's baptism being at the center of the Great Commission. You might talk to the child in terms of his relationship with his parents. The connection between obeying parents and obeying the Lord is easy for the child to make.

- **Matthew 28:19**: "Go ye therefore, and teach all nations, baptizing them in the name of the Father, and of the Son, and of the Holy Ghost."
- **Acts 10:48**: "And he said unto them, Ye know how that it is an unlawful thing for a man that is a Jew to keep company, or come unto one of another nation; but God hath shewed me that I should not call any man common or unclean."

Step Four: It is good to communicate the process of baptism to a child by illustrating what the process entails and what the process represents. Explaining the baptism process to a child should relieve some anxiety about what is an unfamiliar experience, so he will know what to expect and feel safe proceeding with the baptism. What baptism represents is the death, burial, and resurrection of Jesus Christ. It is important when communicating this to the child that you illustrate it clearly.

- **Matthew 3:16**: "And Jesus, when he was baptized, went up straightway out of the water: and, lo, the heavens were opened unto him, and he saw the Spirit of God descending like a dove, and lighting upon him."

- **Acts 8:38**: "And he commanded the chariot to stand still: and they went down both into the water, both Philip and the eunuch; and he baptized him."

- **Colossians 2:12**: "Buried with him in baptism, wherein also ye are risen with him through the faith of the operation of God, who hath raised him from the dead."

Step Five: When dealing with children and their parents, it is not good to pressure them into taking the step of baptism. Remember that it is a process, and every believer grows incrementally. When seeking a commitment from children and their parents, ask for a series of commitments. One way to do this is to ask the question, "Do you understand?" This question can be asked a number of times throughout the conversation. The final point to impress upon the child and parents is that baptism for the new Christian is a public profession of faith. The child being baptized benefits from exercising his faith, while the local church is encouraged by a child's trust in Christ as his personal Savior. The local church then has the opportunity to encourage the child that has been baptized and welcome him into the family of God.

- **Acts 8:12**: "But when they believed Philip preaching the things concerning the kingdom of God, and the name of Jesus Christ, they were baptized, both men and women."

- **Acts 16:33**: "And he took them the same hour of the night, and washed their stripes; and was baptized, he and all his, straightway."

Step Six: While making home visits with families, it is important to ask the parents after a baptism presentation, "Do you have any questions regarding believer's baptism?" Whatever parents answer, this is the appropriate time to ask about their salvation. If they are already saved, ask the parents, "Is there any reason you would not want to be baptized along with your child?" If the parents don't know if they are saved, take the time to present the gospel to them. This is kingdom opportunity time. Take it!

Step Seven: The last objective to accomplish while making a home visit is to ask the children, "Are there friends of yours that you would like us to invite to your Sunday school class or program?" Then ask the parents, "Do you have friends, neighbors, or co-workers that might need special prayer or just a friendly visit?" Children's workers should always carry note cards with them, so they can write down new contacts for the children's ministry.

Group Discussion Questions:

1. What is the difference in a child's motivation to be saved versus to be baptized?

2. Why is baptism called the "second step" of obedience to the Lord?

3. What is the significance of using a "gift from parents" when explaining the difference between salvation versus baptism to a child?

4. What significance does Matthew 28:19 have with regard to baptism?

APPENDICES

5. What two things are accomplished when a new Christian follows the Lord in believer's baptism?

    A. _____

    B. _____

6. What two things should the children's worker ask while finishing up a home visit?

    A. _____

    B. _____

Potential Applications for the Group:

1. Memorize the "planned questions" relating to baptism, so you can use these questions when dealing with children and parents.

2. Memorize the scriptures regarding baptism. As a children's worker, you may be reading upside down, so the child or parent can read along as baptism is presented.

3. Use baptism examples so that this becomes real to the child and parents.

4. Meditate on scripture, recognizing that after salvation, baptism is central in the Great Commission.

5. Make home visits this week with someone who is comfortable presenting believer's baptism to children and parents.

6. Illustrate with your hands the death, burial, and resurrection of Jesus Christ while communicating the symbolism of baptism to at least one child and parent this week.

7. While presenting baptism this week, also present the gospel to at least one parent or set of parents. This can be called "backing into the gospel."

8. This week, ask at least one child and one parent for names and addresses of other children or adults that you can visit.

APPENDICES

APPENDIX M

ADDITIONAL TRAINING: LESSON SIX

TRAINING TEACHERS

Community Group Bible Study Class: Lesson 6

Great Commission & Children's Ministry

II Timothy 2:2: "And the things that thou hast heard of me among many witnesses, the same commit thou to faithful men, who shall be able to teach others also."

Step One: Understand that the biblical model for leadership is faithful believers that can be discipled and entrusted with God's Word to, in turn, disciple other faithful believers.

- **I Samuel 16:7**: "But the LORD said unto Samuel, Look not on his countenance, or on the height of his stature; because I have refused him: for the LORD seeth not as man seeth; for man looketh on the outward appearance, but the LORD looketh on the heart."

- **I Corinthians 11:1**: "Be ye followers of me, even as I also am of Christ."

Step Two: Understand that the Lord's work is not based upon the economy of the world, but rather the economy of God's kingdom. The qualities and actions that are highly esteemed by the world are not the same qualities and actions that are esteemed by the Lord.

- **Matthew 5:19**: "Whosoever therefore shall break one of these least commandments, and shall teach men so, he shall be called the least in the kingdom of heaven: but whosoever shall do and teach them, the same shall be called great in the kingdom of heaven."

- **Mark 10:14-15**: "But when Jesus saw it, he was much displeased, and said unto them, Suffer the little children to come unto me, and forbid them not: for of such is the kingdom of God. Verily I say unto you, Whosoever shall not receive the kingdom of God as a little child, he shall not enter therein."

Step Three: Leadership in ministry comes about when two key biblical principles are applied. The first principle is "followship." The second principle is dominating fears.

- **Matthew 16:24**: "Then said Jesus unto his disciples, If any man will come after me, let him deny himself, and take up his cross, and follow me."

- **II Timothy 1:7**: "For God hath not given us the spirit of fear; but of power, and of love, and of a sound mind."

Step Four: Leadership requires biblical growth in the Word of God and in stretching yourself to more fully apply your God-given talents and abilities to the ministry opportunities that come your way. A clear way to view service and love for God is how you serve people. Spiritual growth comes by study and often comes best by having accountability in your life.

- **Acts 22:3**: "I am verily a man which am a Jew, born in Tarsus, a city in Cilicia, yet brought up in this city at the feet of Gamaliel, and taught according to the perfect manner of the law of the fathers, and was zealous toward God, as ye all are this day."

- **II Timothy 2:15**: "Study to shew thyself approved unto God, a workman that needeth not to be ashamed, rightly dividing the word of truth."

Step Five: The application part of ministry is engaging with parents and children in the first and second steps of their spiritual walk. This may require light biblical counsel with the parents, picking up and dropping off the children, making visits on Saturdays, or any time a need comes up with a family. It takes continual follow-up, including visits and phone calls.

- **Luke 14:23**: "And the lord said unto the servant, Go out into the highways and hedges, and compel them to come in, that my house may be filled. (Though this passage refers to the marriage supper of the Lamb, the application can be made to evangelism.)
- **Proverbs 11:30**: "The fruit of the righteous is a tree of life; and he that winneth souls is wise."

Group Discussion Questions:

1. Based upon **II Timothy 2:2**, what does this passage teach regarding whom we should entrust with passing on the gospel message?

    A. _____

    B. _____

    C. _____

2. Explain how the world's economy differs from the economy of God's kingdom?

   _____

   _____

   _____

3. What are the two biblical leadership principles that were mentioned in this lesson?

   A. _____

   B. _____

4. What are the two first steps taken in a person's spiritual walk with the Lord?

   A. _____

   B. _____

APPENDICES

Potential Applications for the Group:

1. Invite 6–8 faithful believers to the teacher-training Bible study next week.

2. Begin viewing other believers regarding the fruit of their heart rather than their outside appearance or life situation.

3. Begin to view yourself not as a leader of men but rather a follower of Christ.

4. Begin to concisely view your life in terms of the economy of the kingdom of God.

5. Begin to concisely view God as bigger than any fear of man.

6. Be willing to put yourself in a place of ministry where you may not feel comfortable but where God can stretch and mold you for His service and glory.

7. Engage children and parents this week in the two steps of obedience to Him.

APPENDIX N

ADDITIONAL TRAINING: LESSON SEVEN

JOINING THE FAMILY OF GOD

Community Group Bible Study Class: Lesson 7

Great Commission & Children's Ministry

Mathew 16:18: "And I say also unto thee, That thou art Peter, and upon this rock I will build my church; and the gates of hell shall not prevail against it."

Principle One: The local church is God's program and institution for getting the gospel to the whole world. It is the local church that connects the gospel to the world where converts are baptized into membership. It is the institution that was founded upon Jesus Christ and recorded in the Gospels, the book of Acts, and the Epistles.

- **Matthew 3:2; 5-6**: "And saying, Repent ye: for the kingdom of heaven is at hand. Then went out to him Jerusalem, and all Judaea, and all the region round about Jordan, And were baptized of him in Jordan, confessing their sins."

- **Acts 2:41**: "Then they that gladly received his word were baptized: and the same day there were added unto them about three thousand souls."

    A. The local church will rejoice when children come to a saving knowledge of Jesus Christ.

B. The local church is whose membership a new convert is baptized into.

C. The local church is where soul-winners are sent out from. It is the local church where the believers gather, worship, and serve together.

Principle Two: Service to the Lord is a large part of worship and much of what Christians will be doing in heaven. Service to the Lord is a command of the Lord. It is seen in the Great Commission and throughout scripture. It is impossible to love the Lord without service to Him.

- **I Samuel 12:24** "Only fear the LORD, and serve him in truth with all your heart: for consider how great things he hath done for you."

- **John 12:26** "If any man serve me, let him follow me; and where I am, there shall also my servant be: if any man serve me, him will my Father honour."

A. Service to the Lord includes involvement in the children's ministry.

B. Following the Lord involves loving and reaching children that He loves.

C. Serving the Lord through the local church helps to accomplish His will in any one place.

Principle Three: The stewardship of a Christian's life includes your time, abilities, and personal resources. Everything that is given to every believer gives an opportunity to bring glory to the Lord.

- **Deuteronomy 6:5**: "And thou shalt love the LORD thy God with all thine heart, and with all thy soul, and with all thy might."

- **Colossians 3:23**: "And whatsoever ye do, do it heartily, as to the Lord, and not unto men."

- **Leviticus 27:30**: "And all the tithe of the land, whether of the seed of the land, or of the fruit of the tree, is the LORD'S: it is holy unto the LORD."

Group Discussion Questions:

1. What is the main institution that God uses to evangelize the world?

   _____

2. What step of obedience places a new convert into local church membership?

   _____

3. What are the two biblical requirements for church membership?

   A. _____

   B. _____

4. According to the second principle, worship is part of _____ to the Lord.

5. Based upon **I Samuel 12:24** we serve the Lord in _____, with what part of our hearts? _____.

APPENDICES

6. According to **John 12:26**, whom will the Father honor?

   _____

7. Principle Three teaches the stewardship of what three things?

   A. _____

   B. _____

   C. _____

Potential Applications for the Group:

1. Be involved in getting children baptized after they are saved.

2. Seek opportunities and different ways you can serve people.

3. Be a faithful steward of all your time, abilities, and resources.

APPENDIX O

ADDITIONAL TRAINING: ANSWERS ONE

THE BIG PICTURE ACCORDING TO MATTHEW

Training Class: Lesson 1

Answers:

1. Based on these verses, what are the three objectives of the believer on earth?

    A. Evangelize the lost.

    B. Baptize converts.

    C. Disciple all believers.

2. Name four ways this teaching can be applied.

    A. Evangelize

    B. Disciple

    C. Teach

    D. Counsel

3. Based on these verses, what is the motivation for our relationship with the Lord?

    A. Love the Lord.

    B. With all your soul

    C. With all your might

4. What is the scope of the teaching setting?

    A. Sitting in the house

    B. Walking in the way

    C. Lying down

    D. Rising up

5. Whom does this teaching apply to?

    A. Children

    B. Spouse

    C. Circle of influence

TRANSFORMATIONAL TRUTH VOLUME II

APPENDIX P

ADDITIONAL TRAINING: ANSWERS TWO

THE BIG PICTURE ACCORDING TO MARK

Training Class: Lesson 2

Answers:

1. Based on this verse, whom does this apply to? Is the "ye" singular or plural in this passage?

    A. Every believer and every local church

    B. Plural – everyone

2. What was the spiritual state of Jesus's disciples when He gave this charge?

    A. Mourning and weeping

    B. Unbelief

    C. Hardness of heart

3. Was the text describing people that are not even saved?

    Answer: No

4. Were the disciples saying that they didn't believe in the Resurrection? Yet they believed on Christ as the Messiah during His 3½ year earthly ministry. What are the possible causes of the carnal reaction that Christ is alive?

Appendices

    A. Life challenges

    B. Emotional trials

    C. Anger because of the death of a loved one

5. What excuses do people give for not actively being involved in winning the lost?

    A. Fear of rejection

    B. Fear of failure

    C. Unwanted responsibility

6. What are some reasons every Christian can and should be engaged in winning the lost?

    A. We are commanded to win the lost.

    B. We are obligated to give the gospel to the lost.

    C. We should win crowns and give glory to Christ.

APPENDIX Q

ADDITIONAL TRAINING: ANSWERS THRE

THE BIG PRIORITY

Training Class: Lesson 3

Answers:

1. What does the verse teach us about God's priority to reach children?

    Answer: Jesus saw the innocence of children and their willingness to trust Jesus.

2. Why do you think God equates children with the kingdom of heaven?

    Answer: Children are innocent, and their child-like faith is endearing to Jesus.

3. Why do you think the culture's values are different from the kingdom's values?

    Answer: The culture is godless, and the kingdom is all about God.

4. Why do you think children are apt to continue in their faith for the remainder of their lives?

    Answer: One Biblical reason is because of eternal security. Another reason is that habits are formed during childhood.

5. For what reason might God view children as a higher priority in relation to the Great Commission?

    Answer: One reason is that children have longer to live for the Lord; therefore, children have longer to serve the Lord.

6. How do you think children view the gospel differently than adults?

    Answer: Children may view the gospel in terms of being loved by the heavenly Father, while adults may see the gospel as a remedy for sins and life problems.

7. Why do you think King David took the time to teach children about the Lord?

    Answer: King David knew that the children would grow up to be God-fearing adults.

8. What do you think it means to be taught the fear of the Lord?

    Answer: The fear of the Lord could include honor, respect, reverence, and worship.

9. What qualities do you think King David exhibited while teaching the children the fear of the Lord?

    A. Godliness

    B. Humility

10. What do you think the spiritual benefits are in teaching children (in contrast to teaching adults)?

   A. Children learn more quickly.

   B. They have fewer obstacles to faith.

   C. They have a natural love for Jesus.

APPENDICES

APPENDIX R

ADDITIONAL TRAINING: ANSWERS FOUR

THE MASTER'S PLAN

Training Class: Lesson 4

Answers:

1. What are two things that can be done to help understanding while teaching children?

    A. Simplicity

    B. Illustrations

2. What do illustrations do for the child's learning?

    A. They draw the child into the Bible lesson.

    B. They help the child envision the Bible story.

3. What other techniques can the teacher employ to draw the child into the conversation?

    Ask pre-planned questions.

    Tailor illustrations to the child.

4. What are two possible outcomes of asking pre-planned questions?

A. They keep the child focused on the salvation message.

   B. They will help to lead the child to trust in the Lord.

5. What is the main characteristic of God that one wants to impress upon a child?

   Answer: The love of God

6. What is the name of the prayer that one needs to lead a child in?

   Answer: "heaven's prayer."

7. What is the scriptural reason that one would need to give a child after the child prays to ask Jesus into his heart?

   Answer: An assurance of salvation

APPENDIX S

ADDITIONAL TRAINING: ANSWERS FIVE

IDENTIFYING WITH CHRIST

Answers:

1. What is the difference in a child's motivation to be saved versus to be baptized?

    Answer: Accepting God's grace vs. obedience to the Lord is a matter of stewardship.

2. Why is baptism called the "second step" of obedience to the Lord?

    Answer: Trusting the Lord is the first step of obedience.

3. What is the significance of using a "gift from parents" when explaining the difference between salvation verses baptism to a child?

    Answer: A child doesn't pay for a gift; he just receives a gift.

4. What significance does Matthew 28:19 have with regard to baptism?

    Answer: Baptism is a central part of the Great Commission.

5. What two things are accomplished when a new Christian follows the Lord in believer's baptism?

   A. The new believer expresses his faith.

   B. Believers in the church are encouraged.

6. What two things should the children's worker ask while finishing up a home visit?

   - Ask the child if he has friends he wants to have in Sunday school with him.

   - Ask the parents if they have family or friends that need special prayer or a friend's visit.

APPENDICES

APPENDIX T

ADDITIONAL TRAINING: ANSWERS SIX

TRAINING TEACHERS

Training Class: Lesson 6

Answers:

1. Based upon II Timothy 2:2, what does this passage teach regarding whom we should entrust with passing on the gospel message?

   Answer: Those believers who fear the Lord and bear fruits of righteousness and character.

2. Explain how the world's economy differs from the economy of God's kingdom?

   Answer: The kingdom of this world is humanism and selfish gain. The kingdom of God is about reaching children and adults with childlike faith.

3. What are the two biblical leadership principles that were mentioned in this lesson?

   A. Fellowship

   B. Conquer fears

4. What are the two first steps taken in one's spiritual walk with the Lord?

   A. Trusting Christ as Savior

   B. Following the Lord in believer's baptism

APPENDICES

APPENDIX U

ADDITIONAL TRAINING: ANSWERS SEVEN

JOINING THE FAMILY OF GOD

Training Class: Lesson 7

Answers:

1. What is the main institution that God uses to evangelize the world?

    Answer: The local church

2. What step of obedience places a new convert into local church membership?

    Answer: Believer's baptism

3. What are the two biblical requirements for church membership?

    A. Salvation

    B. Baptism

4. According to the second principle, worship is part of _____ the Lord.

    Answer: Service

5. Based upon I Samuel 12:24, we serve the Lord in _____, with what part of our hearts? _____.

   A. Truth

   B. All

6. According to John 12:26, whom will the Father honor? _____

   Answer: Those that serve Him.

7. Principle Three teaches the stewardship of what three things?

   A. Time

   B. Abilities

   C. Reserves

APPENDICES

BIBLIOGRAPHY

Adams, Jay. *Marriage, Divorce, and Remarriage in the Bible*. Grand Rapids: Zondervan Publishing House, 1980.

Anderson, Neil. *Victory Over the Darkness: Realizing the Power of Your Identity in Christ*. Ventura: Regal Books, 2000.

Ashcroft, John. *Lessons from a Father*. Nashville: Thomas Nelson, 1998.

Bahnsen, Greg. *Always Ready: Directions for Defending the Faith*. Nacogdoches, TX: Covenant Media Press, 2011.

Barnes, Albert. *Barnes' Notes, Acts – Romans*. Grand Rapids: Baker Book House, 1884.

Beck, James R. and Bruce Demarest. *The Human Person in the Theology and Psychology: A Biblical Anthropology for the Twenty-First Century*. Grand Rapids, MI: Kregal Publications, 2005.

Berg, Jim. *Changed into His Image: God's Plan For Transforming Your Life*. Greenville, SC: Bob Jones University Press, 1999.

Berkof, Lawrence. *Systematic Theology*. Grand Rapids: William B. Eerdmans Publishing Company, 1939.

Brand, Chad Owens. Perspectives on Election: Five Views. Nashville: B & H Publishing Group, 2006.

Brown, Fred. *Inside The Tulip Controversy: Calvinism Rebuked and Revisited*. Southern Pines: Calvary Press, 1986.

Bryson, George. *The Dark Side of Calvinism: The Calvinists' Caste System*. Santa Ana: Calvary Chapel Publishing, 2004.

Budziszewski, J. *On the Meaning of Sex*. Wilmington:DE: ISI Books, 2012.

Clarke, Adam. *Clarke's Commentary, Vol. VI., Romans – Revelation*. New York: Abingdon Press, 1832.

Clinton, Timothy, and George Ohlschlager. *Competent Christian Counseling*. Colorado Springs: WaterBrook Press, 1984.

Copan, Paul. *Is God a Moral Monster: Making Sense of The Old Testament God*. Grand Rapids, MI: Baker Books, 2011.

Craig, William Lane. *Reasonable Faith: Christian Truth and Apologetics*. Wheaton: IL: Crossway Books, 2008.

Delitzsch, F., and C.F.Keil, *Commentary on the Old Testament, Vol. VII, Isaiah*. Grand Rapids: William B. Eerdmans Publishing Company, 1986.

Dawkins, Richard. *The God Delusion*. Boston: Houghton Mifflin Company, 2006.

Deen, Edith. *All The Women of The Bible*. New York: Harper Collins Publishers, 1983.

DeMoss, Nancy. *Lies Women Believe: And the Truth That Sets Them Free*. Chicago: Moody Publishers, 2001.

DeWeese, Garrett. *Doing Philosophy as a Christian*. Downers, IL: InterVarsity Press, 2011.

Dongell, Joseph R., and Jerry L. Wells. *Why I Am Not A Calvinist*. Downers Grove: InterVarsity Press, 2004.

Douglas, J.D. *The New International Dictionary of the Christian Church*. Grand Rapids: Zondervan Publishing House,1978.

Erickson, Millard J. *Christian Theology*, 2nd ed. Grand Rapids: Baker Books, 1983.

Frame, John M. *A History of Western Philosophy and Theology*. Phillipsburg, NJ: P&R Publishing Company, 2015.

_____. *Apologetics: A Justification of Christian Belief.* Phillipsburg, NJ: P&R Publishing, 2015.

Gangel, Kenneth O., and Warren S. Benson. *Christian Education: Its History & Philosophy*. Chicago: Moody Press, 1983.

Geivett, R. Douglas, and Gary R. Habermas, *In Defense of Miracles: A Comprehensive Case For God's Action in History.* Downers Grove, IL: InterVarsity Press, 1997.

Gent, Jim. *The Local Church: God's Plan for Planet Earth*. Old Bridge: Smyrna Publications, 1994.

Good, Kenneth H. *God's Blueprint for a Church*. Rochester, NY: Backus Book Publications, 1987.

Grudem, Wayne. *Christian Ethics: An Introduction to Biblical Moral Reasoning.* Wheaton, IL: Crossway, 2018.

_____. *Systematic Theology*. Leicester: InterVarsity Press, 1994.

Henry, Matthew. *Matthew Henry's Commentary: Acts to Revelation*. McLean, VA: MacDonald Publishing Company, 1710.

Hoffecker, W. Andrew. *Revolutions in Worldview: Understanding the Flow of Western Thought*. Phillipsburg, NJ: P&R Publishing, 2007.

Ingram, Chip. *Love, Sex & Lasting Relationships: God's Prescription for Enhancing Your Love Life*. Grand Rapids: Baker Books, 2003.

Karssen, Gien. *Her Name is Woman*. Colorado Springs: CO: NavPress, 1975.

Knight, George R. *Philosophy and Education: An Introduction in Christian Perspective,* Fourth Edition. Berrien Springs, MI: Andrews University Press, 2006.

Lightner, Robert P. *The Death Christ Died: A Biblical Case for Unlimited Atonement*, Revised Addition. Grand Rapids: Kregel Publications, 1967, 1998.

Lints, Richard. *Revolutions in Worldview: Understanding the Flow of Western Thought*. Phillipsburg, NJ: P&R Publishing, 2007.

Lockerbie, D. Bruce. *A Passon for Learning: A History of Christian Thought on Education.* Colorado Springs: Purposeful Design Publications, 2007.

MacArthur, John. *Counseling: How to Counsel Biblically*. Nashville: Thomas Nelson Publishers, 2005.

_____. *Think Biblically: Recovering a Biblical Worldview*. Wheaton: Crossway Books, 2003.

McCulley, Carolyn. *Radical Womanhood: Feminine Faith in a Feminist World*. Chicago: Moody Publishers, 2008.

Meister, Chad, and James Dew. *God and Evil: The Case for God in a World Filled With Pain*. Downers Grove: IVP, 2013.

Moser, Paul K. Dwayne H. Mulder, and J.D. Trout. *The Theory of Knowledge: A Thematic Introduction.* New York: Oxford University Press, 1998.

Olson, Roger E. *Arminian Theology: Myths and Realities.* Downers Grove: InterVarsity Press, 2006.

Pearcey, Nancy. *Total Truth: Liberating Christianity from its Cultural Captivity*. Wheaton: Crossway Books, 2005.

Peterson, Robert A., and Michael D. Williams. *Why I Am Not An Arminian*. Downers Grove: Iner Varsity Press, 2004.

Piper, John, and Wayne Grudem. *Recovering Biblical Manhood & Womanhood: A Response to Evangelical Feminism*. Wheaton, IL: Crossway Books, 1991.

Richards, Lawrence O., and Gary J. Bredfeldt. *Creative Bible Teaching*. Chicago: Moody Press, 1998.

Ryrie, Charles C. *Basic Theology: A Popular Systematic Guide To Understanding Biblical Truth*. Wheaton: Victor Books, 1986.

Sell, Alan P. F. *The Great Debate: Calvinism, Arminianism, and Salvation*. Grand Rapids: Baker Book House, 1982.

Shedd, William G.T. *Dogmatic Theology, Vol. II*. Nashville: Thomas Nelson Publishers, 1980.

Smith, Ralph L. *Old Testament Theology: It's History, Method, And Message*. Nashville: Broadman & Holman Publishers, 1993.

Steele, Paul E., and Charles C. Ryrie. *Meant to Last: A Christian View of Marriage, Divorce and Remarriage*. Wheaton: Victor Books, 1984.

Stormer, John A. *None Dare Call it Education: The Documented Account of How Education "Reforms" Are Undermining Academics and Traditional Values*. Florissant, MO: Liberty Bell Press, 1999.

Swindoll, Charles R. *Man to Man*. Grand Rapids: Zondervan Publishers, 1996.

The Holy Bible. King James Version.

Vance, Laurance M. *The Other Side of Calvinism*. Pensacola: Vance Publications, 1991.

Vine, W. E. *Vine's Expository Dictionary of Old and New Testament Words*. Grand Rapids: Baker Book House, 1971.

Webster, Noah. *Webster's Dictionary: A Comprehensive Guide to the English Language for the Home, Office, and School*. New York: Modern Publishing, 1999.

Wright, H. Norman. *Premarital Counseling: A Guidebook for the Counselor*. Chicago: The Moody Bible Institute, 1981.

_____. *Relationships that Work and Those That Don't: The Singles Guide to Looking for Love in All the Right Places*. Ventura: Regal Books, 1998.

APPENDICES

JOURNAL ARTICLES

Chafer, Lewis Sperry. "The Eternal Security of the Believer," *Bibliotheca Sacra* (July 1949): 261.

Chafer, Lewis Sperry. "The Saving Work of the Triune God," *Bibliotheca Sacra* (July 1950): 264.

Henebury, Paul Martin. "Christ's Atonement Its Purpose and Extent, Pat 1," *Conservative Theological Journal* (March 2005):105.

Picirilli, Robert E. "Foreknowledge, Freedom, And the Future," *Journal of the Evangelical Theological Society* (June 2000):262.

Rhodes, Ron. "The Extent of the Atonement: Limited Atonement Verses Unlimited Atonement." *Chafer Theological Seminary Journal* (Fall 1996):6.

Telloyan, Samuel. "Did Christ Die For All?" *Central Bible Quarterly* (Winter 1967):16.

ONLINE SOURCES

Akoue, Vihn Lu.
https://www.researchgate.net/application.ClientValidation.html?origP2019).ath=%2Fpost%2FThe_origin_of_philosophy_What_is_the_origin_of_philosophy (accessed January 14, 2019).

Barna, George "New Marriage and Divorce Statistics Released," The Barna Group (March 2008), Available from http://www.barna.org/barna-update/article/15-familykids/42-new-marriage-and-divorce-statistics-released (accessed Nov 4, 2012).

_____. "What Americans Believe About Sex," The Barna Group. https://www.barna.com/research/what-americans-believe-about-sex/ (accessed April 3, 2017).

Bernard, Saint.
https://en.m.wikipedia.org/wiki/The_road_to_hell_is_paved_with_good_intentions (accessed April 7, 2017).

Carpenter, Kaley M. "Missionary Movement," Association of Religious Archives, http://www.thearda.com/timeline/movements/movement_45.asp (accessed October 8, 2019).

Fischer, Bryan. "Harvard and MIT Scientists: There Is No Gay Gene," American Family Association, https://www.afa.net/the-stand/culture/2019/08/harvard-and-mit-scientists-there-is-no-gay-gene/ (accessed December 8, 2019).

McKinney, Michael. "What Did He Know and When Did He Know It?" (Leadership Now, November 2011) available from http://www.leadershipnow.com/leadingblog/2011/11/what_did_he_know_and_when_did.html (accessed Mar. 12, 2012).

Merriam-Webster, "Merriam-Webster Dictionary," https://www.merriam-webster.com/dictionary/pseudoscience (accessed December 7, 2019).

https://plato.stanford.edu/entries/evil/#RelConGod (accessed October 25, 2019).

The Counsel on Biblical Manhood and Womanhood, "The Danvers Statement, 1987," http://www.churchcouncil.org/iccp_org/Documents_ICCP/English/17_Male_Female_Distinctives_A&D.pdf (accessed April 14, 2017).

Unknown, "Bible History Online," https://www.bible-history.com/old-testament/miracles.html (accessed December 11, 2019).

Transformational Truth Volume II

Follow the

Biblical Teaching

of

Dr. Andrew T. Knight

Books * XM Radio * Online

Children's Ministry Leadership
by Dr. Andrew T. Knight

Dr. Andrew Knight became interested in children's ministry while in Bible College. He worked at a youth camp for two summers during his college years. Dr. Knight's first ministry after college was teaching 5th & 6th grades in a Christian School, as well as running a successful bus ministry. Between two subsequent church plants, it began to occur to Dr. Knight that the Gospel must get deeper into the culture to have a lasting impact. He then pursued a Masters of Christian education as his thoughts about ministry began to move more toward the significance of children's ministry.

Recruiting and Training Children's Ministry Leaders

This book covers precedents for both biblical and historical perspectives for children's ministry, as well as the current cultural context. Advice was drawn from over fifty-five experts in children's ministry. The lesson plans included act as an aid in training parents and ministry leaders for children's ministry. The book concludes with sound analysis and an evaluation of how to better reach the next generation for Christ through children's ministry.

Leadership The Lord's Way
by Dr. Andrew T. Knight

Leadership the Lord's Way *is a biblical philosophy of leadership. This work discusses the organizational culture of the local church. The various types and theories of leadership from almost a century are identified and discussed. A map of strategic planning for local churches is explained and elaborated on. The quantitative and qualitative research on leadership and administration styles are discussed and developed. Practical lesson plans, answer sheets, and suggested applications are found at the end of each of the six chapters. Seven additional training lessons are found in the appendix of this volume. This work will aid in the training of follower first-leaders in the local church, leadership conferences, and in Bible college and seminary classrooms.*

Transformational Truth, Vol. I
by Dr. Andrew T. Knight

Transformational Truth, Vol. I covers a wide number of topics on the subject of presuppositional apologetics. This volume will help to develop one's biblical worldview. Islam and Christianity are compared and contrasted, as well as naturalistic and theistic worldviews. How the apostles in the First century practiced apologetics will be given attention as well as how to apply apologetics in a post-modern culture. This volume will aid in the teaching and training of leaders in the local church, the Bible institute, the Bible College, and the Seminary classroom.

Appendices

To order other books call: 386-220-3141
or visit: www.AndrewKnight.org

TRANSFORMATIONAL TRUTH VOLUME II

INSTITUTE FOR BIBLICAL APOLOGETICS

Register now for these courses!

- Biblical Manhood & Womanhood
- The Problem of Suffering
- Does God Exist?
- Developing a Biblical Worldview
- Answers to Hard Questions

Only $17.76 each!

Start earning your certificate today! Visit www.AndrewKnight.org or call 386-220-3141 to register.

APPENDICES

CENTURION EDUCATION FOUNDATION

www.CEF.gives

Dr. Andrew Knight is also the president of CEF, a mission's foundation in which he has the vision to spread the Gospel across America and around the world.

VISION: The vision of this foundation is to develop an endowment that will support 400 missionary families, placed in 200 countries around the world. With two families in each country, this will provide fellowship and partnership for each missionary family. Church planters will also be trained and funded to plant 250 new Independent Baptist Churches across America.

MISSION: The mission of Centurion Education Foundation is to train and strategically place missionary teams around the globe theologically. While presenting the need for world missions and raising endowments for missions, the foundation's desire is to defend and advance the gospel of Jesus Christ. Dr. Knight has set a goal for the Centurion Education Foundation to raise $440,000,000. Though this may be a twenty-year endeavor, this endowment will perpetuate the gospel by training and supporting 400 missionary families across 200 countries of the world, while training and supporting 250 new churches at a time across America.

DEVELOPMENT METHODS:

- Vehicle Donations
- Property Donations
- Cash Donations
- Corporate Donations
- Will or Living Trust Bequests
- Wealth Replacement Trusts

Call us to discuss how you can help with world missions: 386-220-3141

APPENDICES

BIOGRAPHY OF DR. ANDREW KNIGHT

Author of Transformational Truth Vol. I & II

Dr. Andrew Knight spent twenty years in New England as a church planter, Christian school teacher, and a Christian broadcaster. He is an author, speaker, and lecturer. He has lectured at the Good News Bible College and Seminary located in Telangana, India. He has written extensively on Christian Education, Marriage & Family, Christian Leadership, Presuppositional Apologetics, and Children's Ministry.

After receiving a Bachelor of Bible from Pensacola Christian College, he then earned a Master of Biblical Studies from Emmanuel Baptist Theological Seminary in Newington, CT. He has also received a Master of Religious Education from West Coast Baptist College in Lancaster, CA, and a Master of Biblical Apologetics from Baptist Bible Seminary in South Abington, PA, and a Doctor of Ministry from Luther Rice Seminary in Lithonia, GA. Dr. Knight resides in New Smyrna Beach, FL, and continues to write and speak on these topics.

Dr. Knight is available to speak at your church, seminars, and conferences on these topics:

- Children's Ministry
- Biblical Leadership
- Marriage and Family
- Christian Education
- Presuppositional Apologetics

- Textus Receptus
- Biblical Finances
- Baptist History
- Faith on Fire Testimony

Forums:

- Missions Conferences
- Marriage and Family Conferences
- Competing worldviews
- Men's Conferences
- The Problem of Evil and Suffering
- Biblical Manhood and Womanhood

For ministry information and availability:
Centurion Education Foundation
P.O. Box 87
New Smyrna Beach, FL 32170
386-220-3141
Dr.atknight@gmail.com
www.CEF.gives
www.AndrewKnight.org

www.ingramcontent.com/pod-product-compliance
Lightning Source LLC
Chambersburg PA
CBHW072000150426
43194CB00008B/948